SHARED MADNESS

SHARED MADNESS

TRUE STORIES OF COUPLES WHO KILL

CHRISTOPHER BERRY-DEE

JOHN BLAKE

Published by John Blake Publishing Ltd,
3 Bramber Court, 2 Bramber Road,
London W14 9PB, England

www.johnblakepublishing.co.uk

First published in hardback in 2005
Paperback edition published 2010

ISBN: 978 1 84454 842 2

British Library Cataloguing-in-Publication Data:
A catalogue record for this book is available from the British Library.

Design by www.envydesign.co.uk

Printed in Great Britain by CPI Bookmarque, Croydon CR0 4TD

1 3 5 7 9 10 8 6 4 2

Papers used by John Blake Publishing are natural, recyclable products made
from wood grown in sustainable forests. The manufacturing processes conform
to the environmental regulations of the country of origin.

Photographs © Associated Press plate section pages 1,3,4,5;
© Press Association pages 2,8; © Mirrorpix page 6; © Corbis page 7

To the criminologist, folie a deux is a phenomenon in which two or more individuals, who have a similar delusion or fantasy that remains latent until they meet, together commit crime inspired by this shared delusion or fantasy.

CHRISTOPHER BERRY-DEE

FOREWORD

Apart from a score of psychiatrists and FBI investigators, including John Douglas and Robert Ressler, I have interviewed and corresponded with more serial murderers and mass killers than is healthy for one's mind. At the last count it was around 30, not taking into account the one-off killers and rapists; add these together and the total is probably 70 or more offenders.

To answer a frequently asked question, I would like to confirm that at *no* time have any of these murderous individuals threatened or intimidated me, with the sole exception of the utterly repulsive Kenneth Bianchi, who went berserk after I surprised him with an unannounced visit to his tiny cell in the Special Housing Unit (SHU) at the Washington State Penitentiary. Ken flipped and was furious. He had always told me that he was a 'special' inmate with a large cell and afforded all the mod cons; but he lived in a small 'house', as the inmates call their cells, and was treated just the same as the other prisoners on the tier. Indeed, the regime at the SHU can be likened to the Rule 43 system in the UK. Inmates are incarcerated in these protective units because they fear for their lives. The very nature of their sex crimes makes them targets for the general prison population. Needless to say, I have always treated these people with much respect and, for the most part, they have treated me likewise.

Of course, these killers do lose their temper from time to time, and I have witnessed the 'flick of the switch' personality change from lamb to beast, which can be unnerving; even so, their anger has rarely focused on me. Those of you who have read *Talking with Serial Killers* will know that their anger is directed towards the prison system and society at large, which they perceive, in their warped way, has conspired to put them in their present predicament.

There was one other notable exception. During one of my interviews with Arthur Shawcross, a female film director who should have known better kept breaking into our discussion, which was very unprofessional conduct indeed. Arthur leaped out of his chair and would have assaulted her had the guards and I not intervened. If she had been alone with him, he would have broken her neck in a flash. I took this unwanted intrusion very seriously, especially as this killer was about to admit to two unsolved homicides and it had taken me two years of correspondence to obtain an interview with him. Nevertheless, when he calmed down he finally confessed – a result that pleased the police and the next of kin of the deceased.

Douglas Clark, the 'Sunset Slayer', had been chained to a wall before my interview with him. I can't blame the authorities for this precaution as he had promised to rip the heart out of anyone who upset him and, believe me, he would. But, after 30 minutes of ranting and raving, Doug settled down and was as good as gold.

So I have met my fair share of killers, and this cast of knuckle-grazing voyeurs, perverts, stalkers, serial rapists and homicidal sociopaths contains several familiar names, but is salted with a few that are not. In the USA, the list includes: Kenneth Alessio Bianchi (Washington State Penitentiary, Walla Walla), James Paul (Trenton State Prison, New Jersey), Richard Ramirez (Death Row, San Quentin State Prison, California), Harvey Louis Carignan (Minnesota Correctional Facility, Stillwater), Douglas Daniel Clark (Death Row, San Quentin State Prison, California), Arthur John Shawcross (Sullivan Correctional Facility, Fallsburg, New York), Carol Bundy (Central California Women's Facility, Chowchilla) Cathy May Wood (Central California Women's Facility, Chowchilla), Gwendoline Graham (details of whereabouts restricted), Ronald DeFeo Jr (Greenhaven Correctional Facility, Stormville, New York), Michael Bruce Ross (Death Row, Osborne Correctional Institute, Connecticut), William Heirens (Dixon Correctional Center, Illinois), Joel Rifkin (Riverhead County Jail, Long Island, New York), Patricia Gordy Wright (Central California Women's Facility, Chowchilla).

John Wayne Gacy (executed 10 May 1994, Death Row, Illinois Correctional Center, Menard), Aileen Wuornos (executed 9 October 2002, Florida State Prison, Starke; formerly on Death Row, Broward Correctional Institute, Pembroke Pines, Texas), Theodore (Ted) Robert Bundy (executed 24 January 1989, Death Row, Florida State Prison,

Starke), Kenneth Allen McDuff (executed 17 November 1998, Death Row, Ellis Unit, Huntsville, Texas).

I also spoke to these prisoners who were murdered by fellow inmates: John Gerard Schaefer (hacked to death, 2001, Florida State Prison, Starke) and Jeffrey Dahmer (bludgeoned to death, 28 November 1994, Columbia Correctional Facility, Wisconsin).

Other interviewees were to die of natural causes. Henry Lee Lucas (heart failure, 12 March 2001, Death Row, Ellis Unit, Huntsville, Texas), Ottis Toole (hepatitis, cirrhosis of the liver, 21 September 1996, Florida State Prison, Starke), Angelo Buono (heart failure, 21 September 2002, Calipatria State Prison, California), mobster John Gotti (cancer, 10 June 2002, US Medical Center for Federal Prisoners, Springfield, Illinois; formerly at Marion Federal Penitentiary, Illinois).

The UK killers include serial murderers John Martin Scripps (executed 19 April 1996, Changi Prison, Singapore) and Peter Sutcliffe; gangster Ronnie Kray (died of a heart attack in 1995) and killer Paul Beecham (whose crimes included the murder of his wife and who committed suicide in 2002 after his release on licence); the last three of these I met at Broadmoor Hospital, Crowthorne, Berkshire; murderers Michael Sams and John Cannan, respectively at HMP Full Sutton, North Yorkshire, and the Central Criminal Courts, London. I have corresponded with many more, including the serial killer Dennis Nilsen, who at the time was at HMP Albany, Isle of Wight.

I have met Indian serial killers Renuka Kiran Shinde and Seema Mohan Gavit, at Death Row, Central Prison, Mumbai, plus more killers than I can recall in other establishments, including Sablino Prison for Women, St Petersburg, Russia, and the Crosses Prison in the same city, where I talked with many male inmates.

For years I have been interviewing these evil men and women in my attempts to open up their minds and understand why they did what they did. However, more recently I have taken an interest in couples who kill and this book is the culmination of my research.

ACKNOWLEDGEMENTS

In loving memory of the late and much-missed Joan Odell and, to list the first names that spring to mind, Professor Elliot Leyton and my co-author on several books, Robin Odell – both consummate authorities in their respective criminological fields. Elliot I admire because he says what he says and doesn't give a damn. Robin I thank for all his support and for begging me to moderate my emotions when dealing with murder most foul.

The eminent Professor David Canter, formerly of Surrey University, who had hurt his back and was ensconced on a camp bed when I first met him in Guildford, showed immense interest in the Ken Bianchi autobiography. The fish and chips were OK, David! John Blake was the only publisher who would take on my book *Talking with Serial Killers* when the others fought shy. The very notion that I was to allow serial killers to describe their lives and crimes in their own words sent shock waves through the criminology community, becoming the forerunner of such books and TV documentaries today. Indeed, one international publisher's letter of rejection noted, 'This may upset our older readers', which begs the question, why are they reading true crime in the first instance?

Thanks to my Russian wife, Tatiana, and my great pals Kirstie, Lawrie and Richard Arm. Also, once again, to John Blake and his colleagues who have supported *Shared Madness*.

Finally, to Steve Morris and all of my team at *The New Criminologist* and CRI.

Christopher Berry-Dee

Publisher, *The New Criminologist*
www.newcriminologist.co.uk

CONTENTS

INTRODUCTION

'Folie a deux' means 'a madness shared by two'. The term refers to a delusion affecting two (or more) people, sometimes communicated from one to the other, or the same form of insanity shared by them. In this book our concern is folie a deux that has a murderous outcome or intent. The condition seems to have a strong sexual element and cases are known of two women committing murder together, a man and a woman forming a pair or both sexes acting in a small group. However, while folie a deux can often be found between gay men, the susceptibility to the condition between heterosexual males is very rare, most criminologists agree, and some argue that folie a deux between two males does not exist at all.

Characteristically, folie a deux occurs in pairs of individuals or groups who have become isolated from the world at large. Notorious examples of such groups include Charles Manson's 'family', who committed mass murder in California in 1969, and the Branch Davidian cult, led by David Koresh, which was destroyed in the siege at Waco, Texas, in 1993.

Whether they exist in pairs or in groups, such people lead an intensely inward-looking existence marked by a paranoid view of the outside world. Most couples who commit murder certainly have this kind of insular relationship. Often this inward-looking alliance is based on a shared paranoid disorder in which one partner is dominant and the other or others compliant.

But is it possible for folie a deux to occur in just one person? The question might seem laughable. However, if folie a deux can exist in the minds of two linked people, it is entirely plausible that it could occur in an individual who suffers from multiple personality disorder, for, in genuine cases of this rare condition, two or more 'minds' do exist within one brain.

This book sets out to examine under the glass how folie a deux fuses into a shared motive for murder, whether this is sexual perversity, financial greed, insane jealousy, bitter hatred or a deadly cocktail of several motives, which can only be satisfied when two or more people work together. For example, the combination of murdering for money and committing sado-sexual acts is often found among heterosexual killing teams.

In single, unattached individuals, these motives are merely inert delusions and wishes that can't be acted out. Such a person is like an explosive device that has all of the ingredients in place but lacks a fuse to set it off. To put it simply, we can say that the lone individual does not have the nerve or the willpower to commit the crime, but when his or her fantasies are mirrored and reinforced by those of a willing partner, who additionally provides physical and psychological support, the bomb is armed and ready to explode.

In genuine folie a deux relationships the dominant partner has the stronger delusions and thus becomes the leader, while the other partner has the same delusions to a lesser degree and becomes the follower. (As I suggested above, this dynamic equally applies to groups.) When they join forces, the psychological cocktail is mixed, the cork comes out of the bottle and can't be replaced, and heinous crimes are committed that otherwise would not have occurred.

For just two examples of genuine folie a deux we need look no further than the sado-sexual psychopathic couples Ian Brady and Myra Hindley and Frederick and Rose West. In both pairings the male was the dominant partner. In both we find a strong 'infatuation' element, with the woman seemingly enthralled by her man. And when we examine other genuine cases in this book we will see this male dominance repeated.

However, if we turn to Renuka Kiran Shinde and Seema Mohan Gavit, two of a foursome of serial killers who killed for monetary gain in India, we unearth two women killing as accomplices. Genuine folie a deux this is not.

It has always been argued – quite mistakenly – that folie a deux was evident in the case of Ruth Snyder and Henry Judd Gray, a couple who killed for a mix of financial and sexual motives. Snyder proved, if proof were needed, that women can not only dominate and be more resilient but can also be more deadly than the male. Although at first glance their story seems to be a genuine shared madness, this assumption is incorrect, for the gullible Gray was just a tool in Snyder's grand scheme.

Psychiatrists have established that folie a deux is not due to another mental disorder. By legal and clinical definition it is not madness at all. However, as this book illustrates, it appears in many cases, if not all, where exists in one or both participants a latent psychopathic antisocial personality disorder – again, not madness – which only manifests itself in a destructive manner when the individuals unite. Neither individual has any real structure to their life, or any moral inhibitions: they are able to destroy lives with as much compassion as one would swat an annoying fly, without the least concern about the far-reaching consequences.

Beyond any doubt, however, is the fact that folie a deux is not due to medical, neurological or substance-abuse disorders. That is not to say that these disorders are never present, but that they are neither the cause of nor a contributory factor to folie a deux.

And there is a grey area here, because most criminologists view folie a deux and accomplices as being one and the same phenomenon, whereas a conspiracy between two people can form no part of folie a deux. This is an error that I hope this book will dispel. Of course, when two or more individuals unite to commit murder, or any crime for that matter, there is a conspiracy and they become accomplices in crime, whether it is genuine folie a deux or not.

The pairing of Bonnie and Clyde would not be classified as genuine folie a deux, simply because Clyde Barrow would have gone on to rob banks with or without Bonnie Parker. He did not need her personality to fuse with his own to initiate the explosion which soon led to a spree of robbery and murder.

A person planning to rob a store may enlist a partner in crime to assist in the venture. An individual may coerce a lover into assisting in a murder for an insurance policy payout. By definition they become conspirators and accomplices, but folie a deux plays no part if the two share differing delusions and underpinning motives, as the case of Ruth Snyder and Henry Judd Gray will show us.

As a criminologist I have always had a profound curiosity about couples who kill. My interest was initially sparked when I became involved in a long correspondence with the notorious sado-sexual serial killer Kenneth Alessio Bianchi. He and his cousin Angelo Buono were dubbed by the media the 'Hillside Stranglers'. I met Bianchi on two occasions at the Washington State Penitentiary in Walla Walla, and the information I obtained from him allowed me to discover, as far as I can determine, one of the only two genuine cases in criminal history of what we might call a triple folie or folie a trois: Kenneth Bianchi, Angelo Buono and Veronica Wallace Compton. The other involved Carol Bundy, Jack Murray and Douglas Clark, who also feature in these pages.

Of immense interest to me is the link between Veronica Wallace Compton and Douglas Clark. I interviewed Veronica, or 'VerLyn', at the Washington Correctional Center for Women (WCCW) near Gig Harbor while she was serving 15 years for attempting murder at Bianchi's behest. In her own words she tells her amazing story here for the first time. The full account of Bianchi's and Buono's crimes appears towards the end of this book, and here I was particularly exercised by the question of who was the dominant partner in this killing duo. In fact, I don't think I have met one commentator on these men's heinous crimes who believed, for one instant, that Bianchi was the stronger of the pair.

They always have it that Buono was the leader. I say they are incorrect.

Indeed, I would strenuously argue that, if Bianchi, a stone-cold serial killer, could deceive the very best psychiatrists in the USA into believing he suffered from a multiple personality disorder, fooling them at every turn, then become an ordained priest and a member of the American Law Society at the same time as dragging a leading playing-card company into bankruptcy when he was confined in a close-custody Special Housing Unit, he clearly had his wits about him, whereas Angelo Buono, who could neither read nor write, had not.

From Bianchi's words, again never published before, we can see that, far from being the weaker of the two men, he was far more intelligent, cunning and manipulative than the illiterate Buono, who had a low IQ and a speech impediment. Unlike Bianchi, Buono had never killed before they teamed up, and did not kill, unlike Bianchi, after they parted company. Their story is an unusual, if not unique, example of folie a deux, and without this pairing in Los Angeles the 'Hillside Stranglings' would have not occurred. But there is more to this, for, while Bianchi was awaiting trial in LA for these murders, a young aspiring actress fell in love with him. In her own words, Veronica Wallace Compton tells us her chilling story – I have used her words verbatim – and how she attempted to commit murder for Bianchi by proxy so that he would be released and she could fall into his arms. This is a terrifying plot that even the horror writer Stephen King would be hard pushed to equal.

In those days Veronica, an extremely beautiful woman with a wow factor of ten, was, by her own admission, mentally unstable. While in custody for the attempted murder at

Bianchi's behest, she became a pen friend of the notorious 'Sunset Slayer' Douglas Clark. Letters between the couple showed that Veronica wanted to marry Doug and, if they were both released, open up a morgue together where they could have sex with the dead. When I asked Clark about this, he said, 'The woman was a fuckin' fruit. I wrote her for something to do.'

The final chapter in this book deals thoroughly with what I believe to be the only other example of a 'triple' in criminal history. I stand to be corrected if I am wrong. Carol Bundy, a short, fat, nearly blind intellectual pigmy, had two good-looking lovers in Douglas Clark and Jack Murray. And if there ever was a 'Black Widow', Bundy was a human arachnid. In a nutshell, Bundy and Murray teamed up to commit sexually related serial murder. She shot Murray dead under quite the most obscene circumstances, then teamed up with Clark to start killing again.

Unfortunately, no empirical study of the phenomenon of folie a deux has ever been conducted, so society has no idea how many cases there have been or might be revealed in the future. Nevertheless, in trying to shed a brighter light into the dark recess of this little-understood criminological curiosity, my own studies incline to confirm that in genuine folie a deux relationships between heterosexual men and women the male is always the dominant partner and the crimes are almost always underpinned with strong, if not overwhelming homicidal sexual fantasies and motives.

The same underpinning dysfunctional thinking occurs in genuine folie a deux relationships between two heterosexual men joining to commit sado-sexual serial homicide, as the

Bianchi–Buono and Bittaker–Norris cases will illustrate. I could not, however, find an example of genuine folie a deux between two homosexual men, but readers may wish to study the relationship (not examined in this book) between the bisexual Henry Lee Lucas and the homosexual Ottis Toole and form their own opinion.

There are few known cases of bisexual or lesbian women pairing to commit such serial atrocities, but I can cite the folie a deux that was evident between Cathy May Wood (bisexual) and Gwendoline Graham (lesbian). Wood, who was married, and Graham worked as nursing assistants at a nursing home in Grand Rapids, Michigan. They fell in love, and to cement a bizarre love pact they suffocated five elderly female patients. But their case is quite unique because they did not get their sexual kicks from the act of killing *per se*. Although the police strongly suspected that the two women were killers, there was no conclusive evidence against them and the murderous duo almost escaped punishment. However, the women parted company in acrimonious circumstances, and Wood, the stronger personality of the two, volunteered a statement to investigators which implicated Graham as the prime mover behind the murders and portrayed herself as a helpless accomplice. In return for giving this information, Wood received a lighter sentence.

Many years ago I interviewed Gwendoline Graham, who is serving life in a secure hospital for the criminally insane. A woman teetering on the edge of insanity, she self-mutilates herself almost weekly with cigarette burns and scalding water. She admitted to me that she was desperately in love with Cathy Wood, and would have done anything to keep their relationship alive. This sad, pathetic creature claims that it was Wood's idea to kill the patients. (The case was immortalised in my colleague Lowell Cauffiel's excellent book *Forever and Five Days*.)

My investigations and research have led me to believe that Cathy May Wood's strong personality is that of a control freak and in my opinion she is an obese lump of antisocial garbage. When I interviewed her for the TV series *The Serial Killers* she convinced everyone, except me, with her tears and television debut, claiming that she was the lost soul and innocent party while Gwen Graham was the driving force behind the murders. However, directly after leaving the room, while walking across the prison exercise yard, she became hysterical with laughter, and later boasted to other inmates of how clever she had been in conning us. Wood served ten years and has since been released from prison, proving that a plea-bargain deal pays off.

When a woman does commit serial murder, and Aileen Wuornos is one example, she usually works either alone, as we shall see, or in partnership with a male.

My research also throws light on what we might call 'pseudo' folie a deux. The case of Snyder and Gray illustrates this very clearly, for, when a woman takes the domineering role in such relationships, the associate, male or female, becomes an accomplice, simply a tool to assist the instigator to win her ill-gotten gains – usually for insurance policies or to rid herself of an obnoxious partner or a rival. In examining such cases of pseudo folie a deux in this book, we can see clearly that the interpersonal transactions completely differ from genuine folie a deux. Far from being a meeting of warped delusions, pseudo folie a deux is an issue of mixed motives and disposable accomplices, and invariably gullible accomplices at that.

In compiling this book I have exhumed from the dark cellars of criminal history a number of the most brutal and terrifying homicide cases on record. Several of the examples tell of females who commit murder most foul on their own. I have included these to graphically illustrate that a woman is quite capable of becoming the dominant partner in a male–female killing team and may indeed be more lethal than her partner. My own brief conclusions follow each case history. On my judgements you are cordially invited to form your own opinions. You may agree or disagree with me, but first prepare yourself for some gruesome reading.

Christopher Berry-Dee
Editor-in-Chief *The New Criminologist* and Director of the Criminology Research Institute, January 2005
www.criminologyworld.com

CHAPTER ONE

KELLY O'DONNELL AND WILLIAM GRIBBLE
The 'Jigsaw Murder'

Five female killers are incarcerated on Pennsylvania's Death Row, although their execution dates have not been set.

Brown-eyed, 1.63-metre-tall Delores Precious Rivers, 42, was convicted of the fatal stabbing in January 1988 of disabled 74-year-old Viola Burt in Burt's home in Frankford. Rivers was an in-home nurse for the ailing lady at the time. She was sentenced to death in March 1989, becoming the state's first condemned woman since the USA reinstated the death penalty in 1976.

Beth Ann Markman, aged 49, was sentenced to death for the murder on 30 January 1988 of a 74-year-old man. A Cumberland County jury found William Houseman and Markman guilty of all charges in connection with the death of Leslie Rae White of East Waterford. Markman claimed that

Houseman had forced her into committing murder, and then she denied all knowledge, despite the fact that the victim's DNA was found under her fingernails. The jury deliberated for two hours before convicting both defendants of first-degree murder, kidnapping and abuse of a corpse, plus additional counts of conspiracy in connection with each charge.

Donetta Marie Hill, a crack-addicted prostitute from South Philadelphia, was sentenced to death in April 1992 for the 1990 claw-hammer killings of two customers who foolishly tried to short-change her during a drugs deal. The bodies of Nghia Guy Lu, 72, and Nairobe Dupont, 21, were discovered in their homes by relatives. Hill was expected to be executed on 29 March 2004, but received a stay of execution.

Carolyn Ann King, 32, was sentenced in December 1994 for joining in the killing of florist Guy Goodman, at Palmyra, Lebanon County, in September the previous year.

And finally, the star of our show: 29-year-old Kelly O'Donnell, sentenced in July 1993 for her part in the November 1992 bludgeoning and dismemberment of Eleftherios Eleftheriou, the manager of a pizza parlour in West Kensington, Philadelphia.

On the morning of Friday, 13 November 1992 the Philadelphia police received a 911 call reporting that a shocked citizen had found human body parts in a trash dump. When they arrived at the 3900 block of North Delaware Avenue, officers were shown a bloodstained quilt and a left arm next to a trash bag. Inside another nearby trash bag they found a torso with the head missing. And in a smaller bag there was a blood-covered head with the left eye missing. A short distance away the police discovered a right arm inside another bag. Among papers strewn about the site they found a letter addressed to Agnes McClinchey of 3123 Richmond Street, Philadelphia, and this was their first major clue.

It was obvious that the deceased hadn't committed suicide. So, with little else to assist investigators, the human remains were bagged and tagged before being taken away for examination. Homicide detectives now embarked on the arduous job of attempting to solve the mystery of a very unpleasant crime. The dismembered corpse was later identified as Eleftherios Eleftheriou, and the story of how it came to be in so many pieces is a disturbing tale of violence and animal savagery.

What makes it all the more shocking is that one of the macabre butchers was a woman, and Judge Paul Ribner did not bat an eyelid when he sentenced Kelly O'Donnell to death for murder in the first degree.

O'Donnell, a not unattractive 24-year-old with a history of drug addiction, had a 30-year-old green-eyed boyfriend called William Russell Gribble, who also had had his fair share of problems with drugs. As is usually the case with such people, they suffered from a severe shortage of money, and it was this that would be the motive for the crime.

Early in November 1992 the couple went to stay at 3123 Richmond Street. The apartment at which they stayed was the home of Gribble's mother, Agnes McClinchey, who had given them permission to use it while she was away visiting a friend called Ed Paduski. Also residing at the house at the time was James Matthews, an elderly friend of the owner.

Shortly after 10pm on Wednesday, 11 November, Kelly O'Donnell called in at a pizza shop which was managed by a man of obviously Greek origins, Eleftherios Eleftheriou, whom she knew simply as Terry. As well as running the pizza shop, the outwardly respectable Terry did some drug dealing and, as is often the case with dealers, a little money lending, usually to those who wanted to buy drugs from him. On this occasion O'Donnell took with her a leather jacket to offer as collateral against a loan that she sought from this man.

According to a witness, an employee of the pizza parlour, Terry took a large wad of money from his pocket and gave some of this to O'Donnell. The amount of money involved is uncertain. With the loan transaction completed, the two arranged to meet later that night. Around 1am Terry closed the shop, got into his car and drove to the rendezvous, from where O'Donnell took him back to the apartment on Richmond Street, arriving there at about 1.30am. What happened next is drawn from O'Donnell's confession and her evidence given at the trial, much of which conflicts with the testimony of Gribble, who seemed desperate to shoulder most of the blame.

O'Donnell said that Eleftheriou was looking out of a window when she walked up behind him and hit him over the head with a hammer. He fell to the floor and, as he lay at her feet, she continued raining hammer blows on to his skull. The reason O'Donnell gave for this murderous attack was that the man was, in her words, 'a pervert' and had previously sexually assaulted her. Whether there was any truth in this claim has never been substantiated. Nevertheless, whatever the reason for her action, she now had a very serious problem on her hands. In her boyfriend's mother's home a body was lying on the floor, a body which needed to be disposed of; and an undertaker was obviously not an option on this occasion.

With no other solution springing to mind, O'Donnell said, she grimly realised that she would have to get rid of the pizza man's remains the hard way. Somehow she managed to drag the body down to the basement, and there, in the anaemic half-light, among a clutter of pipes and cables, she dismembered it.

Now faced with the question of what to do with the bits of body – truly a logistical nightmare – she came up with an answer. Dispersal of the component parts of the deceased was effected by the simple, if irreverent, expedient of placing them in black plastic waste bags. Only at this juncture, O'Donnell claimed, did she enlist the assistance of her partner, Gribble. The two of them, using the dead man's car, dumped the bags on North Delaware Avenue, where they were later discovered. Later that same day they used Eleftheriou's car and his credit card to go on a shopping spree to purchase clothing for Gribble's children.

On 13 November, the day after the murder, Agnes McClinchey returned from her visit and entered her apartment. Her home was not quite as she had left it, however, for she found blood on the front door and carpets. As if that were not enough to contend with, O'Donnell told the bewildered woman that she and Gribble had been involved in a murder. Agnes sat down in her chair and, shaking with shock, said that she had heard a radio report which indicated that a man's head had been found on North Delaware Avenue.

For a short while Agnes wandered confusedly around her home, then she overheard O'Donnell telling Gribble to burn Terry's car. This he did, and when he returned Kelly said to him, 'Thank God you didn't get caught.'

5

At 7.30pm that day police officers responded to a report of a car on fire on D Street. When the fire was eventually extinguished, they searched the burned-out vehicle and, not entirely to their delight, found the missing bits of the pizza man's dismembered corpse.

An hour or so later, after much deliberation, Agnes McClinchey went to a call box and telephoned the police. Detectives met her at a nearby gas station, where she told them what she knew of the murder that had taken place in her apartment. Following their discussion with the distraught woman, law officers visited her apartment at 1.30am on 14 November, where they arrested Kelly O'Donnell and William Gribble.

With most of the body parts found, and two suspects in custody, crime scene investigators (CSI) now began a search of the apartment and cluttered basement. In the basement they found a kitchen knife, a chisel and a claw hammer, each of which revealed traces of human tissue and blood. They had the murder weapon and the tools that had been used to dismember the victim's body. Strangely, however, O'Donnell's fingerprints were not on any of the items. Finally the CSI stumbled across the two missing pieces of the human jigsaw puzzle that had until recently been Eleftherios Eleftheriou. A cop found, stuffed inside a pipe, a pencil case containing an eyeball and a penis.

Now that they could relax, secure in the knowledge that nobody was going to turn up with more bits and pieces belonging to the corpse, detectives got down to the business of interrogating the two suspects. However, while the arrests had been made pretty quickly, they found that the task of establishing the truth behind the killing proved at first to be as untidy as the distribution of the victim's body parts. O'Donnell and Gribble made statements in which each accepted personal responsibility for the murder while attempting to exculpate the other.

On the face of it, in her attempt to take all the blame, O'Donnell made a confession that seemed convincing enough. However, from an investigator's point of view, Gribble's was the more credible story.

In his sworn confession he stated that he arrived at the apartment at approximately 2am and saw Eleftheriou and O'Donnell on the couch together. James Matthews was fast asleep in bed. 'Eleftheriou was feeling all over her,' he said, 'and I then freaked.' He hit Eleftheriou once with his fist, grabbed a hammer that lay on a television and beat Eleftheriou some 10–15 times with it until he 'knew the man was dead'. Gribble claimed that O'Donnell left the apartment at some point during the attack and then he dragged Eleftheriou's body behind the property, covered him with a piece of plywood and returned to the house to decide what to do next.

A little later Gribble uncovered Eleftheriou's body, dropped it through an access hole into the basement and began to dismember it. While Gribble was carving up the body, O'Donnell said she felt unwell and they both went upstairs where she called for an ambulance that took her to hospital. Gribble said he then returned to the basement and finished dismembering Eleftheriou, including cutting off Eleftheriou's penis. He then bagged the body parts and cleaned the basement. O'Donnell came back from the hospital a few hours later and the couple slept.

According to Gribble's confession, they awoke early on the

morning of Thursday, 12 November 1992 and loaded the body into Eleftheriou's car. He alone drove to North Delaware Avenue and threw half of the bags from the car into a trash dump, and then took the remainder of the bags back to the apartment.

In the end, Gribble and O'Donnell were both charged with murder, criminal conspiracy, arson and a variety of offences connected to the demise of Eleftherios Eleftheriou. The two butchers were tried together and both waived their right to trial by jury, electing instead to appear before a bench judge. The medical evidence given at the trial makes very disturbing reading.

An assistant medical examiner testified that there were numerous abrasions on the victim's head and these were consistent with blows from a hammer. This witness also testified that one person, acting alone, could not have killed and dismembered the victim's body in a manner consistent with the physical evidence.

The most horrifying aspect of the murder was revealed when, during this witness's testimony, he stated that red abrasions in the areas where the murdered man's head and right arm had been severed indicated that, at the time these parts were removed, the man's heart had still been beating. Whether or not he could feel the pain at any time is not known. The witness went on to say that one person alone would not have been able to remove both the head and right arm in the estimated 15 minutes that it took before Eleftheriou bled to death. In contrast, yellow abrasions in those areas where the remaining body parts had been severed indicated that the victim's heart had stopped beating by the time they were cut off.

The overwhelming evidence was incontestable. Kelly O'Donnell was found guilty of first-degree murder and for this was sentenced to death on 11 August 1994. Initially she was housed on Death Row at the Pennsylvania State Correctional Institute in Muncy, but was later moved to the State Road Penitentiary in Philadelphia. William Russell Gribble was also found guilty and sentenced to death. Nowadays he is on Death Row at SCI-Greene at Waynesburg.

Despite the watertight nature of the case against her, Kelly O'Donnell's story does contain a degree of mystery and some questions remain unanswered, not the least of which concerns her true level of involvement. With both her and Gribble making contradictory statements, the issue was clouded from the start. In his testimony, the medical examiner stated emphatically that one person acting alone could not have carried out both the removal of the body to the basement and the subsequent dismemberment. This implicates both parties at a stage immediately after the murder itself, but it doesn't provide an answer to the question of who performed the killing. In the event, with the court unable to decide between Gribble and O'Donnell, the two were deemed to be involved to an equal degree in a premeditated plan to lure the victim to the apartment to rob and murder him by smashing his skull with a hammer.

There was also compelling evidence of the killing indeed having been premeditated. The motive was more than likely the large roll of cash that the victim was carrying. Testimony from Agnes McClinchey revealed that the tools that had been used as murder and dismemberment weapons were normally kept in the basement and, since the hammer was already in the living room when the attack took place, this supported the prosecution's assertion that it had been placed in the living room in anticipation of the attack on the victim.

The truth of what happened in the Philadelphia apartment building in the early hours of 12 November 1992 may never emerge. There is, however, one certainty: neither Kelly O'Donnell nor William Gribble suffered a miscarriage of justice. They were both as guilty as sin.

Gribble still sits on Death Row and welcomes pen friends. His interests include motorcycles, fishing, boating, all outdoor activities and, like most men, sport. He says, his tongue in his cheek, 'Being on Death Row has limited my laughter, so I'd like to correspond with someone who has a good sense of humour. I'll respond as soon as I receive your letter and I'll try to make you smile.' His address is: William Gribble, CC-7649 Progress Drive, Waynesburg, PA 15370, USA. But, if you are going to drop him a line, you'd better send a letter soon. His execution was scheduled for 28 January 1999 but he received a stay, though for how long, no one knows.

Conclusion

Dubbed the 'Jigsaw Murder' because the body had been cut up and scattered around town like a macabre jigsaw and took some fitting together again, this was a case guaranteed to receive much media attention. The fact that one of the participants was a young woman only served to fuel the ghoulish media coverage. Indeed, because she was a young, not unattractive woman, Kelly O'Donnell's name has become synonymous with the murder, while William Gribble barely receives a mention. What better nightmare to disturb one's sleep than a woman hacking her victim to pieces in an eerily lit basement and placing an eyeball and a penis in a pencil case?

But the truth, I feel, is somewhat different and, although the couple were very much in love, no existence of folie a deux is evident in the 'Jigsaw Murder'. I do not think this was a premeditated homicide, for it was too ill-conceived and bears the hallmarks of a spontaneous, unplanned murder. If the killing had been planned with the motive of robbery, as has always been claimed, the couple chose the most unsuitable location for a bloody crime scene – a family home, with a friend asleep in bed – when they could have met their victim elsewhere.

Eleftherios Eleftheriou had gone to the apartment to complete a drugs transaction with O'Donnell, who was a regular client, and he was killed by the jealous Gribble, who came home and found the man fondling his girlfriend. Therefore I am inclined to accede to the account given by Gribble, which is far more detailed and can be supported as fact. Added to this is the fact that the victim's penis and an eyeball were placed in the pencil case, 'out of spite', according to Gribble. The record does show that Kelly was nauseated by the crime and was admitted for medical treatment during the course of this gruesome crime.

Both offenders took the dead man's wallet, however,

and both were involved in the dismemberment of the corpse, and this is where I say the complicity begins. After reading Gribble's testimony, I suggest that he killed the man but both he and O'Donnell, for their own reasons, decided to shoulder the blame. In several respects my conclusion is not supported by the evidence of the medical examiner, but, having given the matter close scrutiny, I suggest that, faced with a dying and blood-soaked man, O'Donnell had no other option but to assist her boyfriend in clearing up the mess.

CHAPTER TWO

MARC DUTROUX AND MICHELLE MARTIN
The Devils of the Dungeon

Born in November 1956, Belgian Marc Dutroux was one of five children of Victor and Jeanine, who were both teachers. According to his mother, he was 'a black sheep', although she said there was nothing in his background that could have unhinged him. However, his father had suffered bouts of schizophrenia and ruled the house with a fearsome irrational temper. Moreover, one of Marc's brothers, Serge, committed suicide.

When Dutroux was 15 years old his father left home, and from this time the children were raised by their mother. By now the teenager was showing signs of serious mental disturbance. Nevertheless, he appeared to have hobbies and, at school, an aptitude for metalwork if nothing else; he would later use these skills to create a dungeon. Soon after his sixteenth birthday Dutroux was expelled from school for selling pictures of topless women to other pupils. His education completed, he left home and sold his body to wealthy homosexuals. Then, at 19, he married his first girlfriend, Francoise Dubois, and they had two sons.

In 1983 Francoise found him in bed with primary-school teacher Michelle Martin, who subsequently became his second wife. There has been speculation about the relationship between Dutroux and Michelle, a blonde, hard-faced woman who bore him three more children. Was she the compliant or the dominant partner? Equally culpable, like Myra Hindley and Rose West, or foolishly naive, in the mould of Maxine Carr? Or was she ignorant of all the comings and goings, like Sonia, the wife of one of Britain's most sickening serial killers, Peter Sutcliffe?

What we do know is Dutroux received his first jail sentence in 1989: 14 years for a string of aggravated rapes and sexual assaults. In one attack he thrust a knife between the legs of a six-year-old girl to force her to hand over money. In another he videoed a young girl performing sex acts on him. Incredibly, Dutroux was freed in 1992 after serving just three years. He melted back into suburban life, his appetite for young girls even stronger.

The first of several police blunders occurred early in 1995. Local officers, told by three reliable informants that Dutroux, a recently released sex offender, was building a dungeon in the cellar of one of his five houses, did nothing. Nor, incidentally, did detectives investigate how a self-employed electrician could have bought five houses, or how several large cash deposits, some as much as £30,000, had found their way into his bank account.

In June 1995, in a grim pre-echo of the murder of Jessica

Chapman and Holly Wells in Britain, two girls, Julie Lejeune and Melissa Russo, both aged eight, were snatched as they walked hand-in-hand towards their home in Liege. In Britain and the USA such an incident would have resulted in nationwide news coverage. In Belgium the case was treated with apathy. Despite the reports of his dungeon, five months elapsed before police troubled themselves to visit Dutroux's home. When their search was conducted, officers heard young voices screaming but believed Dutroux's explanation that they were those of his own children having fun. They were not the sounds of childish fun: they were the pitiful screams of Julie and Melissa.

During their search of the house, police found a speculum – a medical instrument used in the examination of bodily orifices – but accepted Dutroux's explanation that it belonged to his wife, Michelle. They also discovered videos marked 'Laurel and Hardy and Disney', which they did not play. Had they done so, they would have seen Dutroux raping his victims. In the event, he remained at large (apart from serving a three-month sentence for theft) and his torture chamber went undiscovered for a further 14 months.

By this time Julie and Melissa had starved to death and been buried in Dutroux's back garden. Each body weighed little more than two stone and there was not a morsel of food in the digestive systems.

Two teenage friends, An Marchal, 17, and Eefje Lambrecks, 19, who were snatched as they hitched a ride back to their hotel after a hypnotist's show in Ostend in the summer of 1995, had also been abused and killed. Their bodies, which were unearthed the following year in one of Dutroux's gardens, lay alongside that of a man called Weinstein. The autopsy proved that he had been tortured by a chain tightened around his testicles. Dirt found in his lungs showed that he had been buried alive.

Only two of Dutroux's victims escaped death. Twelve-year-old Sabine Dardenne was bundled into a white van as she cycled to school in May 1996 and imprisoned in the dungeon for 80 days. Laetitia Delhez, 14, was snatched as she left a swimming pool and kept for six days in the same cell before being released.

It was while he was snaring Laetitia near Belgium's border with Luxembourg that Dutroux was spotted by a student who noted part of the white van's number plate. The details were fed into the national police computer and, to the lasting shame of the police, the name that flashed up on their screens was that of Dutroux, the man they had been repeatedly warned about and whose home they had already searched.

In August 1996 this sedate, cobbled-together little country, where nothing ever seems to happens, received a wake-up call when a huge digger started churning up the garden of a peeling clapboard house in a working-class suburb of Charleroi and grim-faced officers wrapped up two emaciated bodies in tarpaulin and carried them away. In custody was 39-year-old Marc Dutroux, such a cold-hearted and sickening pervert that he could scarcely have been invented. Here was a beast who stood comparison with Fred West and Ian Brady: guilty of a plethora of crimes, including kidnap, false imprisonment, torture, rape and murder.

The police must have hoped Dutroux's disastrously belated arrest would draw a discreet veil over yet one more mishandled investigation in a country known for its abysmal criminal-justice system. In the event, it sparked a national outcry. Hundreds of thousands vented their outrage by marching on the Palace of Justice in Brussels. Child-protection groups were formed; police officers and justice officials resigned; and it seemed that the government might fall. Since the mistakes were partly caused by a lack of co-operation between police in the French and Flemish parts of Belgium, a new national police force was devised. But how can the public feel confident when the investigation was so fundamentally flawed? It is said, for example, that no DNA tests were conducted on the 5,000 human hairs found in the dungeon – checks that could reveal precisely who 'visited' the imprisoned girls. Then there is the controversial treatment of Regina Louf, a witness who claimed to be able to give crucial evidence concerning events in the 1970s and 1980s when sordid, drug-fuelled, debauched sex parties were arranged for rich and privileged Belgians, society figures who were supplied with young girls.

Louf's story is jaw-dropping. When she was 12 her parents began sending her off for weekends with a family friend who made her participate in paedophile sex parties where torture and sado-masochism were routine. Those who raped her and other adolescent girls included judges, a prominent banker and one of Belgium's most prominent politicians, who has since died.

'It was highly organised,' Louf said. 'Big business. A lot of money was involved.'

Louf also described, in chillingly precise detail, how a 15-year-old girl named Chrissie Van Hees (whose body was found dumped in 1984) was murdered for kicks at one of these 'parties'. Within months of coming forward, however, Louf had been publicly discredited as a 'fantasist' by the Prosecutor General, who announced that her evidence would not be heard. A judge who did give her credence was replaced, as was the police team who took her statements. Faced with such inexplicable behaviour, the Belgian public rightly asked who could be relied upon to reveal the truth about Marc Dutroux and his chamber of horror.

But eventually, on 17 June 2004, justice was seen to have been done in the Dutroux case. After a 15-week trial Marc Dutroux was sentenced to life imprisonment for a catalogue of kidnap, child rape and murder that had appalled the world. His estranged wife, Michelle Martin, was convicted of imprisonment that led to the deaths of Julie Lejeune and Melissa Russo.

However, another outcome of the trial provoked scepticism. No firm evidence was found of the criminal network which Regina Louf had alluded to and which, according to Dutroux's testimony, had manipulated him. On the contrary, the murderer was characterised by the prosecution as an 'isolated predator'.

Conclusion

A grim and disturbing example of genuine folie a deux with the dominant figure a male, the compliant follower his wife. Marc Dutroux and Michelle Martin are cast from the same mould as Fred and Rose West and Ian Brady and Myra Hindley, yet their case is perhaps even more sickening because it took eight years to bring the killers to trial. Even in a country strangled by red tape and where police incompetence delayed prosecution, why did justice have to wait so long?

CHAPTER THREE

FREDERICK AND ROSE WEST

The Dread Secrets of
25 Cromwell Street

They were seemingly an ordinary family, living in an ordinary house in an ordinary English street. In their neighbours' eyes quiet, decent folk with a simple way of life, Fred and Rose West were a well-liked couple. There was curtain-twitching and whispers about the number of nocturnal male and female visitors to their home, but nothing to arouse alarm. Besides, it had been going on for years.

But on 24 February 1994 things changed for ever. That morning police arrived at the Wests' house and began to reveal the full horror of what lay beneath 25 Cromwell Street, Gloucester, uncovering what would be reported globally as the most twisted and brutal serial-killing double act in criminal history.

Rose West, born in 1953, was not at all typical of the inward-looking and paranoid personality essential to a genuine folie a deux, although she had suffered a traumatic childhood of systematic sexual abuse and bullying at the hands of her father. In 1969 her mother decided that she could take no more and left her husband with Rose and her two young brothers. It was later that year that Rose met her destiny in Frederick West.

By the time 27-year-old Fred met Rose, aged 15, he had been married with two children and it is now thought that he had already committed two murders, although no evidence exists. Fred and his wife, Rena, had split up and he had taken both children, Charmaine (from an affair Rena had had earlier) and Anne-Marie (their own child), to live with him. Rose acted as a stand-in mother.

Life was not kind to Charmaine: being neither Fred's nor Rose's child, she was tortured and horrifically abused. Police believe that Fred killed and disposed of Charmaine, and when Rena came looking for her he did the same to her. Neither disappearance was reported and when police questioned Rose she told them that Charmaine had 'gone off with her mum'.

With Fred's own background that of an abused child who went on to indulge in warped sexual behaviour, and Rose already experimenting with prostitution, a dangerous chemistry was brewing. Then, in 1970, the couple were married and moved into 25 Cromwell Street. The bomb was fused. For the next 24 years Fred and Rose West kidnapped, raped, tortured and sexually abused a string of female victims. Eventually they were accused of murdering ten women and young girls over a 16-year period ending in 1987.

The Wests took great joy in luring vulnerable runaway girls into their clutches with offers of lifts, lodgings or jobs as nannies. Once inside the 'House of Horrors', the victims were stripped, bound with tape, raped, tortured and then killed.

Often they were invited to lodge with the Wests, and before long the sadistic couple forced their prey to act out their warped sexual fantasies with them. Each girl was subjected to a terrifying ordeal before being killed and hacked to pieces by Fred, who disposed of the evidence in various parts of the house: under the patio, in the cellar and beneath the floorboards were some of the places where police found body parts.

The first person to go missing and arouse police interest was Fred West's second daughter and first child with Rose. Sixteen-year-old Heather had been made a virtual recluse by the taunting and sexual molestation she endured from her mother and father. She disappeared on 17 June 1987 after school. When police started to make enquries, the Wests said that Heather had left home to go and work at a holiday camp in Devon. But an in-joke began to develop among the West children. They would mutter about Heather being 'buried under the patio' at 25 Cromwell Street.

Fred and Rose West were sent for trial but, miraculously, were acquitted after two of the two witnesses refused to testify. However, a diligent policewoman had other ideas. Detective Constable Hazel Savage had gained the confidence of the Wests' five children during the trial and little by little she began to gather information on their parents. On 23 February 1994 she obtained a search warrant for the couple's home and the following day police sealed off the property and began to excavate the garden. There they dug up the remains of 16-year-old Heather, who had 'vanished' seven years earlier. Further excavations in the garden and under the house produced eight more female bodies, including Rose's stepdaughter, Charmaine. A tenth was found under the kitchen of the Wests' former home at 25 Midland Road, Gloucester.

The couple's fate was sealed and Fred West was to face two further charges of murdering his ex-wife and a babysitter and burying them in fields near a house in which he had lived many years earlier. However, on 1 January 1995 he took the coward's way out, escaping his imminent trial by hanging himself at Winson Green Prison in Birmingham. On 22 November the same year Rose was convicted of ten murders and the following day sentenced to life imprisonment.

The authorities believe that Fred probably killed more women than they know about, while Rose, a self-confessed prostitute, still maintains her innocence. At the time of writing, the whereabouts of nine other missing women who frequented 25 Cromwell Street are being investigated.

Conclusion

A classic example of genuine folie a deux. Fred West, who may well have murdered before he fell in with Rose, had a disturbed childhood and at an early age started to fantasise about rough sex. Rose, who had also suffered a dysfunctional childhood, was running on parallel tracks. A chance meeting led to their sharing their almost identical sickening delusions of rough and extreme sex that culminated in an explosion of sado-sexual serial homicide.

As a reasonably good-looking male, Fred West never had trouble finding partners of both sexes – there is solid evidence that he was bisexual. Rose, by contrast, despite having a high sex drive, was sexually starved. An extremely ugly duckling and overweight, she was totally unable to form meaningful relationships with the opposite sex. For this reason she would have considered Fred a good catch, and to keep him she would be willing to please him in any way she could.

I suggest that the male in this murderous partnership was dominant and the female his eager accomplice. Without Fred as a companion, it is doubtful that Rose would have committed murder. Together they lit a fuse, both becoming addicted to perverse sex, abduction, rape, torture and serial murder.

CHAPTER FOUR

CHRISTINE AND LEA PAPIN
The Lambs Who Became Wolves

In February 1933 the whole of France was horrified to learn of an unspeakably savage double murder that had taken place in the north-western town of Le Mans, already renowned for its motor-racing circuit. Two respectable, middle-class women, Madame Lancelin and her daughter, Genevieve, had been murdered by their maids: two sisters who lived in the same house with them.

The maids had not simply killed the Lancelins, but had gouged their eyes out with their fingers while they were clinging on to life, then used a hammer and knife to reduce their terrified victims to a bloody pulp. In both cases there were no wounds to the body. Apart from some gashes to the daughter's legs, the full force of the attack was directed at the heads, and mother and daughter were left unrecognisable.

For many years I have studied the 'mechanics' of homicide. It is now agreed that an examination of the injuries suffered by victims, along with consideration of the varying types of instruments and weapons used to commit murder, can help investigators to narrow down a list of suspects, and, more specifically, point to the killer's modus operandi and mindset. For an example, and one that applies in the Papin case, we may look to the heinous murders committed by Harvey Louis Carignan, aka 'Harv the Hammer'. I spent many years corresponding with Harvey before meeting him at the Minnesota Correctional Facility at Stillwater in 1996.

A large man, built like an ape, Harvey – whose full story is told in my book *Talking with Serial Killers* – killed all of his 30-plus female victims by smashing their heads to unrecognisable pulp while leaving the rest of the body untouched. Why he targeted the head had always been a mystery, not only to the prison psychiatrists, but also to 'Harv the Hammer' himself. However, he had always hated women with a passion, because 'they played mind games with my head'. This throwaway comment proved to be the answer I had been searching for. He was destroying the part of the human body which he perceived to be the cause of all of his life's problems. An excellent parallel might be the mindset of the Papin sisters when they beat their victims' heads to a pulp.

Adding the bizarre to the horrifying, the Papin sisters made no attempt to escape and were found together in bed, naked in each other's arms. This naturally added a dimension of scandal and titillation to the case. Were the maids having a sexual relationship? If so, it was both incestuous and lesbian.

Overnight the sisters, Christine, 27, and Lea (pronounced 'Lay-ah'), 21, became infamous, and the public was inflamed in a way that rarely happens unless a particularly brutal and large-scale massacre takes place. The tabloids went berserk, calling the sisters colourful names like the 'Monsters of Le Mans', 'The Lambs Who Became Wolves' and the 'Raging Sheep'. Suddenly the names of Christine and Lea Papin were known throughout the land.

Almost as striking as the horrifying murders was the contrast between the sisters' violence and their reserved demeanour. They had been with their employers for seven years and had always been quiet, hard-working and well behaved. Their work references described them as 'neat, industrious and proper'. Needless to say, they had no criminal record. They always spent their spare time together, appeared to have no vices and were regular churchgoers. Yet, suddenly and without the slightest warning, these two quiet maids had turned into monsters.

While most of France simply wanted to lynch the sisters, others were intrigued and wanted to understand what had happened. And they had plenty of grist for their intellectual mill. Theories abounded, focusing mainly on the idea that the murders had been an expression of class warfare. The psychoanalysts also weighed in, finding fertile material in the eye-gouging and the apparent sexual relationship between the sisters. Almost eight months elapsed between the murders and the trial, providing ample time for fevered imaginations to dream up theories.

Even while in prison awaiting their trial, the accused managed to provide more food for thought. Christine spent much of her time crying out for her younger sister and begging to be reunited with her. She rolled around on the floor in apparent paroxysms of sexual agony and sometimes expressed herself in sexually explicit language. At other times she seemed to experience hallucinations and visions. During one such attack, in July 1933, she attempted to gouge out her own eyes and had to be put in a straitjacket; all of which pointed to a very disturbed mind.

The following day Christine called for the investigating magistrate and gave him a new statement in which she said that she had not told him the whole truth before; that she had killed Madame and Mademoiselle Lancelin on her own as a result of a kind of 'fit' coming over her; and that Lea had not taken part in the murders. The investigating judge dismissed this statement as merely a spurious way of trying to set Lea free, and the jury at the trial treated it with equal contempt. Moreover, Lea persisted in saying that she had taken part in the murders.

The trial, held in September of that year, was a national event, attended by a vast number of members of the public and press. Police were called in to deal with the crowds outside the packed courthouse. There were moments when the judge had to threaten to clear the court in order to control the emotional reactions of the people in the public gallery, particularly when the eye-gouging was described. Naturally enough, the girls denied having had a sexual relationship, but they never attempted to deny the murders.

Not surprisingly, they were found guilty of murder and Christine was sentenced to death on the guillotine. As the sentence was pronounced, she fell to her knees and had to be assisted by her solicitor. Lea was found guilty of the murder of Madame Lancelin but was not charged with the murder of Genevieve, because doctors concluded that she had died before Lea had joined in the attack. The younger sister was sentenced to ten years' hard labour; in her case the jury had found extenuating circumstances in that she had been completely dominated by the overweening Christine.

Christine's sentence was later commuted to life imprisonment, the normal procedure in the case of women in France at that time. However, her condition deteriorated rapidly in prison. Profoundly depressed at being separated from her beloved Lea, she refused to eat and her condition grew ever worse. She was transferred to the asylum in Rennes, but she never showed the slightest sign of improving as time went by and died in 1937. The official cause of death was cachexia, or wasting away.

Lea, by contrast, continued to be her usual quiet, mild-mannered self while in prison and was released after eight years, having gained remission for good behaviour. She was then joined by her mother, Clemence, and they settled in Nantes, south of Rennes, where Lea worked as a hotel chambermaid under the assumed name of Marie.

The Papin case is a psychological one as much as a criminal one, and it has already been noted that the psychoanalysts had a field day with the sisters. Looking at them from a modern perspective, however, it is clear that Christine would nowadays be diagnosed as a paranoid schizophrenic. In the 1930s there was no effective treatment for her malady, but these days she would be treated with tranquillisers and probably have a longer life, if not a happy one. Lea, on the other hand, never showed signs of being psychotic and there is no reason to believe that she was. She appears to have been very timid, anxious and prone to panic states when under stress, and probably suffered from anxiety disorders. Also, she was of rather low intelligence and dominated by her elder sister.

During the trial, doctors testified that Lea's personality seemed to have disappeared completely into Christine's. Lea was, by all accounts, a shy, good-natured and gentle person. Employers never had a bad word to say about her, whereas Christine had a 'difficult' personality and more than once had been dismissed for insolence. Lea's tragedy was that she was so dominated by Christine. If she had been separated from her at an earlier stage, she certainly would have led a blameless life and never passed through a prison gate. One perceptive employer had in fact suggested to Lea's mother that she should place the girls in separate jobs because Christine was a bad influence on her younger sister but, unfortunately for Lea, the suggestion was ignored.

That the sisters had severe problems is not surprising in view of the family history, in which bad blood ran through every generation. Their paternal grandfather had been given to violent attacks of temper and epileptic fits. Some relatives had died in asylums or committed suicide. Their father, Gustave Papin, had had a drinking problem and had also raped their sister Emilie when she was nine years old. This attack had precipitated their parents' divorce, after which Christine and Emilie had lived in an orphanage at Le Mans for several years. Lea had been looked after by an uncle until he had died, then she too had been placed in an orphanage until she was old enough to work. Their mother had visited them regularly during this time but there was always a certain degree of friction between her and Christine. About two years before the murders there was a complete rift between the girls and their mother, apparently caused by disagreements over money. Afterwards their mother wrote to them on occasion, but was ignored.

The one constant in the lives of the sisters, and their only enduring emotional tie, was their mutual devotion. They worked together whenever they could and it was for this reason that they ended up in the Lancelin household in 1926. Christine started working there first and within a few months persuaded the Lancelins to take on Lea as well. Christine worked as the cook and Lea as the chambermaid. It seems that their contact with the family was minimal and their employers rarely bothered to talk to them. They shared a room on the top floor of the Lancelins' three-storey terraced house and kept largely to themselves. They went to Mass every Sunday, but appeared to have no interests apart from each other.

Psychologically, the girls became enmeshed in a condition that owes its name to the French language: folie a deux – literally, madness in a pair – also known as shared paranoid disorder.

According to statements made by some witnesses, Christine became increasingly agitated and manic in the months leading up to the murders. Her condition was obviously worsening, and on the evening of 2 February 1933 her madness finally came to a head. She attacked first the mother and then the daughter, gouging them with her fingers. At some stage she was joined by Lea and the attack was continued with a hammer and knife, as well as a pewter pot that stood in the hallway. It seems to have lasted for approximately 30 minutes, after which the victims were beyond recognition. The sisters then washed the blood from themselves, went to their room, undressed, climbed into bed and waited for the police to arrive. They made no attempt to escape and no attempt to disguise their deeds.

Although their story is not widely known outside France, the Papin sisters have had, over the years, an impact matched by few people, criminal or otherwise. Plays, films and a never-ending stream of articles and books have been devoted to them. Even most celebrities can't boast of a record like that, and probably only Jack the Ripper has provoked a greater outpouring. The first such work was Jean Genet's play *The Maids*, which was first produced in 1947, when Lea was still alive and probably working in the hotel in Nantes. The Papin sisters have a remarkable capacity to intrigue people, fascinating them and provoking them to intellectual and creative efforts.

In 1966 the French writer Paulette Houdoyer produced a book, *L'Affaire Papin*, which told the sisters' story in an unfortunately novelistic format. Apparently as a result of this book, Lea was interviewed by a journalist from *France-Soir*. In this interview we learn that she experienced vivid visions of Christine appearing before her in spirit form and was certain that her sister was in paradise. She still kept old photos of Christine, as well as an ancient trunk crammed with beautiful dresses that the girls had made for themselves before the murders. She also stated that she was saving to return to Le Mans and rejoin her other sister, Emilie, who had become a nun at the age of 16, but there is no evidence that she did so. The interview in *France-Soir* is the last record of the lives of Lea and Christine Papin.

It was thought for many years that Lea had died in 1982 at the age of 70, but the French film-maker Claude Ventura recently repudiated this idea. In the course of making his documentary film *En Quete des Soeurs Papin*, he found various anomalies in the official records. This led him to the astonishing discovery that Lea had not died in 1982 but was still alive when he was making his film, released in 2000.

As late as December of that year, Lea was said to be still alive in a hospice somewhere in France. She was half-paralysed and unable to speak as the result of a stroke. She would have been 89 at the time. There has been no further news of her since then.

Conclusion

Most criminologists agree that genuine folie a deux existed between Christine and Lea Papin, but is this view correct? There seems to be no real evidence that the sisters conspired to kill their employers, their actions being initiated by the psychotic and stronger Christine, while Lea was the weaker person who stood on the sidelines, and the court's verdict acknowledged this. So it is probable that Christine, with her unbalanced mind, would have resorted to murder at some time with or without her sister's collaboration.

CHAPTER FIVE

DEBRA BROWN AND ALTON COLEMAN
The Midwest Monsters

The only good thing to emerge from the trial and conviction of Debra Brown and Alton Coleman is that they are no longer at large to repeat their monstrous crimes. In a cross-country binge of up to eight murders, seven rapes, three kidnappings and 14 armed robberies, they left a trail of repugnant and perverted acts of sadistic violence that ended when they were arrested following the abduction of two little girls in Indiana.

On 18 June 1984, seven-year-old Tamika Turks and her nine-year-old niece, Annie, were walking from a candy store to their home when Brown and Coleman confronted them. The two persuaded the children to walk into nearby woods to play a game. Once there, they removed Tamika's shirt and tore it into small strips which they used to bind and gag their little victims. The terrified Tamika began to cry. Infuriated by this, Brown held the child's nose and mouth closed, while

Coleman stamped on her chest before strangling her to death. After being carried a short distance, Annie was forced to perform oral sex on both Brown and Coleman. Then the man raped her. The two perverted monsters finally choked the little girl until she became unconscious. When she awoke, they were gone.

Police discovered Tamika dead in bushes close by. She had been strangled with an elastic strip of bed sheet. (The same fabric was later found in the apartment shared by the killers.) Annie had received cuts from the rape so deep that her intestines were protruding into her vagina.

This was not the first of such crimes committed by this evil pair: evidence of a strikingly similar murder, in Ohio, was admitted at the trial and probably had some effect on the verdict. Coleman was executed on 26 April 2002 at the Southern Ohio Correctional Facility, Lucasville. As of 3 July 2004, Brown is on Death Row at the Indiana Women's Prison, Indianapolis.

Conclusion

Once again, cast almost exactly in the same mould as Hindley and Brady and Rose and Fred West, we find two people who harboured extreme sexual and violent fantasies which lay dormant until they teamed up into a classic folie a deux relationship.

CHAPTER SIX

LYNDA LYON BLOCK AND GEORGE SIBLEY JR

Husband and Wife on the Run with Guns

This is the story of the only husband and wife in America sentenced to die by electrocution for a crime they say they did not commit. George Sibley Jr and Lynda Lyon Block said they shot and killed a very bad cop. The State of Alabama said it was murder, but the couple argued that it was self-defence, the dead officer being the only other witness to how the shooting began and that the officer's personnel file, which they claim would have shown a long history of abuse of the public, was not shown to the jury. It was a predictable verdict: guilty of capital murder. The sentence was death in the electric chair, and Lynda Lyon Block, silver-haired with a pleasant face, was executed on 10 May 2002.

The 54-year-old and her common-law husband were on the run after failing to appear on a charge of domestic violence. They stopped in the town of Opelika, with Block's nine-year-old son in the car, so that she could use the telephone in a Wal-Mart parking lot, and it was then that things started to go wrong.

Police sergeant Roger Lamar Motley had just finished lunch and was out shopping for supplies for the jail when a woman came up to him and told him there was a car parked in the lot with a little boy inside. The woman was worried about him and afraid that the family was living in their car. Would he check on them?

Motley cruised up and down the rows of cars and finally pulled up behind a Ford Mustang. Sibley was inside with the boy, waiting for Block to finish a call to a friend from a payphone in front of the store. Motley asked Sibley for his driver's licence. Sibley said he didn't need one and was trying to explain why when Motley put his hand on his service revolver. In response Sibley pulled out a gun. Motley uttered a four-letter expletive and spun away to take cover behind his car. Sibley crouched by the bumper of the Mustang, and people in the parking lot screamed, hid beneath their cars and ran back into the store as the two men began firing at each other.

Preoccupied by the threat in front of him, Motley did not see Block until the very last moment. She had dropped the phone, pulled a 9mm Glock pistol from her bag and was running towards the scene firing. Motley turned. Block remembered later how surprised he looked. She kept on firing. She could tell that a bullet had struck the officer in the chest. Staggering, Motley reached into the car. Block went on firing, thinking he was trying to get a shotgun. But he was grabbing for the radio. 'Double zero,' he managed to say – the code for help. He died in a nearby hospital that afternoon. Later, in letters to friends and supporters, Block described Motley as a 'bad cop' and a wife beater with multiple complaints against him. She said she was prohibited from bringing up the police sergeant's record in court. However, his personnel file reveals no mention of any misbehaviour and his wife says he was a kind, patient man.

Block and Sibley received death sentences. True to their 'patriot' ideology, Block waived her appeals. She refused to accept the validity of Alabama's judicial system, claiming that Alabama never became a state again after the Civil War. To further aggravate matters, she was completely unco-operative with her court-appointed attorney, who nevertheless tried to work against her death sentence. Hers was to be the first execution of a female in Alabama since 1957, and she became the ninth female executed in the US since reinstatement of the death penalty in 1976. However, there are always two sides to a story, and perhaps this is the time to consider the somewhat romanticised account of the episode that Block gave shortly before her execution in the electric chair.

'It was fate – and a libertarian philosophy – that brought George and me together at a Libertarian Party meeting in Orlando, Florida, in 1991,' Block said. 'George had been attending for a year when I entered the meetings for the first time. I was immediately at home with the small but active group of intellectual activists, and George and I were among a smaller group that together attended political rallies.

'A year later, my marital problems came to a head and my husband agreed to leave the house to our son and me and to start divorce proceedings. At that time, needing to enlarge my fledgling publishing business, I accepted an investment partnership offer from George, who had seen my potential as a writer and publisher, and who had also seen a business opportunity for himself.

'Our partnership, which had begun as friendship, soon blossomed into romance – a true libertarian relationship of two highly intellectual, fiercely independent individualists who live passionately. We soon realised that we were soul mates – totally compatible in every way. We married in 1992 and our love and friendship has grown continually.

'George helped me launch a new magazine – *Liberatus* – and we published hard-hitting articles about political corruption. We pioneered a revocation process that eliminated driver's licences, school-board surveillance on my home-schooled son, IRS demands, and state revenue notices. Every document we filed was challenged by the various agencies, but, after we sent them legal proof of our right to revocate, they went away. We taught others this process in papers, video and seminars. We spoke on local talk radio. The local, state and federal agencies began to notice the influx of revocation documents from Florida.

'Our hell began, not with the agencies, but with Karl, my ex-husband, who had decided to sue me for possession of the valuable house. He petitioned the judge to allow him back into my house until the case was settled, a preposterous idea. George urged me not to go to Karl's apartment to try to reason with him, knowing Karl to be a violent-tempered man. But I was desperate to keep my home and was prepared to offer him a deal, so George went with me. Karl let us in to talk, but he became angry at my attempt to bargain. In a rage, he lunged at me. George managed to pull him off, but Karl had sustained a cut from a small knife I had pulled out and held up as a warning just as he had grabbed me. The cut was not large or deep, and, when we offered to take him to a medical centre, he refused, though he did allow us to bandage the cut.

'George and I were arrested in our home at 2.30am that same night. Karl had called the police and told them we had broken in and attacked him. George and I had never been arrested before, never been in any trouble other than traffic tickets. We were in shock – George's face was pale and grim, and I felt faint when the deputy began to read us our "rights". They put us both, handcuffed, in the back seat of a patrol car and we tried to console each other. We agreed not to make any statements until we got a lawyer. I told him tearfully how sorry I was that he got pulled into this mess between Karl and me, and he assured me that it was all right, that he didn't blame me. I would have gladly borne the ordeal myself to spare him this. At the jail, as George was taken away, he looked back at me one last time and said, "I love you, Lynda." Those words sustained me through the next five days of hell.

'Because we were charged with "domestic violence", George and I could not make bond [bail] without a hearing, and we had to wait five days for that. I was placed in a cell with 30 other crying, arguing, loud-talking women. I chose a top bunk on the far end, and sat and cried. I was terrified, because I had recently been interviewed on the radio about apparent inconsistencies in the jail accounts, and the sheriff had ordered the radio station padlocked that night.

'I could not eat those five days. The meat stank, and the vegetables and whipped potatoes were watery. I lived on whatever cartons of milk I could trade for my trays. I was astounded that the long-timers would eagerly bid for my tray, and I managed to get paper and pencil as well. Writing helped me keep sane. I was able to converse with some of the women who recognised me as "fresh meat" and protected me from the lesbians and bullies. I called my mother to see how my son was doing, and she told me that Karl said he would make sure I went to prison and that he didn't want his son. When I began crying, the others stopped talking and looked at me. A large, black woman came over and hugged me to her ample bosom, and I felt a strange kinship to these thrown-away, forgotten wives, daughters and mothers.

'The most humiliating experience was the strip search. When ordered to strip for a body search, I froze. I had never undressed for anyone except my husband and doctor. Silent tears ran down my face as I disrobed, then turned to squat so they could see if I had any drugs protruding from my rectum. When I dressed, my face was red with shame. I felt violated, mentally raped. I never did get over that.

'George and I did get out on bond the fifth day. We were sure that our ordeal was over and that we would soon prove our innocence at trial. We were so naive.

'It soon became evident that politics had entered our case. When our trial date arrived, we felt unprepared. George and I immediately fired our attorney and asked the judge for a continuance to prepare for trial. He said no – we either plead "Nolo contendere" [No contest] or go to trial that day; and, if we were convicted, we would be sent directly to prison for a mandatory three-year term. We felt we were forced to sign "No contest".

'We were still determined to fight it; we had a month before sentencing. We filed papers arguing we had been denied a right to a fair trial, sending copies to the Governor, Lt Governor,

Chief Judge of Florida, Attorney General, and the Sheriff. Friends and supporters flooded these officials with faxes calling for an investigation, throwing their offices in an uproar according to a secretary in the Chief Judge's office.

'We didn't show up for sentencing; fearing Judge Hauser was going to send us to prison anyway. We had three days to file a temporary restraining order in federal court, but the man who had promised to draft the document never did, and a capias was issued for our arrest.

'A friend called me the evening of the third day, his voice shaking. "Lynda, I just heard there's a plan to raid your house. They know you have guns – they're going to use a SWAT team." I was incredulous. "A SWAT team!" His voice became softer, sadder. "You and George have made a lot of important people angry. They're going to kill you and then say you shot at them first." He paused, to let this sink in, then said, "I've put myself at great risk telling you this. Please, get out of Florida. They mean business."

'George had heard this on the speakerphone. His face was as sombre as mine. As a last, desperate attempt to stop this insanity, I called to talk to Sheriff Beary. I had interviewed him when he ran for election. But he wouldn't come to the phone.

'George and I were not criminals and we did not want to become fugitives. But my friend had made it clear we had no choice. At the invitation of a friend in Georgia to stay with him, we loaded our car and George, my son Gordon and I left Florida that night.'

Block's description of the shooting that followed seems accurate:

'We stayed in Georgia for three weeks, but we knew we

couldn't stay longer and endanger our friends. We decided to go to Mobile, Alabama, a large port where strangers come and go every day, and figure out how to straighten out the Florida mess. We stayed in a motel in Opelika, Alabama, while waiting for our friend to turn our remaining silver coin into cash, and then we started out on 4 October 1993 for Mobile. On the way I spotted a drugstore with a payphone in front and suggested to George that we stop there so I could get a vitamin supplement and call a friend in Orlando. After Gordon and I came out of the store, he got back in the car to wait while George and I made the call.

'While I was on the phone, George stood by, watching the traffic and people going by. He noticed one particular woman in a red Blazer pull in beside our car. She got out and looked at our car, a Mustang hatchback, with pillows stacked on top of all our belongings. It later came out at trial that she had presumed that we were transients, living out of our car, with a child obviously not in school. Actually, I always carried my own pillows when sleeping in motels.

'Because I had run out of change for the phone, my call was cut off, so we left. But as we were leaving the shopping centre I remembered my friend had an 800 number and I then spotted a phone in front of Wal-Mart. So George pulled the car into a parking space and he and Gordon stayed in the car while I walked to the store to call. Unknown to us, the woman saw a police officer coming out of a nearby store. She approached him and told him that we were living out of our car and she was concerned about the child. She gave him a description of our car and left.

'Roger Motley was the supply officer for the Opelika Police

Department and hadn't been on patrol for years. He was irritated that he had to stop and check on this situation. He drove his car up and down the aisles, and when he found our car, he stopped behind it.

'I had my back turned while talking on the phone and didn't see the officer pull up. When George saw the officer in the rear-view mirror, he got out of the car, closed the door, and waited to see what the officer wanted. The officer approached George with the typical "I'm the guy with the badge and the gun" attitude. In a curt voice he demanded to see George's driver's licence. George told him he didn't have one, and was prepared to get our legal exemption papers from the car. The officer then decided to arrest George and told him to put his hands on the car. George hesitated, knowing this was an arrest, yet he had done nothing illegal. Motley, thoroughly irritated now, reached for his gun. When George saw him go for his gun, he reacted instinctively and drew his own gun. When Motley saw George's gun, he said, "Oh shit," and, with his hand still on his gun, turned and ran for cover behind the police car.

'When I heard the popping noises, it took me a couple of seconds to realise it was gunfire. I heard people yelling and running to get out of the way. Quickly I turned and saw Motley crouched beside his car, shooting at George. Fear gripped my stomach. I cried, "Oh God, no!" and, dropping the phone, began running, ignoring the people scrambling for cover.

'I saw George standing between the rear of our car and the right side of the police car; he was holding his gun in his right hand, but his left arm was hanging strangely. Motley didn't see me approach, and just as I came to a stop I pulled my own gun and shot several times. He turned to me in surprise, and, as he did, one of my bullets struck him in the chest and he fell backwards, almost losing his balance in his crouched position. His gun was pointed at me and I prayed he wouldn't shoot. Instead, he crawled into the car and, after grabbing the radio microphone, he drove off.

'I immediately ran to our car and got in. The parking lot was quiet – everyone had sought shelter inside the stores. I was shaken, yet incredibly calm. "What happened?" I asked. George's face was extremely pale. "He tried to arrest me for not having a driver's licence." He shook his head in disbelief. "I was going to show him our papers, but he didn't give me a chance – and he went for his gun." He looked at me, his eyes begging me to believe him. "I couldn't just stand there and let him shoot me."

'I did believe him. George is the most honest person I know. He would not have placed himself or us in danger. He took the law seriously. He was never the show-off gunslinger-type and would walk away before being drawn into a fight.

'I told him that I believed him; but that we had just shot a cop and the whole police force would be gunning for us. We had to get out of there fast. It was then I noticed his arm and he raised it up to show me. With characteristic understatement, he said simply, "I've been hit." A bullet had pierced his arm. Although blood was dribbling down his arm, it didn't obscure the hole. I examined his arm and could see that the bullet passed through his forearm and miraculously had not broken any bone or cut through a tendon or artery. I had an advanced medical kit in the car and I knew I could treat it later.

'George manoeuvred our car deftly through the streets, trying to get us out of the area quickly while not attracting attention. I tried to calm Gordon, who was crying and shaking, and I looked at the map for the best route out.

'We had gone only 1/4 mile down the country road when we came upon a rise – and then we saw the roadblock, at least 20 cars. George slowed down, then pulled the car over to the side of the road and cut the engine. He sat in calm resignation, and then looked over at me. I said quietly, "I guess this is it, isn't it?" He nodded, then we both looked out at the policemen, detectives, deputies coming at us from all directions, guns drawn, shouting, "Get out of the car and put your hands up!" It was an incredible, surrealistic scene, as though I was experiencing a virtual-reality game where I could feel the action and motion, but then the game would end and I would go back to living my real life again. My son's sobs brought me abruptly back to reality.

'I rolled down my window and put out my raised hand. "Stop!" I shouted. "I have a child in the car!" I could plainly see the closest officer's face turn pale, and he quickly spoke into the radio on his shoulder. "There's a child in the car!" he shouted. The Opelika Police never told these Auburn Police this. The word was quickly passed and then he said, "OK, ma'am, we won't shoot. You can let the child go."

'I talked to Gordon, calmed him down, then I opened the door and let him out, told him to be a good boy and that they would take care of him, and pointed him toward a plain-clothes policeman. I gave him a last kiss, holding his handsome nine-year-old face in my hand, to get a last picture in my mind of the child I may never see again. I watched him walk quickly away to the beckoning officer and I felt as though my heart would break.

I had planned his conception, had nurtured him through sickness, and home-schooled him. No one could have possibly loved a child as much as I loved mine, and he was walking out of my life only half-grown, unfinished.

'As soon as Gordon was taken away, the police then shouted at us to surrender. I turned to George and asked, "What do you want to do?" He had lost a lot of blood and was pale and tired. "I don't know." I made a decision for us. I told the officer, "We are not surrendering. You will have to kill us first."

'For four hours George and I sat in the car and talked. I held my gun where the officers could see that we were not going to surrender peacefully. The officer continued to talk to me to get information about us. George and I spent the time talking about the shooting, as he explained to me what happened. We discussed our plans for our future together, all gone. We discussed the probability that, if the officer died, we'd be charged with capital murder and executed. If we decided to fight in court, it could take years. We knew we did not want to spend the rest of our lives in prison for an act of self-defence. We knew that it would be our word against a cop's word, and we had already seen how the justice system worked. We then talked about suicide.

'My religious belief is that suicide is wrong, but now I was faced with the total hopelessness of our situation. I told George that the only regret I had in all this is that I would not be able to raise my son. We discussed all our options.

'As dusk settled in, we saw the SWAT team position themselves around us. The regular police had pulled back an hour earlier. A negotiator got on the police car hailer and tried to talk us into surrendering. We said no, that if they tried to come after us we would shoot ourselves. He then tried to bargain with us. What did we want? I printed my answers on notebook paper with a marker and George held it out his window for them to read – to talk to my son, to talk to the press and to talk to clergy of my religion. He agreed to all these things (he lied – they did none of them), but we had to surrender first.

'Finally, the showdown came. The SWAT teams had us surrounded. We were told that, if we did not surrender in five minutes, they would lob tear gas through the windows of the car and take us anyway. George and I had been sitting with our guns in hand. We had planned to shoot ourselves in the head at the same time. George looked at me with such sorrow and asked, "Would you mind if I stayed in the car and shot myself while you surrender? At least you could have some decision in Gordon's future."

'I looked up at him with surprise, my eyes filling with tears at the thought that this honest, loving, gentle man who had waited over 40 years to find the right woman and found me, spending all those years in patient waiting, should now die alone with a bullet to his head.

'"No," I said firmly, "I'm not going anywhere without you. Either we surrender together or we die together. I'll follow you, George – whatever you want, I'm leaving it up to you."

'A totally surprised expression came to his direct, penetrating gaze. Until that very moment, he had not realised the depth of my love for him; that I would rather stay with him, even in death, and that I would trustingly place my life in his hands.

'"If we surrender, it will be years before this is resolved."

'"I know," I said, "but at least we'd be fighting this together."

'He then took my left hand in his right, stained with blood where he had tried to staunch the wound, and raised my hand to his lips. "No," he said with renewed determination. "We will surrender so we can fight this. We have to do whatever we can to see that Gordon is taken care of, and to prove our innocence – if only for his sake." For the first time in months, hope was in his voice: "We will fight this to the end, and, if they still execute us, we'll die knowing we fought for what was right." He then gave a tired smile.

'"Yes," I said with respect and admiration for my husband. With a look of tenderness I'll always remember, he leaned forward and kissed me, a gentle, parting kiss, perhaps the last we would ever share. Then, at a nod from him, we laid down our guns and exited the car with our hands up.'

Sibley remains on Death Row at Holman Prison, near Atmore, Virginia. It could be several years before his appeal is decided.

Conclusion

Nowhere in this story is there a single element of folie a deux. Here we have a loving couple who became involved in a downward spiral which culminated in the shooting of a police officer. The crime was not premeditated: the discharging of firearms was a spontaneous act to avoid being arrested while on the run.

The shooting of a police officer is first-degree homicide and demands the death penalty in US states that endorse execution, so Block's fate will have come as no surprise to the reader. Some might be swayed in the couple's favour by her Bonnie and Clyde-like account, but there is too much icing on the cake for me. The questions I ask myself are: why are such a 'decent' couple on the run with firearms? And why carry such weapons unless one is prepared to use them? This aside, they were clearly devoted to each other and Sibley loves and honours his wife's memory to this day.

CHAPTER SEVEN

LOIS NADEAN SMITH
Mean Nadean

Lois Nadean Smith had gained a reputation for having a foul temper since high school. She was nicknamed 'Mean Nadean', and with her podgy face, shifty eyes and uneven teeth, her looks certainly earned the sobriquet.

At the age of 61 Lois Smith, a former minister's daughter, was convicted of the murder on 4 July 1982 of 21-year-old Cindy Baillee in Gans, Oklahoma. Cindy had been the girlfriend of Smith's son, Greg Smith. Along with Greg and another woman, Mean Nadean picked up Baillee from a motel in Tahlequah early on the morning of the murder. As they drove off, Smith challenged Baillee about rumours that Baillee had arranged for Greg's murder – charges that she denied. Smith choked Baillee and stabbed her in the throat as they drove to the home of Smith's ex-husband in Gans.

There Smith forced Baillee to sit in a recliner and taunted her with a pistol, before firing several shots at her. Baillee dropped to the floor, and, while Greg reloaded the pistol, Smith laughed and jumped on Baillee's neck. She then fired four shots into her victim's chest and two into the back of her head. An autopsy revealed nine gunshot wounds to Baillee's body.

For her last meal in the death house at the Oklahoma State Prison in McAlester, Smith requested barbecued ribs, onion rings, strawberry and banana cake, which she washed down with cherry lemonade. At 9pm CST, on 4 December 2001, as she lay strapped to the gurney waiting for the lethal injection, she made a final statement: 'To the family I want to say I'm sorry for the pain and loss I caused you. I ask you to forgive me… To live is Christ. To die is to gain. To be absent from the body is to be present with the Lord, thank you Jesus.'

Three minutes later she was dead.

Conclusion

Straightforward homicide and not folie a deux. 'Mean Nadean' was a stone-cold killer, with no mitigation in her favour at all.

CHAPTER EIGHT

LAWRENCE SIGMUND BITTAKER AND RAY LEWIS NORRIS
A Strictly Male Folie a Deux

Lawrence Sigmund Bittaker was serving time for rape when he met Ray Lewis Norris at the California Men's Colony in San Luis Obispo in 1978. They recognised soul mates in each other, for they enjoyed the same sick sexual fantasies, and they soon became inseparable fellow cons. While still confined they hatched a grisly plot to kidnap, rape and murder teenage girls 'for fun' as soon as they were freed. Their plan was to kill at least one girl from each teenage year, 13–19, and videotape the murders.

Paroled on 15 November 1978, Bittaker began making preparations for the crime spree, including the purchase of a van that he dubbed 'Murder Mac'. Norris was released on 15 June 1979, and, after a period of observation at the Atascadero State Mental Hospital, he joined up with his sidekick at a motel in Los Angeles.

Nine days later, on 24 June, Cindy Schaeffer, aged 16,

vanished after a church service at Redondo Beach, never to be seen alive again. She was bundled into the back of the van and driven up into the mountains, where Bittaker and Norris repeatedly raped her before jointly strangling the girl with a wire coat hanger. Her body was dumped in a nearby canyon.

On 8 July they transported another victim, 18-year-old Andrea Joy Hall, along the Pacific Coast Highway to a spot where she was subjected to repeated sexual abuse before Bittaker rammed an ice pick through her ear and into her brain.

On 2 September 13-year-old Jacqueline Leah Lamp and 15-year-old Jackie Gilliam were picked while hitching a ride in Redondo Beach. After two days of torture, their bodies were thrown over a cliff.

At Halloween the same year the pattern of abduction and sexual torture was repeated. This time 16-year-old Shirley Ledford was abducted and her body left on the front lawn of her house in Sunland, where it was found by horrified neighbours. Strangled with a coat hanger, she had first been subjected to sadistic and barbaric abuse. Her breasts and face were mutilated, her arms slashed, her body covered with bruises.

Bittaker and Norris were arrested on charges stemming from an earlier assault, carried out on 30 September in Hermosa Beach. According to reports, their female victim had been sprayed with Mace, abducted in a silver van and raped before she managed to escape. The woman ultimately failed to make a positive ID on the two men, but the arresting officers discovered drugs in their possession and held both in jail for violation of parole.

Norris started showing signs of strain in custody. At a preliminary hearing in Hermosa Beach he offered an apology 'for my insanity' and was soon regaling officers with tales of brutal murder. According to his statements, the girls had been approached at random, photographed by Bittaker and offered rides, free marijuana or jobs in modelling. Most turned down the offers, but some were abducted forcibly, the van's radio drowning out their screams as they were driven to a remote mountain fire road for sessions of rape and torture. Videotape recordings of Jacqueline Lamp's final moments were recovered from Bittaker's van and detectives counted over 500 photos of smiling young women among the suspect's effects.

On 9 February 1980 Norris led deputies to shallow graves in San Dimas Canyon and the San Gabriel Mountains, where the skeletal remains of Lamp and Gilliam were recovered. An ice pick protruded from Gilliam's skull and the remains bore other marks of cruel mistreatment.

Charging the prisoners with five counts of murder, Los Angeles County Sheriff Peter Pitchess announced that Bittaker and Norris might be linked to the disappearance of 30–40 more young women. By 20 February the stack of confiscated photographs had yielded 19 missing girls, but none was ever traced, and Norris had exhausted his desire to talk.

On 18 March Norris pleaded guilty on five counts of murder, turning state's evidence against his accomplice. In return for his co-operation he received a sentence of 45 years to life, with parole possible in 2010. Bittaker – nicknamed 'Pliers' for his favourite instrument of torture – denied everything. At his trial, on 5 February 1981, he testified that Norris first informed him of the murders after their arrest in 1979. A jury chose not to believe him, returning a guilty verdict on 17 February. On 24 March, in accordance with the jury's recommendation, Bittaker was sentenced to die. The judge also imposed an alternative sentence of 199 years and four months in prison, to take effect in the event that Bittaker's death sentence is commuted on appeal. This twisted sado-monster is still on Death Row and awaiting his appointment with the executioner.

Conclusion

Although sick and evil characters, it is doubtful that these two men would have committed serial homicide if they had not entered into a folie a deux relationship. However, realising while in prison that they shared the same fantasies, they planned their murderous campaign in some detail before their release. So this is a genuine example of folie a deux, the more so because, while committing these brutal and sadistic crimes, they revelled in spurring each other on, like the Wests and Brady and Hindley.

CHAPTER NINE

RENUKA KIRAN SHINDE AND SEEMA MOHAN GAVIT
The Mumbai Child Killings

I have visited Death Rows across the world, from Changi Jail in Singapore to the Ellis Unit in Texas, but nothing could have prepared me for the stench and squalor of Death Row at Central Prison, Mumbai, formerly Bombay, where I was to come face to face with the two most heinous serial killers in India's history. What made this brief encounter even more sickening was the fact that they are both women.

There are ten cells on Mumbai's Death Row. This brick corridor, from which the black paint is peeling, has no windows on the right, and there is a row of barred, black-painted cells on the left. There is one door leading into the corridor and one door out, the second just a few steps from the ancient triple gallows. The air is suffocating, with a stench of urine, faeces, cheap disinfectant and human sweat.

At the end of the 'Row' two women sit in their 'units' on concrete slabs that serve as beds. There are no mattresses, only straw, changed once a week. In colder weather the two killers are allowed a grey blanket to keep out the chill. There are neither chairs nor a table; their only 'luxuries' are a filthy toilet and a washbasin. Recreation is allowed once a week: a walk in the confined yard and a shower.

Prison regulations permit no physical or verbal contact with the residents of Death Row; not even the guards are permitted to speak with the inmates except to discipline their charges. So these two women remain silent, forbidden even to communicate with each other. Each is shackled by a chain leading from an ankle to the wall. This restraint stays on day after day, year after year. There is just enough slack to reach the food hatch, but no more. There are no books, no newspapers, no radio or TV.

Seema Mohan Gavit looked at me with inquisitive eyes. Once a dark-haired beauty, she now looked like an old lady, her features withered and drawn. She stared at my unfamiliar face. There was no warmth, no emotion at all – just the gaze of the living dead. Renuka Kiran Shinde was asleep, or feigning sleep, curled up tight in a ball, her back towards me; only her shallow breathing hinted that she was alive. I stayed for three minutes, then I was gone.

With the notable exception of the USA, the Western world has rejected the death penalty. Even Russia, a one-time devotee of capital punishment, has abolished execution, although this was done to further its alignment with Europe. Improving its criminal-justice system allowed it to sign the European Convention on Human Rights and enjoy the resultant economic benefits. However, outside Europe, there are many countries that are not disposed to embrace such humane principles, instead seeing the ultimate form of punishment as a useful expedient for a range of offences. In these countries Death Row and execution are often the consequences of a guilty verdict and will remain so for the foreseeable future.

India is just such a state, and since the beginning of 2001 the condemned cells in Mumbai have housed the two women I was allowed to see there. These monstrous killers of children carried out a series of murders and abductions that rightly earned them the death sentence.

It was on 28 June 2001, at Kolhapur, that Renuka Kiran Shinde, 29, and Seema Mohan Gavit, 25, were sentenced to death. According to reports, these two sisters, together with their mother, Anjanabai, and Kiran Shinde, Renuka's husband, had been charged with abducting 13 children between 1990 and 1996, using them for criminal purposes, murdering nine of them and disposing of the bodies.

There is no doubt that, had these crimes taken place in the West, they would have received massive exposure in the press and broadcast media and would have come to be regarded as being among the worst enormities to have been perpetrated against children in the 20th century. The story of this family's involvement in a grisly saga of abduction, torture and murder begins in the 1960s, when a runaway girl, twice-married Anjanabai, took to the life of a prostitute and thief. She gained notoriety among the police for picking pockets, snatching bags and other forms of theft, including stalking railway platforms to seek out well-off victims.

In the 1980s Anjanabai began to rob women who had children with them. She would select victims in crowded places and smear a dab of ointment on the child. This preparation was a healing balm which caused sufficient irritation to make the child cry, and, as the mother bent down to comfort her offspring, Anjanabai would snatch the woman's bag or any gold chains she was wearing.

Around 1990 Anjanabai was joined in her life of crime by her two teenage daughters, Renuka and Seema, together with Renuka's husband, Kiran Shinde. This quartet would kidnap children and use them as decoys while they stalked their victims. The gang kept the abducted children in two flats in Maharashtra, treating them with appalling cruelty, starving and torturing them. This regime took its toll on the health of the infants and eventually rendered them useless for their role in criminal activities. When this happened to a child, it would be killed. It becomes all the more horrifying when it is realised that most of the children were less than three years old.

One child, Santosh, only 18 months old, had his head smashed against an iron bar. Four-year-old Pankaj Mhamulkar was hung upside down and had his head banged against a wall several times simply because he had become too friendly with neighbours.

The four monsters were eventually exposed in October 1996. Anjanabai held a grudge against her ex-husband, Mohan, because he had remarried. She kidnapped his elder daughter, Kranti, aged nine, and killed her. Not content with this, the gang returned to kidnap the second of Mohan's daughters, but his wife recognised them and contacted the police. The gang were arrested and the investigators recovered the remains of five of the murdered children.

Anjanabai, the matriarch of this vile and murderous family, died of a brain haemorrhage while in custody in December 1997. However, her two daughters were tried and convicted, both receiving the death sentence that she too would have undoubtedly faced had she survived. Kiran Shinde was pardoned as he had turned informer.

Asked exactly how little Santosh was used and abused, Shinde said Anjanabai, who had the child in her arms, banged his head on the road in front of a man whom Seema had tried to pickpocket. When the man saw blood oozing from the baby's head, he panicked and let Seema go. Shinde said he was at home with his son in Pune when the incident took place. After that the foursome travelled to Kolhapur in April 1991, where they continued their pickpocketing spree at the Mahalaxmi temple and the central bus stand.

One night Anjanabai killed Santosh and the gang abandoned his body near the central bus stand. Asked why Santosh had been killed, Shinde said the child was seriously wounded and would not stop crying. 'Renuka said the boy was of no use to us now and that he will keep on crying and might get us caught. Therefore we killed him,' he confessed.

The judge, G.L. Edke, described the case as falling within the ambit of 'rarest of the rare', one that involved extreme cruelty and brutality, the punishment for which could only be death by hanging. It is only the fourth time that women have received the death penalty in India and the sisters showed no emotion or remorse on hearing the verdict, which was delivered in a packed courtroom.

A request was made to the court by Sharmila, the mother of one of the child victims, that both accused should not just be hanged but also made to suffer a slow death. And who would argue with this grief-stricken woman?

Conclusion

A mild element of folie a deux exists in this case in which there was a meeting of four perverse criminal minds. Yet here I lean towards the notion of 'accomplices', as the principal motives for killing were financial gain and expediency. The 'tools' they were using, to good effect, were babies and very young children. When these were no longer considered efficient, they were disposed of with as much compassion as a safecracker dumps an empty acetylene bottle. My personal opinion after seeing the autopsy photographs? No rope could be long enough!

CHAPTER TEN

CHRISTA GAIL PIKE AND TADARYL DARNELL SHIPP
The Devil's Daughter

When she was sentenced on 29 March 1996, 21-year-old Christa Gail Pike became the youngest woman on Death Row. The crime that earned her this distinction was one of the most savage and evil single killings in the history of Tennessee. Pike's murder of her 19-year-old love rival is a disturbing story of uncontrolled violence with sexual undertones and satanic connections.

Christa Pike had been brought up with little parental guidance and what there was is hard to understand as being in her best interests: when she was only 14 her parents had allowed her to have a sexual relationship with her live-in boyfriend. Moreover, with their permission, she had dropped out of high school, although later she enrolled on the Job Corps Program in order to receive her diploma.

It was while attending the Job Corps Center in Knoxville that Christa met two other youngsters and close friendships developed. Tadaryl Darnell Shipp was 16 and came from Memphis. He and Christa began dating. The other friend was 18-year-old Shadolla Renee Peterson, and the two girls became almost inseparable.

Around the same time Colleen Slemmer appeared on the scene. She was a year younger than Christa and the two did not get on at all. The cause of the animosity was Christa's jealousy over Colleen's interest in Tadaryl. This festered within her until she became openly hostile towards the younger girl, calling her names and starting malicious rumours about her. After the two eventually had a fight, Christa made up her mind to really teach her rival a lesson. She and Shadolla Peterson conspired to get Colleen alone at a deserted spot on the University of Tennessee's Agriculture Campus and give her a beating.

Such schemes are not unusual among adolescents, but the outcome of this one was so terrible that it provoked horror and revulsion among the people of Knoxville.

The intended beating and humiliation took place on the cold, damp night of Thursday, 13 January 1995. Shortly before 9pm Christa Pike, Shadolla Peterson and Tadaryl Shipp left the Knoxville Job Corps Center. As they were leaving, Pike persuaded Colleen Slemmer to join them on the pretext of smoking some marijuana together as a peace pact.

After some debate it was decided that they would all go to an abandoned steam mill on the campus. According to one description of this place, it was so secluded that a person could scream at the top of their lungs and not be heard elsewhere. Nearby there were thick bushes and all around lay a mess of old building materials, including lumps of asphalt and big pieces of plastic.

When the quartet arrived at the mill, Colleen began talking with Tadaryl. Christa flew into a rage. Screaming obscenities, she dragged her rival away from him and the attack began. Colleen was taken completely by surprise. Her first reaction was to try to get away and she ran off down a muddy track. But, in the dark, she slipped and fell, allowing Shipp to catch up with her. The young man hauled her back before her tormentor, who resumed her onslaught.

The element of surprise had given Pike the upper hand. Now, to further demoralise her frightened, unwilling adversary, she made Colleen take off her sweater and bra, so that, bare-breasted, the girl would not try to run away again. Then she and Shadolla Peterson began to hit their terrified and humiliated victim with their knees and fists. Shipp turned away, but Colleen clung to him in the hope that he would somehow stop what was being done to her. But the unpleasant youth was having none of that, and pushed her away, slapping her when she wouldn't let go of his arm. All the while, Pike was punching and kicking Colleen, who eventually fell to the ground, where she lay weeping and clutching her stomach. Then the killing began.

Pike pulled out a small meat cleaver and slashed her victim's forehead. In great pain, Colleen covered her face with her hands and begged Pike to stop and try to resolve the issue without any more violence. Her pleading was useless. Pike slashed Colleen's pants open with the cleaver, taunting her with remarks about having sex with Shipp as she did it. The distraught girl struggled to her feet and made a dash for freedom but Pike threw a rock, which hit her on the back of the head, and she fell to the ground. Shipp picked her up and carried her back to the bushes, where the depraved and merciless attack continued. It was then that a box-cutter was produced.

For some 30 minutes or so Colleen was stabbed and slashed hundreds of times with the knife and the meat cleaver. Then Pike and Shipp, working together in an act of appalling savagery, carved a pentagram into the girl's chest.

Throughout this terrifying ordeal, Colleen remained alive. She continued to beg for her life and tried to sit up, even though her throat had been cut, but she was pushed back amid a barrage of taunts from Pike. Eventually, however, after her head had been pounded with chunks of asphalt, the teenager's struggles ceased.

Realising that their battered and blood-drenched victim was close to death, Pike and Shipp each grabbed one of her feet and dragged her towards some trees, where they left her body on a pile of dirt and debris. They gathered up her clothes and threw them into the surrounding bushes. After washing some of the blood from their hands and shoes, they discarded the box-cutter.

Leaving the scene of their terrible crime behind them, the three killers began to make their way back to the Job Corps Center and Pike returned the cleaver to the student from whom she had borrowed it. Then all three went to a Texaco service station on nearby Cumberland Avenue to wash off the remaining blood and change their clothes, before returning to the Job Corps Center around 10.15pm.

Some time later Pike went to the room of her friend and fellow student Kim Iloilo, where she brandished a piece of Colleen Slemmer's skull and proceeded to give a graphically detailed account of the atrocity that she and the other two had carried out. She told Iloilo that Colleen had begged them to stop cutting and beating her but that she hadn't stopped because her victim had continued to talk. The triumphant killer told her horrified friend that she had thrown a large piece of asphalt at Colleen's head and, when it broke into smaller pieces, had thrown those at her as well. She went on to explain that a meat cleaver had been used to cut the victim's back and a box-cutter to slit her throat. Pike ended by saying that a pentagram had been carved on to the dead teenage victim's chest and forehead. All the time she was narrating the tale, she was dancing in a circle around the room.

The next morning, during breakfast at the Job Corps Center, Iloilo saw Pike and asked her what she had done with the piece of Colleen's skull. Pike replied that she still had it and then said, 'And, yes, I'm eating breakfast with it.'

Later in the day, according to court records, the garrulous Pike made a similar statement to another student, Stephanie Wilson. She pointed to brown spots on her shoes and said, 'That ain't mud on my shoes, that's blood.' She then pulled a napkin from her pocket and showed Wilson a piece of bone which, she assured her, was a piece of Colleen Slemmer's skull. Pike went on to say that she had slashed Colleen's throat six times, adding that her blood and brains had been pouring out at the time that she had looted the piece of skull as a grisly trophy of the macabre orgy.

Both witnesses testified that the ghoulish braggart was in an extremely happy and triumphant mood as she told them of her crime.

At the time that Christa Pike was relating details of how she had overcome her love rival, horrified and sickened officers from the University of Tennessee Police and the Knoxville Police Department were taping off the area around the butchered remains of Colleen Slemmer. Her corpse, naked from the waist up, had been found at 8am. Her discarded bra and sweater were found in nearby bushes. At first Terry Johnson, the officer who had discovered the body, believed that he had found the remains of a dead animal. It was only after a closer inspection, when he saw the victim's clothes and her naked breasts, that he realised it was the body of a human female.

The savagery of the slaying and its location caused panic in some of the university's 26,000 students and 2,000 flyers were very quickly posted around the campus advising them not to walk alone at night or take short cuts.

It was not long before the Knoxville Police Department came to the conclusion that the murder was the work of satanists. The pentagram carved on Colleen's chest was the source of this idea, which was not without foundation. Evidence shortly came to light which demonstrated that Pike and Shipp had shown some interest in satanic worship, although it is doubtful that this was to any profound extent.

On the Saturday, two days after the killing, Pike and Shipp were arrested after calls to the police from informants who had listened to Pike's boasting. In confessing to the crime, the two implicated Peterson, whose arrest followed quickly.

In their search of Pike's room, police found a copy of *The Satanic Bible* and a silver figurine of Satan. A visit to Shipp's room revealed other evidence of satanic worship. Most damning of all, however, was the evidence found in Pike's leather jacket: a piece of Colleen Slemmer's skull.

Pike's 46-page statement, dictated to Detective Randy York, contains details of the murderous events which make chilling reading, for they highlight the immense evil displayed by Pike and her two accomplices.

In her statement Pike said that she had begun to cut Colleen across the throat when the victim sat up and begged for her life. Her response was to cut her throat several more times. At one point she could hear her victim 'breathing blood, in and out' and that she was 'jerking' as she lay on the ground. Out of control by now, the killer had simply kept on 'hitting her and hitting her and hitting her' before asking, 'Colleen, do you know who's doing this to you?' The dying girl's only response was to make groaning noises.

Knox County's Medical Examiner, Dr Sandra Elkins, who performed the autopsy on Colleen Slemmer's body, testified that she had attempted to catalogue the slash and stab wounds on the girl's torso by assigning a letter of the alphabet to each one. However, there were so many that eventually she decided to list only the most serious and major wounds. She explained that, to catalogue every wound, she would have been required to 'go through the alphabet again and stay in the morgue for three days'.

Among the major stab wounds and slashes that Dr Elkins noted was a six-inch gaping wound across the middle of Colleen Slemmer's neck. This had penetrated the fat and the muscles of the neck. There were another ten wounds on the victim's throat and slash wounds to her face.

But another of Dr Elkins's observations was perhaps the most chilling of all. Because the area round each wound was red in colour, she concluded that it was certain that Colleen

Slemmer was conscious throughout the time that she was being cut, slashed, punched and kicked. Blood in the sinus cavity and the appearance of some of the wounds bore further testimony to that. The young victim would have slipped into unconsciousness only after her skull had been hit by the large lump of asphalt.

Soon after Pike and Shipp had confessed to their involvement, a grotesque episode occurred as the police put the finishing touches to their investigation. Pike was taken to the murder scene, where, before a video camera, she re-enacted her role in the murder.

Tried in Knox County, Tennessee, in March 1996, Christa Gail Pike was found guilty of first-degree homicide and conspiracy to commit first-degree homicide.

While it would be foolish to imagine that there could be an easier, less painful way to dispense justice in these matters, many of the proceedings seem calculated to ride roughshod over the sensibilities of the bereaved and can be downright harrowing in their lack of sensitivity. Moreover, there are few examples that can compare to the treatment of Colleen Slemmer's mother, May Martinez, at the behest of Christa Pike's legal team. For Colleen's skull, which was introduced as evidence at the original trial, was still being retained in 2004 and will be until Pike has exhausted every possible angle of the appeal system, a process that could easily last another decade. Until that time the murdered girl's mother must endure the anguish of having her daughter's remains subjected to this impersonal, irreverent, almost sacrilegious treatment. All the while, she is tormented by the fact that she can't bury Colleen's skull with the rest of her body and finally lay her daughter to rest beside the remains of the girl's father.

Although Pike was sentenced to death, Tadaryl Shipp, because of his age, was sentenced to life imprisonment, with the possibility of parole. Shadolla Peterson, however, despite her active participation in the atrocity, escaped with a derisory six years' probation and walked free.

It is seldom understood just how much an enormity of this magnitude can blight the lives of the victim's family and loved ones. May Martinez has had her life destroyed and lost her home as a result of having to spend time and thousands of dollars travelling to and attending innumerable court hearings involving the three murderous conspirators and in attempts to overturn Tennessee's court rulings concerning evidence and obtain her daughter's skull. In a tragic irony, her house, in Jacksonville, Florida, was repossessed on Thursday, 13 January 2000, the fifth anniversary of her cherished daughter's brutal murder.

May Martinez has pursued every option in her attempts to ensure that her daughter's killers receive the fullest punishment and that Shipp is never released on parole. For all her endeavours, it is doubtful that she will ultimately succeed: cold pragmatism suggests that, before he reaches the age of 40, Shipp will almost certainly be deemed to have atoned for his crime and allowed to walk free.

By contrast, the fate of Christa Pike will be an appointment with the executioner, although the precise date has yet to be determined at the time of writing. The Court of Criminal Appeals rejected attempts by her defence team to have the death sentence overturned. Their argument centred on supposed procedural errors during the trial and the sentencing. Later, at a hearing in the Supreme Court of Tennessee at Knoxville, on 5 October 1998, the judges affirmed the earlier judgment, saying, 'After reviewing the record, we have determined that none of the alleged errors have merit. Moreover, the evidence supports the jury's findings as to the aggravating and mitigating circumstances, and the sentence of death is not arbitrary or disproportionate to the sentence imposed in similar cases, considering the nature of the crime and the defendant. Accordingly, the judgment of the Court of Criminal Appeals, upholding the defendant's convictions and the sentences, is confirmed.'

Pike's lawyers assert that they have a few options still open to them, but, realistically, their only chance rests on the fact that in more than 40 years Tennessee has executed only one murderer. Otherwise all that they will achieve is to postpone the inevitable and so prolong unnecessarily the pain and anguish that, since 1995, have been heaped relentlessly on May Martinez and the rest of Colleen Slemmer's family.

At the time of writing, the angel-faced Pike, now 28, shares her Death Row accommodation at the Tennessee Prison for Women with Gaile Kirksie Owens, who, at the age of 32, hired Sidney Porterfield to beat her husband, Ronald, to death at their home in Bartlett, Tennessee, on 17 February 1985. The couple's two young sons were in the house at the time.

Conclusion

Not folie a deux. The psychotic Christa Gail Pike found in Tadaryl Shipp a lover who shared the same interest in satanism, but the overriding factor is that she was overtly jealous of any other female who appeared to vie for his company. It is doubtful that the murder of Colleen Slemmer was premeditated: rather, here we have an act of explosive homicidal fury, fuelled by profound jealousy, as in the case of Kelly O'Donnell and William Gribble.

In this case it is difficult to find one ounce of mitigation, for the suffering, both physical and psychological, inflicted on an innocent and terrified young woman is almost beyond comprehension.

CHAPTER ELEVEN

SUSAN MINTER AND MICHAEL WHITE

Accomplices

Thirty-six-year-old Michael White and Susan Minter, three years younger, were lovers. Both divorced, they met in January 1987 while working at a care home in Prescott, Arizona, and Susan was the one with the brains and ambition. She was also enjoying a relationship with David Johnson, a miner, who lived in Bagdad, Yavapai County, where he worked for the Cyprus Bagdad Copper Company of Boulder Creek.

White knew of the affair, and eventually he and Minter conspired together to kill Johnson and collect on his insurance policy. The plan, masterminded by Minter, was simple. She would marry Johnson and have him name her as his beneficiary. The unsuspecting man would then be killed.

Accordingly, on 20 November 1987, Susan Minter became Mrs David Johnson and almost immediately had herself and her children made beneficiaries. The sum involved was $65,000.

The two conspirators were not the type to let the grass grow under their feet. On the day before the wedding, White bought a .357-calibre Magnum revolver from a pawnbroker in Bagdad and, three weeks later, on the evening of 12 December, stationed himself outside the newlyweds' home, armed with the gun and waiting for Johnson to return from work. Johnson arrived and, using a potato for a makeshift silencer, White shot him in the face and back. Bemused neighbours, alerted by muffled gunshots, saw a man run to a green Oldsmobile, climb in and drive off into the night.

Despite the calibre of the bullets, which were fired at point-blank range, Johnson was not dead. Bleeding badly, he called out for help. Inside their home, his new bride assisted her mortally wounded husband by thoughtfully locking the doors to make sure that he could not get in. After a few minutes he staggered to a neighbour's house, where he managed to describe his attacker as 'a masked man with a gun' before expiring.

Johnson's widow managed to convince police that the man whom they were seeking was her ex-husband, Clifford Minter. She claimed that Johnson had managed to tell her this, despite their having been on opposite sides of a locked door. In any event, the police believed her and a description of both Clifford Minter, as well as the green Oldsmobile seen by neighbours, was broadcast on the police radio to all units. White was stopped in the Oldsmobile soon afterwards by a patrol car, but after giving a plausible alibi he was allowed to go free.

Police investigators tracked down and interviewed Clifford Minter, who had a solid alibi for the time of the murder. They went on to discover the full extent of the relationship between Michael White and the widow Johnson. Both were arrested and charged with first-degree murder.

More damning evidence turned up in the form of the murder weapon and it was revealed that White had sold it to a pawnbroker in Phoenix a week after the shooting. When the gun was recovered, traces of potato starch were found on the barrel: moreover, a bag of potatoes was found in White's car, along with ammunition, and traces of potato were found at the murder scene.

The evidence was conclusive and the two murderous lovers were convicted of the killing of David Johnson. Instead of a handsome payout from the insurance company, Susan Johnson was rewarded with a life sentence. For White, the penalty was even greater: he was sentenced to death on 8 August 1988. Interestingly, he was offered a choice in the method of his execution, the unattractive options being to die by gas or by lethal injection – he went for the latter.

This case aroused much debate, largely centred on the perceived injustice of the disparity of the sentences handed out. Some argue that there was a strong case for Susan Johnson to receive the death penalty, given that she was the instigator and played a significant role in the killing. The controversy will undoubtedly continue long after White has been dispatched.

At his appeal before five justices at the Yavapai Superior Court, Michael White's sentence was affirmed. However, Chief Justice Thomas A. Zlaket, who dissented, said, 'I believe that Susan is more culpable than White.' He went on to say, 'This case does tend to make a mockery of equal treatment under the law. She lives, he dies.' Justice Stanley G. Feldman concurred with this view.

Conclusion

This case may be compared to that of Snyder and Gray, for again we see that the female can be more lethal than the male. Here we find no folie a deux, but a straightforward accomplice scenario.

CHAPTER TWELVE

CYNTHIA COFFMAN AND JAMES GREGORY MARLOW
Death Row Couple

Born in 1962, Cynthia Coffman was the privileged daughter of a St Louis businessman and was raised by her parents as a devout Catholic. Abortion was unthinkable when she got pregnant at 17, and she was forced into a loveless marriage, enduring five years of domestic captivity before she left home and drove west. Travelling with little more than the clothes on her back, Cynthia wound up in Page, Arizona, working as a waitress in a diner and moving in with a local man several weeks later.

In the autumn of 1985 the couple were evicted from their small apartment after numerous complaints from neighbours about their drunken all-night parties. On 8 May the following year they were pulled over by the police for ignoring a stop sign in Barstow, California. An officer found a loaded derringer and a quantity of methamphetamine in Cynthia's purse, but she was released on her own recognisance on bail and the charges were later dropped. However, her lover wound up serving six weeks in the county jail, and it was during one of Cynthia's visits that she first met his cellmate, the man who would irrevocably change her life. The result was a shared and deadly madness.

James Gregory Marlow was doing time for the theft of his sixth wife's car when 24-year-old Cynthia walked into his wasted life. Born in 1957, he had been a dedicated thief from the age of ten. In 1980, aged 23, he had been dispatched to Folsom Prison, Texas, for a series of burglaries and knifepoint robberies. Marlow served three years, earning himself a reputation as 'The Folsom Wolf' for proudly wearing tattoos of the neo-Nazi Aryan Brotherhood.

It was love at first sight between this Lothario and his cellmate's girlfriend. On Marlow's release in mid-1986 they instantly forgot Cynthia's partner and before long set off for California. Marlow had relatives near the border with Mexico, so they began working their way through the family tree, sponging room and board where they could and repaying their hosts' generosity by stealing any valuables when they were finally asked to leave.

Word soon spread on the grapevine that these two guests were a hazard and in time Marlow's relatives began to turn them away with angry words or pocket change, depending on their frame of mind. Things got so bad that the couple were reduced to sleeping in the woods. Cynthia contracted head lice and James was forced to bathe in kerosene to rid himself of hungry mites.

As dawn broke on 26 July 1986, Coffman and Marlow were burgling a house in Whitley County, Kentucky, taking a good haul that included cash, jewellery and a shotgun. Days later they arrived in Tennessee and were married. Cynthia celebrated the occasion by having her buttocks tattooed with the legend 'I belong to the Folsom Wolf'. That done, they drifted west again, in search of easy prey.

On the evening of 11 October 32-year-old Sandra Neary left her home in Costa Mesa, California, to obtain some cash from the ATM outside her bank. She never returned and police found her car in a local parking lot. On 24 October her strangled, decomposing corpse was discovered by hikers near Corona, in Riverside County. Four days later the killers struck again.

Thirty-five-year-old Pamela Simmons was reported missing in Bullhead City, Arizona, on 28 October, and her car found abandoned near the police headquarters. Detectives theorised that she had been snatched while drawing money from an ATM.

On 7 November 20-year-old Corinna Novis vanished in similar circumstances in Redlands, California. This latest victim had been kidnapped from an urban shopping mall in broad daylight.

Five days later Lynel Murray's boyfriend was worried when the 19-year-old psychology student failed to keep a date after work. He found her car outside the dry-cleaning shop where she worked in Orange County, California, but it was the next day before her naked, strangled body was discovered in a motel room at Huntington Beach. In addition to the kidnapping and murder, there was evidence of sexual assault. Police were praying for a break, and when it came the mystery unravelled swiftly.

First, Corinna Novis's chequebook was found in a trash dumpster at Laguna Nigel, tucked inside a fast-food takeout bag along with papers bearing the names of Cynthia Coffman and James Marlow. Around the same time the couple were linked to a San Bernardino motel room where the manager had found stationery bearing practice versions of Lynel Murray's signature. A glance at Marlow's criminal record did the rest, and a state-wide alert was issued for the two fugitives.

On 14 November 1986 police were summoned to a mountain lodge at Big Bear City, California, where the proprietor identified his latest guests as Marlow and Coffman. A hundred-strong posse, finding the building empty, fanned out with dogs through the woods for a sweep that paid off around three in the afternoon when the suspects were found hiking along a mountain road. Coffman and Marlow surrendered without a fight. They were both wearing outfits stolen from the dry-cleaning shop where Lynel Murray worked.

Within hours Coffman led officers to a vineyard near Fontana, where they found Corinna Novis, sodomised and strangled, lying in a shallow grave. Marlow and Coffman were formally charged with her murder on 17 November and held over for trial without bond. If any further proof of guilt were needed, homicide investigators told press that the fingerprints of both defendants had been found inside Corinna's car, and Coffman had been linked to the pawnshop in Fontana where the victim's typewriter was pawned. However, 32 months would pass before the killers stood trial, and in the meantime they experienced a falling-out, blaming each other for their plight.

During one jailhouse visit Coffman's lawyer asked if there was anything she needed from the outside world. 'Yeah,' she told him, pointing to her backside. 'You can find someone to help me lose this damn tattoo!'

The couple's trial for murder began on 18 July 1989, in San Bernardino County. Both defendants were convicted across the board, and sentenced to death on 30 August. Cynthia Coffman became the first woman sentenced to die in California since the state restored capital punishment in 1977. Nevertheless, it seems unlikely that she will actually be put to death in liberal California, but the 1992 execution of Robert Alton Harris cancelled all bets, making anything possible. She remains on Death Row at the time of writing.

James Gregory Marlow is currently on Death Row at San Quentin State Prison, California.

Conclusion

This is an unusual case of folie a deux, for the motive for the couple's crimes was financial, not sexual. There is no doubt that Cynthia Coffman would have ended up in prison at some time – mixing with criminals always seems to have the same result. It would also be fair to surmise that Marlow too would have spent much time locked up at the taxpayers' expense.

With Marlow the dominant partner, they started off by sponging from his relatives and friends until, rejected on all sides, they reached the bottom of the ladder and were driven to sleeping in the wild. There was only one way up: violent crime, and this became serial murder. Fate had brought them together in a deadly folie a deux.

CHAPTER THIRTEEN

KARLA FAYE TUCKER AND DANNY GARRETT
The Houston Pickaxe Murders

The youngest of three daughters, Karla Faye was born to Larry and Carolyn Tucker on Wednesday, 18 November 1959, in Houston, Texas. Larry worked as a longshoreman and Carolyn was a housewife who stayed at home in their house on Hewitt Street, with the three baby girls, Kathy Lynne, two years old, Kari Ann, aged one, and the new baby, Karla Faye.

The Tucker family at that time enjoyed a modest but comfortable standard of living. They owned a small holiday home on Caney Creek, Brazoria, and during Karla Faye's early years the family would spend their vacations and frequent weekends there. Those times, with her two sisters and the family's German shepherd, were 'the happiest times of my life', Karla Faye later recalled.

'We were a family and we used to go to the bay house and do neat things with the dog and the boat and water skiing and fishing and stuff,' she said in a television interview. 'But it didn't last very long.'

In fact, it lasted only a handful of years. Larry and Carolyn's marriage was far from stable: they divorced and remarried several times before they eventually threw in the towel.

When Karla Faye was ten, the family finally disintegrated and her parents went their separate ways. Infidelity was to blame, but whether both partners were guilty is not clear. There is no doubt, however, that Carolyn had enjoyed the odd foray into another man's bed and proof of her ways was to emerge during the divorce proceedings.

Karla Faye was an extremely self-conscious child. Although both of her sisters were blonde, blue-eyed and fair-skinned, she was not. She was a brown-eyed brunette and this marked difference from her siblings made her feel like an ugly duckling and something of an outsider. Added to this, she had great difficulty in communicating with children outside her family.

The confused youngster's problems weren't made any easier when, at the time of the divorce, Carolyn decided to unburden herself of a secret. She told ten-year-old Karla Faye that she had been born as the result of an extramarital affair, so her father was not Larry.

This news was quite devastating to Karla Faye and, despite the fact that Larry had always accepted her as his own daughter, she was never again able to consider herself as being truly a part of that family. This feeling of not belonging greatly affected the pre-pubescent girl, and from that time influenced profoundly the way in which she approached life.

A major outcome of the divorce was that Larry was given custody of the three girls, despite the fact that they had really wanted to be with their mother. Although well intentioned and conscientious, Larry wasn't really up to the task of bringing up three daughters on his own. Working two shifts, he was seldom at home in the evenings. The girls took advantage of their freedom, and Karla Faye, who had begun to smoke marijuana with her sisters, dropped out of school during seventh grade.

By the time she was 11 she was taking heroin. Years later, in an interview that she gave to *LifeWay Church* magazine, she summed up the situation by saying, 'My father couldn't control us real good. He tried to discipline us but we were just too much, just too much.' With only her elder sisters to turn to for guidance and companionship, Karla Faye began to associate with people who were too old for her. As she recalled, 'My sisters always hung around with older people. There was a lot of drugs.'

With the drugs, almost inevitably, there came sex. Her sisters' friends were mostly bikers who belonged to a gang called the Banditos and held parties at which drugs of all types were available in abundance and which often developed into orgies. It was with one of the bikers that Karla Faye, aged 12, enjoyed her first full sexual experience.

Looking for her sisters one evening, she called at the biker's home. Her sisters weren't there and, rather than carry on searching for them, she accepted his invitation to join him in 'shooting up some smack'. Once the heroin had begun to work, the biker took his 12-year-old companion for a ride on his motorbike. They rode until they came to a suitably secluded place and there, high on heroin, Karla Faye surrendered her virginity and enjoyed 'sex on high' for the first of what would become countless times.

The downward spiral that was Karla Faye's life continued, unchecked, until her father faced up to the realisation that he could not control his daughter and sent her to live with her mother, who was, by then, living in the town of Genoa, Texas.

Since her divorce, Carolyn Tucker had kept body and soul together by following the oldest profession in the world. She was still a young woman in her twenties, and prostitution allowed her to maintain herself in a reasonably comfortable lifestyle. Suddenly presented with the responsibility of giving a home to her out-of-control daughter, Carolyn took a pragmatic view of the situation. She made no shamefaced attempt to conceal the nature of her occupation. Instead, she responded with gusto and organised a similar career for her teenage charge.

Karla Faye described the way in which her mother set about arranging her career training. 'She took me to a place where there was all men and wanted to school me in the art of being a call girl. I wanted to please my mother so much. I wanted her to be proud of me, so, instead of saying no, I just tried to do what she asked. The thing is, I knew, deep down inside, that what I was doing was wrong.'

At the age of just 14 and under the expert tutelage of her maternal mentor, Karla Faye embarked on a life of prostitution, which she sustained on a robust diet of amphetamines and alcohol. It was a lifestyle that she found enjoyable. She kept it up for the next two years, until she met and married a mechanic by the name of Stephen Griffith.

The marriage was, on the face of it, much the same as any other teenage pairing. They were generally a happy couple and Stephen found much that he admired in his young wife. The quality that he admired most, even though it was far from conventional, was Karla Faye's ability to pack a punch. In an interview with the *Houston Chronicle*, he said, 'We fought a lot. I've never had a man hit me as hard as she did. Whenever I went into a bar, I didn't have to worry because she had my back covered.'

Eventually, however, Karla Faye became bored with married life and decided to move on. After leaving her husband, she drifted back into prostitution, working an area in Quay Point, Houston, where another prostitute, Shawn Dean, befriended her and the two became very close.

Among the people that Shawn introduced to Karla Faye was a drug pusher named Danny Garrett. Although there was an age difference of 14 years, Karla Faye and Danny got on well and in time began to live together. Karla Faye found Garrett easy-going; he was aware that she was a prostitute and made no issue of it. Not only that, he was always on hand to keep her well provided with the wide range of drugs that she now used: amphetamine, cocaine, Valium and other drugs were all available in abundance from Danny and were washed down with copious amounts of alcohol. All in all, life with Danny suited Karla Faye right down to the ground and they stayed together in that lifestyle for a few years, until 13 June 1983. On that day they were to carry out an act of terrifying proportions that had an impact from which they would never recover.

At that time they were living in a small house in Houston. Although Danny was working as a bartender, he was still very much involved in the provision of drugs. Karla Faye had maintained relations with her two sisters, Kari Ann and

Kathy Lynne, and she had organised a birthday party to celebrate Kari Ann's birthday over the weekend of 11–12 June, at the house where she lived with Danny. However, this was no ordinary party; when she had asked her elder sister what she would like, Kari Ann had replied that she would like a sex orgy. When it comes to an orgy, few people would have the first idea of how to even begin; not so Karla Faye. She responded to the request by organising precisely what her sister had asked for. Accordingly, Danny had provided the mountain of drugs that such an occasion demands and, with a house full of like-minded friends, all of them eager to shed their inhibitions and their clothes, Kari Ann's birthday wish came true.

For almost three days the naked guests, their mood fortified by copious amounts of drugs washed down with beer, whisky and tequila, enjoyed themselves and pretty much whoever happened to be next to them. While they may not have been A-list celebrities, they were all well known to the Tucker sisters, sharing the girls' enthusiasm for drugs, booze and group sex.

According to what she told *LifeWay Church* in 1990, Karla Faye had been keeping her energy levels high by downing cocaine and home-made amphetamines in liberal quantities. 'I had been doing a considerable amount of coke and bathtub speed,' she said. She went on to explain, 'I'm a very hyper person and doing speed always skitzed me out – made me go crazy. That night [Sunday, 12 June] we were cooking speed and we started shooting it because it was there, and I loved the needle in my arm; what one would call a needle freak.'

These remarks demonstrate vividly the ignorance that is

common among low-life drug users about the chemicals they hungrily ingest. Karla Faye and her friends were taking on board grossly excessive amounts of strong stimulants without the slightest concern over the effect, blind to anything beyond their immediate desires. There is a downside to such drug consumption and, for Karla Faye, the consequences of her intake of coke and speed, not to mention the alcohol, would be catastrophic.

During the weekend's excesses they gossiped with Karla Faye's friend Shawn Dean about the recent break-up of her marriage to a biker by the name of Jerry Lynn Dean. It seemed that Jerry Lynn was in the habit of knocking Shawn about and she had finally walked out on him after his latest bout of violence. As Shawn sat pouring out her anger and grief to Karla Faye and Danny, she could have had no idea of just how terrifyingly violent would be the upshot of this conversation with her friends.

Karla Faye regarded Shawn as her closest friend and, with her emotions distorted by the drugs with which she had bombarded her nervous system, she began to brood darkly on Shawn's predicament. And the more she brooded, the more exaggerated and melodramatic became her views on the matter. She disliked Jerry Lynn Dean in any case and Shawn's plaintive lament simply served to increase her dislike of the man until it had become a seething hatred. At one point she even threatened to get into her car and drive round to his home to beat him up.

In her account of events, Karla Faye said, 'I saw what he had done to her and I was really mad at him because I was really protective of her. I thought, Yeah, I'll get even with him. My idea of getting even with him meant confronting him, standing toe to toe, fist to fist.'

Around nine on Sunday evening it was time for Danny to go to work. He made an attempt to sober up and Karla Faye drove him to the bar where he worked. After arranging to pick him up around 2am she drove back home to resume listening to Shawn's drunken litany of complaints about her former husband, a tirade which ended only when the wronged woman fell into a deep stupor. As Shawn slept, Karla Faye continued chewing over the matter with another friend, Albert Sheehan. She explained that her hostility towards Jerry Lynn Dean had begun some months earlier, when Shawn had brought him over to introduce him. He had wheeled his bike into her house, to prevent it being stolen, and when Karla Faye arrived home it was to find the machine dripping oil on her carpet. Understandably annoyed, she asked the couple to leave and had ended up having a row with Jerry Lynn.

There had been several other incidents that had made things worse between them, including one occasion when the biker had stuck a knife through a photo of Karla Faye and her mother that Shawn carried. He had done this because he didn't like his wife associating with such a woman. Jerry Lynn's dislike of the friendship wasn't entirely unreasonable as the two women had recently used his bank card to clean out his account. Relations between Karla Faye and Jerry Lynn couldn't have been much worse.

When 2am came around, Karla Faye got into her car and drove off to pick up Danny at the bar. Albert Sheehan had come along with her and they got there as Danny was locking up. Moments later he was in the car and telling them of the idea he had thought up to hit Jerry Lynn Dean where it would hurt him most: his Harley-Davidson.

According to the account given by the writer Joseph Geringer, Danny had said, 'Been giving the situation some thought and I say we go, tonight, now, to steal the sonofabitch Jerry Dean's bike.'

Needless to say, the idea went down well with his two friends. The trio returned home and told Shawn what they were planning to do. She, in turn, told them that Jerry Lynn would be asleep by that time. The three changed their clothes, dressing in black from head to toe. Before leaving, they gathered up a shotgun and a .38-calibre pistol. They later insisted that the guns were there only for protection and that they had no intention, at that stage, of killing the wife-beating biker.

Jerry Lynn lived in a ground-floor apartment in an area that was rough and rundown, even by Quay Point standards. The three conspirators reasoned that it would be easy to break into the place as the police didn't cruise the area unless they were specifically told to do so. Making it easier still was the knowledge that Jerry Lynn was in the habit of smoking a couple of joints before turning in and so would be out like a light.

As they reached the building where Dean lived, Danny took charge. He told Albert to stay outside in the car, to keep an eye out for police. Moments later he and Karla Faye were at the grimy front door of the apartment, relieved that there was no overhead light shining on the proceedings. Within a few seconds Danny had slipped the lock on the front door and they were inside.

The room they entered was in complete darkness, but they knew they had the right place because of the smell of burned engine oil that pervaded everything. There was no sound to suggest that anyone was awake, so Danny switched on a flashlight that he had brought along. By its anaemic beam they could see that the room, as well as smelling like a garage, actually looked like one. Standing on a tarpaulin that seemed to serve as a carpet, Dean's bike was partially dismantled and the various components of his pride and joy were spread out over the floor, along with a collection of greasy tools. Leaning against one wall, incongruously, stood a shovel and a pickaxe.

The difficulty in which the couple now found themselves was that, with the bike in pieces, they could no longer steal it. Yet that didn't mean that they couldn't do anything at all. By stealing some of the key components, they could cause Dean no end of problems, not to mention considerable expense. But it was not to be. Suddenly, taking them completely by surprise, a light came on in an adjoining room and the door began to open. They scarcely had time to take it in when a gravelly voice called out, 'Who the hell's out there?'

It was a voice that Karla Faye recognised instantly as Dean's. She froze momentarily, then gathered her senses and moved into the bedroom. Through a crack in the curtains, light was filtering in and she could see the silhouette of someone sitting up. This, she saw, was Dean and she sat down on the bed, legs astride him and told him to shut up. Puzzled, the biker said, 'Karla, we can work it out. I didn't file charges.' He was referring to Karla Faye and Shawn having emptied his bank account.

In the darkness, Dean grabbed Karla Faye's arms and the two began struggling. Danny reacted quickly. After grabbing a hammer from the toolbox, he charged back into the room, where he could make out the shadowy figure of Dean, and hit him full on the head with it. Dean's attempt to rise was brought to an abrupt halt as his head was jolted backwards by the blow. As Karla Faye switched on the light, Danny followed up with a series of hammer blows. Blood began to run from Dean's nose in two crimson rivulets, followed by a similar flow from the corners of his mouth, all four tributaries merging as they reached his chin.

In Karla Faye, standing in the doorway, the sight of Danny raining hammer blows on his hapless victim produced a curious effect. She felt a wonderful, exciting, tingling sensation in her thighs. Fascinated and aroused by the surreal scene that was taking place before her, she stood rooted to the spot. Moments later a strange sound emanated from the battered Dean that took Karla Faye by surprise and unnerved her. 'It was a gurgling sound. It was coming from Jerry,' she told the court. 'Danny walked out of the room and I was standing there. I kept hearing the sound. All I wanted to do was stop it. I saw a pickaxe leaning up against the wall. I reached over and grabbed it. I swung it; hit him in the back with it. He kept making that noise. When Danny came in, I told him to make him stop making that noise. Danny took the pickaxe, swung it several more times, hitting him in the back. Then he turned him over and hit him in the chest and the noise stopped.'

And then, as Danny left the room, Karla Faye saw the girl. There, in the bed, to the side of Dean, trying desperately to remain hidden beneath the covers, was a young woman dressed only in a T-shirt. Her name, it would later emerge, was Deborah Thornton and until a few minutes earlier she had been sleeping peacefully next to Dean. Now, her eyes filled with terror, she cowered among the disarrayed bedding, wanting to scream but rendered mute with fear.

The sight of the terrified girl acted like an exciting surge of electric energy on Karla Faye. For a moment she stood motionless, taking in the scene. Then, like a sprinter rising from the starting blocks, she propelled herself back into the room where the motorcycle and the tools lay. Grabbing the pickaxe, she darted back into the bedroom and approached the bed. Dean, his head battered almost beyond recognition, lay completely still, another gurgling sound coming involuntarily from his mouth. Danny had stopped his furious assault and stood watching Karla Faye as she raised the pickaxe above her head before swinging it downwards at Deborah Thornton. As the point of the pickaxe pierced her shoulder, the defenceless woman gave a single scream and grabbed the weapon.

Lying there on the bed beside the bloody mess that was Jerry Lynn Dean, with a pickaxe penetrating her, Deborah Thornton knew that there was no way out of this nightmare. 'Oh, God, it hurts,' she gasped. 'If you're going to kill me, then please, hurry up' were the last words she uttered before Karla Faye brought the vicious weapon down again and again, each blow finding a different part of Thornton's body to impale on its murderous spike, each fresh wound spouting blood that sprayed the two killers.

Spurred on uncontrollably by a delicious sensation in her legs that she had never before experienced, Karla Faye, wielding the pick like a medieval battleaxe, punctured the quivering, squishing, blood-drenched remains of her victim, more than 20 times, as Danny whooped encouragement.

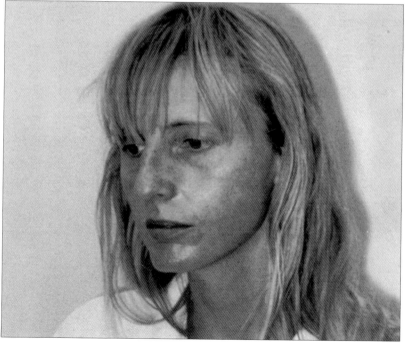

Marc and Michele Dutroux, as they were arrested in 1996, in connection with the murder of several children in Belgium.

The portrait of Fred and Rosemary West that was released at the time of their arrest.

Alton Coleman and Debra Brown arraigned before the Bench in
Cincinnati on 10 January, 1985.

Lynda Lyon and
George Sibley in
prison in April 1996.

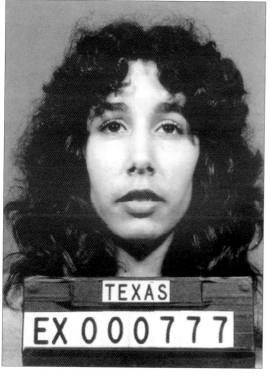

Daniel Garrett in court and Karla Tucker in late 1984.

Percy Thompson and his wife Edith, who was to be charged with his murder.

Martha Beck in court and Raymond Fernandez in prison in 1949.

Myra Hindley and Ian Brady in the late 1960s.

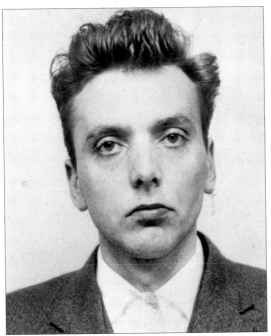

Laughing, he threw a blanket over his murderous girlfriend's head, inviting her to do her work blindfold. To her insane delight, the wonderful sensation became more acute. She later told friends that she had enjoyed the most massive, intense orgasms, three of them, as, sightless, she plunged the pickaxe into flesh.

With Deborah Thornton's body a mass of bloody puncture wounds stretching from her shoulders to her legs, Karla Faye turned to the inert but still gurgling Dean, the man for whom she felt the deepest hatred. Having raised her blood-soaked weapon, she drove it with enormous force into her enemy's chest. Pulling the spike free, she mutilated his helpless corpse with another 20 savage blows before bringing her frenzied assault to an end.

It was Jerry Lynn Dean's workmate George Turner who discovered the butchered bodies, at 7.30am, and phoned the police. Shortly afterwards Detectives Bill Owen and Chet Thomas arrived at the apartment. Inside they found a shocked Turner, who identified Dean's corpse but was unable to shed any light on the identity of the dead woman, although she was later identified by a relative as Deborah Ruth Thornton, aged 32, after her picture had appeared in the local press.

The walls and ceiling of the murder room were spattered with blood and the two corpses were sprawled on the blood-drenched bed. According to court papers, Deborah Thornton was found with the pickaxe sticking out of her chest, its spike embedded in her heart.

At first the investigating officers had great difficulty in finding anything that would help them to find the killers. However, a month later, during an unrelated, unsolved investigation, Detective Sergeant J. Mosier came upon Danny Garrett's name and recognised it as one of those questioned about the double killing. Mosier knew Garrett and managed to contact his ex-wife, who agreed to ask discreet questions of her former in-laws. As a result of this a man who was a relative of Garrett came forward and, after much heavy persuasion, agreed to be wired up with a microphone, a tape recorder and a radio transmitter and to go and talk with Garrett and Tucker.

Police officers waited outside the house, listening to and recording all that was said. During the conversation Karla Faye was asked if it was true that she had become sexually aroused with every blow that she struck with the axe. 'Hell, yes!' she was heard to reply.

On Wednesday, 20 July 1983 police arrested Danny Garrett and Karla Faye Tucker, along with Albert Sheehan. Karla Faye and Danny had actually gone home and bragged about their exploits to the remaining party guests, most of whom were quick to relate what they knew when the police started to round them up. Sheehan, in particular, was more than willing to co-operate with the law, eventually turning state's evidence and walking free.

In September, Danny Garrett and Karla Faye Tucker were indicted for the murders. Karla Faye pleaded not guilty and in April 1984 was tried before a jury in the 180th Judicial District Court of Harris County. The trial judge was Patricia Lykos.

Tucker was found guilty as charged on 19 April and six days later was sentenced to death. After sentencing she was taken to Mountain View Prison, at Gatesville, Texas, where, as prisoner no. 777, she spent the next 14 years. During that time she underwent a change of character, becoming a devout Christian and attracting a great deal of publicity as she fought to have her sentence commuted to life imprisonment.

In November of the same year, Daniel Ryan Garrett was tried separately but suffered the same verdict as Karla Faye. He too was sentenced to death, on Thursday, 29 November, but, unlike his partner in crime, he didn't see his sentence carried out. His liver, damaged by years of drug abuse, failed him and he died in prison in 1994.

Karla Faye Tucker died by lethal injection in Texas on 3 February 1998. She was pronounced dead at 6.45pm. Just before she died, she made a last statement:

'Yes, sir, I would like to say to all of you – the Thornton family and Jerry Dean's family – that I am so sorry. I hope God will give you peace with this. Baby, I love you. Ron, give Peggy a hug for me. Everybody has been so good to me. I love all of you very much. I am going to be face to face with Jesus now. Warden Baggett, thank all of you so much. You have been so good to me. I love all of you very much. I will see you all when you get there. I will wait for you.'

Conclusion

This bloodbath – the pickaxing to death of two young people half-asleep in their warm bed – stuns the mind into insensibility. Bitter hatred is writ large across the mind of Karla Faye Tucker, proving that hell hath no fury like a woman scorned.

Not folie a deux. Danny Garrett was, I believe, just an accomplice to the brutal act. However, spurred on by a woman who he believed loved him, he went along for the ride. It was to cost him dearly.

The media clamoured over this case like rats around trash, not least because Karla Faye Tucker admitted that with every blow she experienced an orgasm – a damning admission indeed. Mitigation rating: a dysfunctional childhood maybe, but on a scale of ten, minus ten.

CHAPTER FOURTEEN

FRANK ANDERSON AND KIMBERLY LANE

A Kid's Crush

Thirty-year-old Leta Kagen lived in a trailer home 24 kilometres west of Kingman, in Golden Valley, Arizona, along with her 15-year-old son Robert Delahunt and Roland Wear, aged 50.

During the summer of 1996 Bobby Poyson, 19, had turned up at Leta's door homeless and hungry. She had taken pity on him and given him a home. The young man had been living in the trailer for some weeks when two strangers turned up. Frank Anderson, 48, and his 14-year-old girlfriend, Kimberly Lane, had been neighbours on another trailer park and had run away together. They had been hitch-hiking in the area when Leta agreed to let them stay for a few days.

Despite the seemingly romantic picture of two lovers on the run, the true nature of the relationship between Anderson and his underage lover was unsavoury and sordid. Kimberly had an IQ of 84, which is on the wrong side of mediocre, and the maturity of a ten-year-old. During the days that followed, the newcomers spent a lot of time talking with Bobby Poyson. He and Anderson were old acquaintances. Anderson confided that he was trying to get to Chicago, where he had connections with organised crime, and the three conspired to kill Leta, Robert and Roland in order to steal Roland's pickup truck, which they would use to drive there.

The first to be killed was going to be Robert. Kimberly was the bait. Slightly younger than Robert but sexually more experienced, she lured him to a nearby travel trailer with the promise of sex. It was an offer the teenager could not refuse, but it was the biggest mistake he ever made in his short life.

When Robert reached the trailer it was murder rather than sex that was on the agenda. Anderson was waiting for him. The teenager was no match for the mature man who attacked him, but he fought desperately. Using a bread knife, Anderson cut the youth's throat from ear to ear, and still Robert struggled. Poyson arrived on the scene and, while Anderson held Robert down, Poyson drove the bread knife into the victim's ear so hard that it emerged through his nose. Robert somehow did not die, continuing to fight tenaciously until Poyson finally ended his life by crushing his skull with a cinder block. The teenager had defended himself against his brutal attackers for an astonishing 45 minutes and it is impossible to imagine the intense pain and terror he was subjected to as he lost this unequal battle.

Back in their trailer home, Leta and Roland had heard nothing of Robert's dreadful murder and went to sleep, unaware of the danger they were in. Outside, the murderers cleaned themselves up and located a .22-calibre rifle belonging to Roland. But they couldn't find any ammunition, so Bobby Poyson borrowed a couple of rounds from a girl in a nearby trailer. Then they cut the phone line to Leta's home. Using a lantern for light, the killers entered her trailer and Poyson shot her in the head, killing instantly the woman who had shown him so much kindness. Roland awoke and Poyson fired at him, shooting him in the mouth. The bullet did not kill Roland, so, while Poyson clubbed him about the head with the rifle, Anderson bludgeoned him with the lantern.

Like Robert, Roland fought fiercely for his life. The struggle spilled out into the yard, where Anderson finally crushed the victim's skull using the cinder block with which Poyson had murdered the teenager. The killings had taken almost five hours to carry out. Roland's last words were, 'Bobby, stop. Bobby, don't. I never did anything to hurt you.'

Their grisly task accomplished, Poyson, Anderson and Lane set off for Chicago in the pickup, leaving behind the corpses of three people who had provided hospitality and kindness. The bodies were found on 16 August by Leta's former husband. Seven days later Poyson was arrested at a homeless shelter in Evanston, Illinois, and he now has a roof over his head: a cell on Death Row. Both he and Anderson received the death sentence for their callous, barbaric crimes.

The juvenile seductress Kimberly Lane was convicted of murder and sentenced to life in prison. However, this was overturned on appeal and in January 2002 she received a sentence of only eight years.

107

Conclusion

A 14-year-old girl falls for an older man and is willing to do whatever he wishes. Rather than folie a deux, this case was more an infatuation, as the Appellate process recognised.

CHAPTER FIFTEEN

EDITH THOMPSON AND FREDDIE BYWATERS

A Double Hanging

There is no smoke without fire and often when passions blaze out of control murder is the result. Edith Thompson was an attractive 28-year-old who was married to Percy Thompson, a shipping clerk four years her senior. The couple had no children and Edith had a good job as the manageress of a milliner's shop in London, so they enjoyed a comfortable life.

However, Edith was having an affair with 20-year-old Frederick Bywaters, a ship's steward. Their relationship had started in June 1921 when he accompanied the Thompsons on holiday to the Isle of Wight. He moved in as a lodger while waiting for his next job on board ship, but meanwhile was thrown out by Percy for getting too friendly with Edith after witnessing a violent row between the couple and later comforting her. He saw Edith secretly from time to time until eventually they booked into a hotel under false names.

Freddie Bywaters was an impulsive young man. On 4

October 1922 he lay in wait until just after midnight for Edith and Percy, who were returning home to Ilford, Essex, after a night out at a theatre in London. When they got back he stabbed Percy several times. Edith was said to have shouted, 'Oh don't! Oh don't!'

Bywaters ran off and Percy died at the scene. Edith was hysterical but when she calmed down the police questioned her and she alleged that a strange man had stabbed her husband. A neighbour of the couple, Fanny Lester, told officers that Bywaters had lodged with them and they also learned that he worked for the P&O shipping line.

The police discovered letters that Edith had written to Freddie and soon arrested him and charged him with Percy's murder. Edith was arrested soon afterwards and charged with murder and, alternatively, with being an accessory to murder. She did not know that Bywaters had been arrested, but when she saw him in the police station later she said, 'Oh God, why did he do it?' and claimed, 'I didn't want him to do it.'

Bywaters explained his actions to the police as follows: 'I waited for Mrs Thompson and her husband. I pushed her to one side, also pushing him into the street. We struggled. I took my knife from my pocket and we fought and he got the worst of it… the reason I fought with Thompson was because he never acted like a man to his wife. He always seemed several degrees lower than a snake. I loved her and I could not go on seeing her leading that life. I did not intend to kill him. I only meant to injure him. I gave him the opportunity of standing up to me like a man but he wouldn't.' The defendant stuck rigidly to this story during his trial, which opened at the Old Bailey on 6 December 1922.

Edith had written no fewer than 62 intimate letters to Bywaters and stupidly they had kept them. In these she referred to Bywaters as 'Darlingest and Darlint'. Some of them described how she had tried to murder Percy on several occasions. In one apparently referring to an attempt to poison him, she wrote, 'You said it was enough for an elephant. Perhaps it was. But you don't allow for the taste making it possible for only a small quantity to be taken.' She had also tried broken glass and told Bywaters that she had made three attempts, but that because Percy had discovered some in his food she had had to stop.

Edith had sent Bywaters press cuttings describing murders by poisoning and had told Bywaters that she had aborted her own baby after becoming pregnant by him.

At the trial Bywaters refused to incriminate Edith and when cross-examined told the prosecution that he did not believe that Edith had actually attempted to poison Percy but had rather a vivid imagination and a passion for sensational novels that extended to imagining herself as one of the characters.

Edith had been advised by her counsel not to go into the witness box but decided to do so and promptly incriminated herself. Asked what she had meant when she had written to Bywaters asking him to send her 'something to give her husband', she said she had 'no idea', an answer that was found unconvincing.

In his summing up the judge described Edith's letters as 'full of the outpourings of a silly but, at the same time, a wicked affection'. Mr Justice Shearman's summing up was fair in law, but he made much of the adultery, for he was obviously a Victorian gentleman of high moral principles. However, he also instructed the jury, 'You will not convict her unless you are satisfied that she and he agreed that this man should be murdered when he could be, and she knew that he was going to do it, and directed him to do it, and by arrangement between them he was doing it.'

The jury were not convinced by the defence case and took just over two hours to find both defendants guilty of murder. Even after the verdict was read out Bywaters continued to defend Edith loudly. Nevertheless, the judge had to pass the death sentence on both of them as required by law. Edith was taken to Holloway and Bywaters to Pentonville, prisons less than a kilometre apart in north London, and placed in the condemned cells.

Each lodged an appeal but these were dismissed. Edith Thompson was an adulteress, an abortionist and possibly a woman who incited a murder or, worse still, had herself tried to poison her husband. At least this is how she was judged by the morals of the time – that is, until she was sentenced to death. The public and the media, which had both been so against her, now did a complete U-turn and campaigned for a reprieve. A petition to spare Edith containing nearly a million signatures was produced. However this, even together with Bywaters's repeated confession that he and he alone killed Thompson, failed to persuade the Home Secretary to reprieve her.

At 9am on 9 January 1923 both prisoners were hanged by the neck until they were dead. Bywaters met his end bravely, still protesting Edith's innocence, while she was in a state of total collapse. She had dramatic mood swings even up to the morning of execution as she expected to be reprieved all along. A few minutes before they entered the condemned cell the execution party heard a ghastly moan come from Edith's cell. She was semi-conscious as the hangman, John Ellis, strapped her wrists, and according to his biography she looked dead already.

Edith was carried the short distance to the gallows by two warders and two assistants and held on the trap while Ellis did his work. Depending on whose version of events you believe, a considerable amount of blood dripped from her after the hanging. Some, including Bernard Spillsbury, the famous pathologist who carried out the autopsy on her, claim it was due to her being pregnant and miscarrying. Others claim it was caused by an inversion of the uterus, but the authorities claimed that nothing untoward happened at all.

She had been in custody for over three months before the execution, so would have probably known if she was pregnant. Under English law the execution would have been stayed until after she had given birth. In fact, Edith would have almost certainly been reprieved. She had everything to gain from claiming to be pregnant, so it is surprising that she didn't if she had indeed missed two or three periods. However, she had aborted herself earlier, which may have damaged her uterus, and this, combined with the force of the drop, may have caused it to invert. Whatever the truth, this hanging seems to have had a profound effect on all those present. Several of the prison officers took early retirement. John Ellis retired in 1923 and committed suicide in 1931.

Edith's body was buried 'within the precincts of the prison in which she was last confined', in accordance with her sentence, but was reburied in 1970 at Brookwood Cemetery, Surrey, when Holloway Prison was being rebuilt.

Conclusion

In what appears at first to be a clear-cut case of folie a deux, we find in the end nothing more than two besotted lovers. So, almost shared madness. Tragically for both of them, Edith Thompson and Frederick Bywaters were executed because of the naivety they shared. The fact that Edith sent love letters in which she claimed to have tried to poison her husband with glass did not help her case one bit. The fatal act – the killing of a man in the street – by Bywaters was a cowardly act, which the jury recognised. But it was the act of one person.

CHAPTER SIXTEEN

MARTHA BECK AND RAYMOND FERNANDEZ

The Lonely Hearts Killers

Thirteen-year-old Martha Seabrook had already grown prodigiously fat when her brother raped her in 1933. This unpleasant incident may account for her later almost insatiable appetite for the bizarre in sex and her longing for a life of romance. It may also have lain at the root of her increasingly callous view of her fellow human beings.

She married three times, the last time to Alfred Beck in 1944. Each of the three lasted for a very short time. During this period she trained as a nurse, then as an undertaker's assistant. After several years of washing dead bodies she was appointed superintendent of a home for disabled children in Pensacola, Florida.

Raymond Fernandez, six years Martha's senior, was born in Hawaii of Spanish parents. Raised in Connecticut, he lived for some time in Spain, where he had married and fathered four children, all of whom he had long since abandoned.

During the WWII Fernandez had served – briefly but apparently with some distinction – with British Intelligence, though a head injury sustained in 1945 seems to have unhinged an already none too stable personality. He began to study black magic and claimed to have an irresistible power over women. Whatever the reason, this philanderer is thought to have charmed his way into more than a hundred women's hearts, homes and bank accounts over the next couple of years and swindled them all.

Fernandez's modus operandi was simple. Each of his victims was selected from 'Lonely Hearts' ads in newspapers and that is how, towards the end of 1947, he met Martha Beck, and murder was added to fraud and deceit. The relationship ran into trouble early on as a result of Beck's fanatical demands on Fernandez's fidelity, for she went to extreme, often burlesque lengths to ensure that he did not consummate any of the similar liaisons into which he entered. In one instance she insisted on sleeping with one of the victims to make sure there was no nocturnal fun and games. All the while Fernandez remained a difficult consort to control and his frequent falls from grace soon made him the focus of Beck's violent temper.

In December 1948 Fernandez made the acquaintance of a 66-year-old widow from New York named Janet Fay. Having plundered her savings by promising marriage, he invited her to the Long Island apartment that he shared with his 'sister' (Beck) and strangled and bludgeoned her to death. The body was later buried.

Mrs Delphine Downing, a young widow with a two-year-old daughter, Rainelle, was the next victim, only weeks after Mrs Fay was disposed of. She took Fernandez as her lover –

much to Beck's annoyance – and he moved into Delphine's home in Michigan. After robbing her of what money and possessions they could, Beck and Fernandez forced sleeping pills down Delphine's throat and shot their unconscious victim through the head. To stop little Rainelle crying, Beck drowned her in the bath. The two bodies were buried in the cellar under new cement. However, after suspicious neighbours reported the disappearance of Delphine and her daughter to the police, the murderous career of Beck and Fernandez came to an end.

The couple were arrested and, when it was realised that Michigan could not implement the death penalty, extradited to New York. Both prisoners confessed to the Fay and Downing murders, but stubbornly denied the other 17 of which they were suspected. The trial became a cause celebre, not so much because of the murders themselves, but because of Beck's regular dispatches from jail to the press detailing her and her lover's sexual exploits.

Despite serious doubts as to Fernandez's state of mind, the so-called Lonely Hearts Killers were judged sane and found guilty. Still expressing their undying love, Beck and Fernandez were executed in the electric chair at Sing Sing Prison, New York, on 8 March 1951. There was a slight hitch when it was discovered that Beck was too fat to fit in the chair. She had to be seated on the arm rests for her flight to eternity.

Conclusion

This is not an easy case to categorise, though on balance I see it as folie a deux. Beck had an insatiable desire for unusual sex and no doubt developed a sexual fascination with dead bodies. If any motive dominated in her, it was that she was desperate to find a hard-working and faithful husband, as her extreme possessiveness testifies. Beck would have done anything to keep her husband, even theft and murder, and to such acts she may have been his accomplice, but whether a willing or a reluctant one is not clear.

For his part, Fernandez was a consummate philanderer and con man, and marrying Martha Beck could never have changed his ways, despite her persistent complaints. His motive was simple: financial gain.

While their motives may have differed, it's certain that without each other they would not have committed acts of theft and murder.

CHAPTER SEVENTEEN

MYRA HINDLEY AND IAN BRADY
THE MOORS MURDERERS

If ever a killing couple deserved to be hanged, it was the sado-sexual psychopathic duo Myra Hindley and Ian Brady. Britons jailed for life serve on average about 12 years in prison, but such was the depravity of the 'Moors Murders' that later Home Secretaries stated that Brady and Hindley (until her death in 2002) were among a small group of lifers – Rose West is another – who should never be released.

Public opinion in Britain certainly supports him on this issue, as evidenced by the hatred that Brady and Hindley engendered both for their crimes and their behaviour during their trial and subsequently. The Moors Murders recall Fred and Rose West in that the impetus for these horrific acts was the powerful physical and psychological bond between the two killers: the folie a deux that led them to commit crimes that they would probably never have carried out as individuals.

Glasgow-born Brady was a quiet, brooding stock clerk who admired the Nazis and was heavily influenced by the writings of Nietzsche and the Marquis de Sade. In 1961 his employers, Millwards Merchandisers in Manchester, recruited a new secretary, Myra Hindley, who harboured a crush on Brady for a year until he finally responded to her interest.

They became lovers and she was putty in his hands, listening without reproach to his talks on Nazism and Nietzsche, changing the way she dressed to please him and eventually agreeing to take part in a murder spree with him. Hindley always portrayed herself as a gullible, easily led and totally manipulated young woman – she was 19 when she met Brady – who fell under the spell of an evil man and simply went along for the ride. But there has always been strong evidence – including the harsh tone of her voice on the couple's ghoulish tape recording of the murder of Lesley Ann Downey, and Brady's claims that she insisted on strangling the little girl herself and enjoyed toying in public with the silk cord she had used – that Hindley was far more than a passive accomplice.

The killings began on 12 July 1963 when Hindley lured Pauline Reade into her car as the 16-year-old walked to a dance at a railwaymen's club in Manchester. Brady later said she was lured on the pretext of helping Hindley find an expensive glove on nearby Saddleworth Moor and was offered a stack of records in return. When Hindley and the girl arrived on the moor they met Brady, who had ridden there on his motorbike. Depending on whose account you believe, Pauline was then taken off to a remote spot either by Brady alone or by both of them, where she was raped, beaten and stabbed before being buried.

MYRA HINDLEY AND IAN BRADY

The couple repeated the method roughly every six months, picking up 12-year-old John Kilbride at a market in Ashton-under-Lyne; Keith Bennett, also 12, as he walked to his grandmother's home in Longsight; and finally ten-year-old Lesley Ann Downey. Each time they elaborated on the process, taking more time over it, drawing out the agony for their victims and maximising their own perverted pleasure. Pornographic pictures of Lesley Ann which had been taken by Brady and Hindley were later found, along with the tape cassette, in a luggage locker at Manchester Central Station.

However, in 1965 the couple made a fatal mistake: they let a third person into their dark secret. Brady had been grooming Myra's brother-in-law, David Smith, for several months and was confident he could trust the 17-year-old to not only keep a secret but also become an active member of their killing club. But Brady miscalculated badly. While Smith appeared to have been brainwashed by him, noting in his own diary, 'Rape is not a crime, it is a state of mind. Murder is a hobby and a supreme pleasure', in reality he was just a naive teenager who was simply mouthing phrases because he admired the older man and wanted to be his friend.

All that changed on the night of 6 October 1965, when Smith called at Brady and Hindley's home at 16 Wardle Brook Avenue in the east Manchester suburb of Hattersley. Smith was confronted by Brady axing to death 17-year-old Edward Evans, a stranger whom he had met earlier that evening in a local pub. Terrified, Smith agreed to help tidy up the mess and hide the body in an upstairs bedroom, and tried to join in as Brady and Hindley joked about the killing. Having convinced them he would keep his mouth shut, Smith left the house and went straight back to his young wife, Maureen, Myra's sister, and told her everything.

She persuaded him to call the police and the following morning Brady and Hindley were arrested at their home and Evans's body was found upstairs. Brady was immediately charged with murder, but Hindley was not charged until four days later, after a notebook containing a 'murder plan' was found in her car.

Smith told police that the couple had bragged about having killed other youngsters and buried them on the moors to the east of the city. Greater Manchester Police began a huge search of Saddleworth Moor and over the next fortnight recovered the bodies of Lesley Ann Downey and John Kilbride. Although they suspected Brady and Hindley had also killed Pauline Reade and Keith Bennett, they had no bodies and no other evidence.

In April 1966 the couple went on trial at Chester Assizes accused of three murders. They both denied all charges and tried to shift the blame on to Smith, but the jury saw right through their charade and convicted Brady of all three murders and Hindley of two. Hindley was also found guilty of harbouring Brady in connection with the John Kilbride murder. They were jailed for life with a recommendation that they serve a minimum of 30 years.

Initially the couple's sordid love affair remained strong despite their enforced separation and they requested permission to marry, which was denied. Over the years, however, they grew apart, as Brady accepted his guilt and his fate, while Hindley continued to protest her innocence and increasingly blamed him for his role in her downfall. In 1970 she broke off all contact with Brady and the following year began a campaign for her release, which was soon taken up by civil rights campaigner Lord Longford.

Then, in 1986, Hindley changed her strategy. She realised she would never be released until she confessed to her crimes and tried to help find the two missing bodies. This she did and in July 1987 police unearthed the remains of Pauline Reade on Saddleworth Moor. But successive home secretaries, both Conservative and Labour, said that Hindley should never be released.

Her supporters claimed this was unjust because the judge set a tariff of 30 years and they said it should not be for politicians, who might be swayed by public opinion, to override the recommendations of the judiciary or the parole board.

Early in 2002 the European Court of Human Rights made a ruling in the case of another lifer that appeared to set a precedent. Hindley claimed she was a completely reformed character who did not pose a threat to children or society in general. But her victims' relatives actively lobbied against her release and there remained genuine fears that if she were freed her life would be in danger because of the public's hatred for her, especially in the Manchester area. Myra Hindley died in November 2002 from a chest infection that developed after a heart attack.

Brady meanwhile has sought permission in vain to be allowed to starve himself to death. He has also written a book, *The Gates of Janus*, which he claims gives an insight into the mind of a serial killer. He is legally barred from receiving any profits from sales of the book.

More than 30 years after the Moors Murders, the names of Ian Brady and Myra Hindley remain perhaps the most reviled in Britain. Even after her death, Hindley provokes stronger emotions than her partner, because people find it difficult to understand how a woman – and apparently a sane woman – could be involved in such atrocious crimes against children. However much she tried to minimise her involvement in the murders, the fact is that without her Brady would have found it much more difficult to commit the crimes.

It was Hindley who helped entice the children into the car and Hindley who drove the vehicle on to the moors, for Brady could not drive. At the time of writing Brady is at the secure Ashworth Hospital, and has repeatedly said he does not wish to be released – his only wish is to be allowed to die. Over the years he has launched a number of legal actions, albeit unsuccessfully, to ensure his wishes are met.

Conclusion

Folie a deux is in abundance here, given the powerful, all-consuming sexual elements. As with Frederick and Rose West, two fantasy-driven minds nurturing the same latent delusions fused when Brady and Hindley joined together. Without doubt, Brady was the stronger character and he found a subservient partner in his new girlfriend, Myra, who, like Rose West, would do anything to please her man – even murder. It is doubtful that, as individuals, they would have translated their fantasies into murder, but once the cocktail of their warped personalities was mixed they were a lethal team.

CHAPTER EIGHTEEN

CHARLENE AND GERALD ARMOND GALLEGO
A Bit of Rough

Although their murderous career rivals those of most other serial sex killers, the acts of depravity committed by Charlene and Gerald Gallego have gone largely unnoticed since their arrest and trial more than 20 years ago. Just why this should be so is something of an enigma, for they hold a unique place in the annals of American crime.

A report on multiple killings that was compiled in 1987 by an FBI task force stated that at any given time there were more than 5,000 serial killers operating in the USA. Strikingly, not one husband-and-wife partnership was mentioned in the document, yet, a mere seven years earlier, the Gallegos, a deeply twisted pair of psychopaths, had committed their final killing and would, over the following four years, be involved in trials in which the courts were treated to revelations of the most appalling nature.

This lethal partnership had begun in an inauspicious way.

CHRISTOPHER BERRY-DEE

When Gerald met Charlene for the first time it was in a rather seedy bar in Sacramento, California's capital city, in 1977. He found the short, teenage-looking woman with blonde hair very attractive and she, in turn, thought him 'a very nice clean-cut fellow'. Gerald was 31 and Charlene ten years younger, but already she had two failed marriages under her belt. A few days later he sent her some flowers and within weeks they were living together.

Gerald Armond Gallego was born in Sacramento on 17 July 1946. His father, Gerald Albert Gallego, was a violent psychopath who was executed by gas on 3 March 1955 after committing three murders, two of the victims being policemen. Eight years old at the time, Gerald Jr wasn't told how his father died. However, he appears to have been a chip off the old block because two years later he was arrested for first-degree burglary while armed with a deadly weapon. This wasn't just an isolated incident either, for when still only 12 he was sent to a reform school, Fred C. Nelles School for Boys, after being convicted of having forcible sex with a six-year-old girl. After 23 months the priapic adolescent was released on parole to find that his mother had moved away without leaving a forwarding address for him.

His mother's departure was probably born out of her realisation that her son would never be anything other than trouble, given that the family was bursting at the seams with psychopaths and violent thugs. At the time of Gerald's release from the reform school, three cousins on his mother's side were serving life for murder and his half-brother was serving 15 years to life for shooting an assistant in a liquor store during a robbery.

CHARLENE AND GERALD ARMOND GALLEGO

It has to be said that Gerald's mother herself was no angel. Raised in a family that counted murderers and child molesters among its number, Lorraine Pullen Bennett Gallego earned a meagre living working as a prostitute in Sacramento's skid row. Unsurprisingly, Gerald came into contact with aspects of his mother's unorthodox occupation. As a boy during the 1950s he served as a runner for various pimps and it was probably in these circles that he developed his generally less than chivalrous attitude towards women.

Undaunted by his mother's unsubtle attempt to abandon him, Gerald tracked her down and persuaded her to let him share her home once again. Shortly afterwards, however, he was given five years in an adult jail for a string of burglary offences, but served less than three years. By the time he met Charlene he had been arrested 27 times and had seven convictions to his name, even though he had served only six years in total behind bars. And, in addition to having such a distinguished curriculum vitae as a felon, he was a veteran of five failed marriages.

Charlene had enjoyed an upbringing that was as respectable and privileged as Gerald's was disreputable and deprived. Born into a wealthy middle-class family, the daughter of Charles and Mercedes Williams, she came into the world on 10 October 1956. Her father had worked his way up in the grocery business, advancing from supermarket butcher to an executive position with a national grocery chain. Charlene was an only child and grew up in Arden Park, an upmarket area of Sacramento. According to an account of her life by the writer Brian Marriner, she was an intelligent girl with an IQ of 160. Enjoying the benefit of a good education, she was an accomplished violinist and at the age of 17 won a place at San Francisco's Conservatory of Music.

Despite, or perhaps because of, her comfortable upbringing, Charlene was very much a rebel and at the age of 15 she enjoyed a brief love affair with a black law student. In 1971 that sort of thing was still capable of causing a scandal in the USA. By the time she ran into Gerald six years later, this attractive, short, slightly built, young woman had two short-lived, unsuccessful marriages under her belt.

In any event, when the paths of these two individuals from markedly different backgrounds eventually crossed, the mutual attraction they experienced developed into a relationship that would devastate their own lives and leave in its wake the corpses of at least ten sexually brutalised victims.

At first it is difficult to imagine just what it was that drew Charlene to the brutish and uncultured Gerald, other than the strong sexual attraction of 'a bit of rough'. Her track record in such matters suggests she had a libido that in many respects matched his, and their early months together seem to confirm that in this respect they were tailor-made for each other. Gerald's morals were those of an oversexed farmyard animal and he had shown an unhealthily active interest in sex from early childhood. He had been sent to the reform school on account of a serious sexual matter. What is certain in all this is that for eight years he carried on a sexual relationship with his own daughter, Mary Ellen until she was 14. Revealingly, Charlene was fully aware of this and, far from condemning it, used it as a source of inspiration for the couple's own sex life.

During the early months of their relationship the Gallegos lived in north Sacramento, at 2067 Bluebird Lane. At first

Gerald appeared to be the dominant partner. Something of a control freak, as a lover he would dispense a violent beating to his woman and follow this with a long sex session. Charlene was happy to go along with this treatment, but she was far from keen when it came to accommodating Gerald's special sexual preference and she was forced to endure the indignity and pain of anal intercourse. Despite this, she seemed to be besotted with her brutal lover and he in turn, believing that he held the reins, was content with their life together. But he was never in charge to the extent that he imagined, as events were to prove.

Gerald had a girlfriend, a 16-year-old go-go dancer. However, he received something of a surprise when he found that he wasn't the only one at 2067 Bluebird Lane to be enjoying the girl's sexual favours. One afternoon in the summer of 1978 he returned home early from work to find his girlfriend and Charlene in bed together with a vibrator. To Gerald, this was an attack on his position of supremacy in the relationship with the two women and he reacted in the only way he knew. He went wild, throwing his adolescent, go-go-dancing girlfriend out of the window before beating Charlene black and blue. Ironically, had he paused to consider the less violent options, Gerald might have resolved the issue in a way that would have been sexually gratifying to all three and would have prevented the damage that would result from this incident.

The episode had a profound effect on Gerald's confidence and from this time onwards he would experience difficulty in obtaining an erection when making love to Charlene. The only activity that seemed to turn him on was anal penetration but

Charlene voiced her protests loudly enough to make him feel guilty and ashamed of his inability to perform vaginal intercourse. Nevertheless, the relationship survived.

In July 1978, prompted by Charlene, Gerald invited his daughter, 14-year-old Mary Ellen, around for the weekend of his birthday. She arrived with a girl of the same age, and during their stay Gerald celebrated his being 31 by sodomising Mary Ellen and forcing her friend to perform oral sex on him.

The birthday episode worked wonders for Gerald, for he found that he was able to enjoy normal intercourse with Charlene for some weeks afterwards. Noting the welcome effect on their sex life, Charlene reflected that Gerald had had no difficulty at all when it came to having sex with their young guests and she wondered if his performance would be maintained if he were to have regular stimulation in the shape of teenage girls. She mulled the idea over and eventually proposed that they kidnap girls for use as sex slaves, so as to ensure that Gerald would experience no further erection problems. Gerald reacted sceptically, asking what was to stop any such girl from going to the police after they had finished with her.

Charlene's response was succinct and cynical and showed that the balance of power had shifted between them. She simply said that dead girls can't talk.

By now Gerald was persuaded by the confidence in Charlene's voice and her enthusiasm for the outrageous scheme. To him, the idea was wonderful, the ultimate sexual fantasy, and all the more exciting because it sprang from his own partner's fertile imagination.

Almost immediately the couple began to plan their

campaign with great thoroughness. On a local firing range Charlene learned how to shoot a pistol, achieving a very high standard of marksmanship. Then the pair bought a white Dodge van, which they fitted out to suit their sinister purpose: in the back went a bunk, a propane cooker and a fridge; the windows were replaced by black, one-way glass.

With the van ready, the pair set out to find their first victims. On 12 September 1978 they parked in a shopping mall in Sacramento and waited until they saw two attractive young girls. Charlene got out of the van and approached the two, Rhonda Scheffler, 17 and married, and her friend, 16-year-old Kippi Vaught. The offer of some heroin was just the bait that was needed and the girls followed Charlene to the van. Inside, they were confronted by Gerald, who slammed the doors shut behind them and at gunpoint ordered them to sit still while he bound their wrists and ankles with tape. Moments later, with Gerald at the wheel, the van exited the car park and headed towards the foothills of the Sierra Nevada, 80 kilometres away.

When they reached their destination, a clearing screened from the road, Gerald stopped the van and ordered the two terrified girls out. He told them to strip off their clothes, which they did. At the same time, Charlene undressed, not wanting to be left out of the proceedings.

For several hours Gerald and Charlene raped and tortured their first sex slaves, leaving bite marks all over the girls' bodies, Charlene becoming particularly aroused by savagely biting their nipples. Then, when they had had enough of their victims, Gerald hit them over the head with a jack handle and seconds later shot them both in the head at point-blank range.

Leaving the bodies where they lay, the Gallegos drove off, full of excitement and euphoria over their new way of enjoying sex. For Charlene it had been the most sexually fulfilling moment of her life.

Back in Sacramento, Rhonda Scheffler's husband had reported her and Kippi missing. However, the police took no action and it was 48 hours before the girls' bodies were found, by two illegal Mexican immigrants who were working as ranch hands.

The bodies were examined and the pathologist's report provided grim evidence that the murders were the work of more than one person. Rhonda Scheffler's body revealed semen in her anus, her mouth and her ear. A deep bite on her left buttock was very close to her anus, while her right nipple had been almost bitten off. She had been killed by three gunshots to her head.

Kippi Vaught had endured almost identical treatment. Her left nipple was almost severed from her breast, and it was later established that Charlene had bitten it while Gerald sodomised the youngster. Kippi had also been killed by three shots to the head and it was with the same weapon, a .25-calibre pistol. What was of most significance to the investigators, however, was that the teethmarks on the girls' breasts were made by two different people.

Even then, the investigating team from the Sacramento County Sheriff's Department didn't for one moment suspect that the killers were a man and a woman. Instead, they suspected that two black men were responsible.

Two weeks after the killings Gerald married Charlene. He took this step to reinforce their relationship because he realised that she could, if she wished, turn him in to the police. His decision shows how much Charlene had come to dominate the relationship. The marriage served to bring her parents into the picture, and, while they were by no means enthusiastic about their new son-in-law, they understood that their daughter was infatuated with the man and accepted the union.

It was at this time that Gerald's daughter, Mary Ellen, told her grandfather that her father had raped and sodomised her. Enraged, he went straight to the police. Mary Ellen and her friend gave statements and a warrant was issued for Gerald Gallego's arrest.

This latest predicament eventually caused Charlene to tell her mother of the position and to ask for her help in getting Gerald out of the mess in which he found himself. Her mother proved to be as resourceful as Charlene herself. She told Charlene to steal the birth certificate of her cousin, Steven Robert Freil, a California Highway Patrolman who looked like Gerald. With this certificate Gerald was able to assume a new identity by obtaining a driving licence and other necessary documentation and using his mother-in-law's address as his own.

Gerald's mother-in-law now had a hold over him, which she used to make him take a regular job. She also bought him a new car and promised that, if he could maintain his reformed behaviour, she would provide the down payment on a house. Underlying her generosity was the plausible threat that, if he didn't keep Charlene happy or if harmed her in any way, she would have no hesitation in handing him over to the police. Gerald had no option but to go along with her demands.

Life for the Gallegos went on in the same way for months.

Then, in the late spring of 1979, Charlene began to hint that she wanted them to go out and capture another couple of sex slaves. It didn't take a lot to persuade Gerald and the couple decided on 24 June 1979 for their mission. Both armed with pistols, they made their way to the next state, Nevada, and headed for Reno. It was the day of the Nevada State Fair and they had no trouble parking unobtrusively among hundreds of other vehicles.

They waited until late in the afternoon and then Gerald spotted two young girls that he found attractive. As before, Charlene made the approach to their victims, offering Sandra Kaye Colley and Brenda Judd $20 each to place leaflets under windscreen wipers. Aged only 13 and 14, the two girls were runaways who were happy to take up the offer of some money and they made their way with Charlene to the white Dodge van to collect the leaflets. However, when they entered the van they were greeted by Gerald, who told them to remain still while Charlene bound their hands and feet with tape.

Out in the desert, the girls were stripped naked. Charlene was still taking her own clothes off when she saw Gerald already having sex with the girls. She threatened to shoot him if he didn't wait for her and he agreed to let her have the girls on her own for 20 minutes, to make up for his greediness. During that time Charlene bit off both girls' nipples.

After inflicting sexual torture lasting several hours, their passions sated, the Gallegos dispatched the two victims with bullets to the head. While Gerald dug a grave for the bodies, Charlene dipped her finger in the blood of one of the dead girls and on the victim's stomach drew a heart pierced by an arrow. Beside this she wrote the initials 'GG' and 'CG'.

CHARLENE AND GERALD ARMOND GALLEGO

After burying the bodies, the killers spent several hours disposing of evidence and cleaning the van. Their tasks finished, they ate breakfast.

Days later Charlene announced to Gerald that she was pregnant. He was not at all happy to hear this news and, once he had calmed down, told her to get an abortion. This she did, paying for it herself. Shortly afterwards Charlene shaved off her pubic hair to please Gerald. He was highly aroused by this, telling his wife that it made her look like a ten-year-old and calling her Mary Ellen during lovemaking.

There is no doubt that Gerald's unhealthy sexual preference was for very young girls, and the closer Charlene could get to looking extremely young herself, the more it boosted their sex life. But she couldn't keep up this play-acting indefinitely and it became more difficult as time passed. On top of this, she was being treated for depression and was taking prescription drugs as well as just about every other drug she could get her hands on. Something had to give, but it wouldn't be Charlene.

Once again Gerald was having erection problems. To make matters worse, when he did manage to get one, he was unable to ejaculate. To a man of Gerald's limited intellect, this was a crisis and he became distraught. Again it was Charlene who grasped the nettle, suggesting that it was about time they went out to find two more sex slaves, and on 24 April 1980 they set off in pursuit of fresh victims.

In a shopping mall they came across two girls who were just right. When Charlotte approached them, they were buying erotic lingerie. She discovered that they were Karen Chipman Twiggs and Stacy Ann Redican, both aged 17, and they needed the lingerie because they were hitching a ride to Los Angeles in the hope of landing parts in pornographic movies. Charlene simply offered them drugs and they eagerly followed her to the van. It was the last time the girls would do anything of their own volition.

With the two would-be porn starlets tied up in the back of the van, the Gallegos drove to Limerick Canyon, some 480 kilometres away, stopping off in Reno to buy a claw hammer. At a deserted camping ground they parked and spent the next few hours subjecting the two teenage runaways to every form of sexual abuse that they could devise. When they had finished, the girls were brutally beaten to death with the hammer before being buried in a shallow grave. The site was discovered barely 24 hours later by horrified picnickers.

As the girls had been killed by hammer blows, the police did not at that time establish a link with the four earlier victims, all of whom had been killed with firearms.

After their third double murder the Gallegos spent the night in a motel, where, Charlene recalled, a reinvigorated Gerald was able to perform normal sex with her. The result was that she became pregnant. Charlene was eight weeks into the pregnancy when Gerald resolved to marry her a second time. The couple went to Reno, where, using the name Steven Robert Freil, he became her husband yet again.

Despite Charlene's being sick much of the time, Gerald decided they would honeymoon in Oregon and on 3 June 1980 they set out in the van. Three days into their journey they saw a heavily pregnant young woman hitch-hiking in the same direction and stopped for her.

Twenty-one-year-old Linda Teresa Aguilar, probably reassured by the sight of another woman in a similar condition, accepted the couple's offer of a ride. Within a short time both Charlene and Gerald had sexually abused their passenger before beating her head with a hammer and burying her in a shallow grave. Her body was found three weeks later and the autopsy revealed that the presence of sand in her mouth, throat and windpipe indicated that she had been buried unconscious but still alive.

Less than a month later, back in Sacramento, relations between the Gallegos had once more begun to deteriorate. Twice, on 12 and 14 July, police were called to the house in Bluebird Lane after reports of noisy shouting matches. Chastened by the attention they were drawing to themselves, Gerald and Charlene made up. Gerald's birthday was coming up in a few days' time and Charlene suggested that they mark the occasion by hunting down another pair of sex slaves.

But this time they failed to find any girls suitable for their purpose and instead spent the evening of 17 July at the Boat Inn in west Sacramento. There they struck up a conversation with the barmaid, 34-year-old Virginia Mochel. Virginia evidently appealed to both Gallegos, for they agreed that she would be the victim they would use to celebrate Gerald's birthday. After finishing their drinks they went outside to their car and waited for Virginia's shift to end. When the woman emerged into the car park she was kidnapped at gunpoint and, in a departure from the Gallegos' previous modus operandi, was taken back to their house. It was, after all, Gerald's birthday and something special was called for.

In their own home the couple felt more at ease and certainly more imaginative, for they produced an illustrated book on S&M which they consulted throughout the evening's proceedings. They began their celebrations by stripping off Virginia's clothes and whipping her. Her body stinging from the lashes, she then had to endure the pain and humiliation of being sodomised by Charlene, who used a thick black rubber dildo. Almost demented by the pain of the anal rape, Virginia was then hung up on a hook, her wrists bound, and whipped again. Without the remotest idea why this was happening to her, the pretty barmaid was then made to perform oral sex on both her tormentors while they viciously chewed her nipples. Over the next hour or so she was forced, three times, to perform oral sex on Charlene while being sodomised by Gerald.

After what must have seemed an eternity to their victim, the evil couple came to the end of their terrifying orgy of cruelty. Her body on fire with the pain of her ordeal and humiliated beyond anything she could have imagined, the mother of two begged the Gallegos to end her life. 'Kill me now,' she sobbed.

'Why on earth do you want to die?' asked Charlene.

'Because I can't live after what you've done to me,' Virginia wailed.

Within minutes she had her wish. She was strangled by Gerald, who then put her body in the van and drove to a river, where he dumped it into the water, assuming that it would be carried out to sea. But he was mistaken, for the body grounded on a sandbank in the river, where it lay decomposing until it was discovered two and a half months later.

The police had treated Virginia Mochel's disappearance as simply another missing-person case but that changed when, on 2 October, a skeleton, its hands tied behind its back, was found in the river. Apart from a few teeth and some cheap jewellery, nothing else remained of the former barmaid.

However, after establishing the identity of the corpse, police interviewed as many as they could trace of the customers who had been at the bar on the night Virginia disappeared. They even spoke to the Gallegos, but not as suspects: at that stage detectives assumed the killer to be a male acting alone. Even so, the episode unnerved Gerald and Charlene, for they sold the van and bought a car. Despite this precaution, retribution was not far away.

Craig Raymond Miller, 22, and his fiancee, Mary Elizabeth Sowers, 21, known as Mary Beth, both promising undergraduates, had enjoyed dinner at the Carousel restaurant in Sacramento on the night of 1 November 1980, and were making their way across the restaurant's car park when they were forced at gunpoint to get into the Gallegos' car. A friend who tried to intervene received a slap across his face from a very pregnant Charlene before the car sped away. Having managed to note the car's licence plate, the man phoned the police. Once it was realised that the abducted couple came from wealthy, prominent families – Mary Beth's father was an eminent nuclear physicist – the police threw all their resources into the investigation.

Meanwhile, the Gallegos had driven to a camping site with their two well-heeled captives. On arriving there, Gerald asked Charlene if she would like to have intercourse with Craig Miller but she declined. Gerald's reaction to this was to shoot Miller in the heart three times at point-blank range.

Leaving Miller's body behind, where it was found at 11.30 the next morning, and with Gerald in the back seat fondling the terrified Mary Beth, Charlene drove back to Bluebird Lane. There the attractive Mary Beth Sowers was subjected to appalling sexual abuse by both Gallegos. The next morning the couple drove her into the country. Near Loomis, about 30 kilometres from Sacramento, they stopped and shot her three times in the head. Then Gerald dumped her body in an old mining cavity, where it lay for three weeks before two schoolboys stumbled across it on 22 November.

On receiving a report of the abduction from the dead couple's friend, the police had run a check on the licence number of the car and found it to be registered in Charlene Gallego's name but at her parents' address. Officers immediately went there but all that their visit achieved was to give Mrs Williams an opportunity to call her daughter and warn her. Charlene and Gerald went on the run.

By this time, because the killings had involved the crossing of state borders, the FBI had become involved and one of the first things they did was to tap the Williamses' phone. This allowed the agents access to conversations between the fugitives and Charlene's parents. Agents followed the Williamses to Sparks, a town in Nevada, where the couple wired $500 to their daughter, who was by then in Omaha, Nebraska. On 17 November, when the Gallegos went to collect the money from the Western Union office in Omaha, they were arrested.

During the time before their trial, Charlene did some plea bargaining with the prosecution. She held some good cards, as the prosecution was short of reliable proof in some of the killings, there being no eyewitnesses other than Charlene. Consequently, she was able to secure for herself a 16-year sentence instead of the death penalty, in return for her testifying against Gerald.

In Charlene's version of events, which is summed up by

Brian Marriner, she had been merely an innocent bystander, caught up in Gerald's demands. She admitted luring girls to the van and to being present when the last two victims were killed, but she claimed that she had acted under duress.

On 17 January 1981, while she was awaiting trial, Charlene went into labour and gave birth to a boy whom she named Gerald Armond Gallego, after his father.

Ten months later, on 15 November 1982, the trial for the murders of Craig Miller and Mary Beth Sowers commenced. Gerald had argued that he would not be given a fair trial in Sacramento and had been granted a different venue. As a result, the trial was held in Martinez, a small town in the San Francisco Bay area. The proceedings were remarkable for the six days of cross-examination that Charlene underwent at the hands of Gerald, who had sacked his defence lawyer. The main thrust of Charlene's defence was that she had acted out of her sense of wifely duty and that all her actions were carried out solely in order to ensure his sexual gratification. This situation provided some interesting exchanges.

When Gerald posed the question, 'Can you tell me anything you did to prevent any of those people from being murdered?' Charlene answered, 'I just sat there like a fool. I didn't do a damned thing.'

On being asked by her husband if she considered herself responsible for even a little part of the deaths, she explained, 'All right! My wifely duties were to do your bidding. I had no right to stop you from doing those things or for me to escape. My life with you was a mixture of love and fear and pleasure. I wish I were dead. The only good thing to come out of all this is my son, Gerald junior.'

On the issue of her having lured young, pretty girls to the van in order to fulfil his perverted fantasies, Gerald asked her if she had no sexual fantasies herself. She replied that she hadn't. Gerald reinforced his point by saying, 'Then we, this court and the jury, are to assume that you risked your life and freedom and everything that is precious to a young woman, you risked all that just to help your husband fulfil *his* sexual fantasies?'

'Yes,' she replied.

'And you got nothing out of it except making him happy?'

'No.'

Demonstrating a surprising skill in the art of cross-examination, Gerald asked, 'Isn't it a fact, Mrs Gallego, that you are a lesbian and have had a lesbian relationship while in jail?'

'Well, I may have had what some would describe as a homosexual affair in jail, but I wouldn't call myself a lesbian,' was her awkward response.

In a further attempt to demolish his wife's credibility, Gerald called a female prisoner as a witness. This woman testified that Charlene was indeed a lesbian and an aggressive one too. She asserted that Charlene had threatened her with violence if she didn't comply with her wishes.

As evidence, Gerald produced some letters that Charlene had written to him while they were awaiting trial. These letters were lovingly written and showed that Charlene had been a willing partner in it all.

While Gerald tried to discredit Charlene, the prosecution produced a witness whose testimony, given to the judge in camera, would be used to steer Gerald towards the death penalty. This key witness was his daughter. In her statement, read to the court by the judge, Mary Ellen said that Gerald had told her that it was natural for her to allow him to commit sexual acts with her. Sometimes she had protested about the sexual contacts but had usually obliged. The assaults were committed periodically, sometimes with force, from when she was six until she was 14. Those acts were intercourse, oral copulation and sodomy.

Mary Ellen also stated that Charlene was on occasion present in the apartment when she was being sexually abused.

The trial lasted until late April 1983 and Gerald was found guilty on two counts of first-degree murder. Added to these were two counts of kidnapping. On 2 May the same jury recommended that Gallego be sentenced to death. Accordingly, he was sent to San Quentin's Death Row, although it was regarded as extremely improbable that California would actually carry out an execution. Instead, it was assumed that he would spend the rest of his life in prison.

However, it wasn't all over yet, for, following his conviction in California, Gerald faced a new threat from the state of Nevada, where the authorities were anxious to extradite him for trial in the murders of Karen Chipman Twiggs, Stacy Ann Redican, Brenda Judd and Sandra Colley. The problem for Gerald was that there was little doubt that Nevada would hesitate to carry out the death sentence.

The extradition went through and arrangements were made for the trial. Before proceedings could begin, however, an unusual episode took place when Pershing County, where the trial was to be held, couldn't afford the cost, estimated at around $60,000, of trying their man. When this was announced it engendered a powerful response from the public, who wanted to see justice done. Donations of money flooded in and, by the time the trial began, more than $23,000 had been raised to help defray the costs.

On 24 May 1984 the trial of Gerald Gallego commenced and once again Charlene was the key prosecution witness against her husband. When questioned about the events of the morning of one of the last murders, she gave the following account: 'Well, Gerald woke up that morning and said, "I want a girl." I took it to mean that he wanted to kidnap, rape and kill another girl who fitted his sexual fantasy.'

On her sex life with Gerald, she had this to say: 'It was a problem all the time. He was always trying different kinds of sex, things that hurt me.' On this point the prosecutor pressed for a more detailed explanation asking, 'Are you talking about anal sex, sodomy?'

'Yes,' replied Charlene. 'He couldn't get an erection most of the time. Then, when he *could* do something, he couldn't have a climax.'

Latching on to this, the prosecutor said, 'You're saying that everything was bad in the bedroom and that was the reason he wanted to have what you call love slaves?'

'Yes,' replied Charlene.

Although fighting a losing battle, the defence wasn't prepared to simply roll over and die. In an attempt to show Charlene's evidence in a more pragmatic light they called up a female psychiatrist who, when she took the stand, spoke derisively of the notion that Charlene was just a weak, subservient wife who had been dominated by Gerald. She said, 'Charlene, the woman he was with for many years, has an IQ of 160, which puts her in the top one per cent of the population and, from a psychologist's point of view, she would have had far more control over their relationship than Gerald did.'

Nevertheless, despite the transparently flawed nature of Charlene's testimony, she received only a prison sentence. Her spouse, however, was shown no such clemency. After deliberating for only four hours, on 7 June 1984 the jury found him guilty on two of the counts of murder and recommended the death penalty, later endorsed by the judge.

As a result of this trial Gerald Gallego was sent to Death Row at Nevada State Prison in Carson City. Although not on Death Row, Charlene was sent to the women's section of the same prison. Their son, Gerald Jr, was brought up by Mercedes Williams, Charlene's mother.

In July 1997 Charlene was released from prison. She gave the prison authorities no indication as to where she was going to live but undertook to register as a felon when she settled somewhere. Her mother was not forthcoming with any clue as to her daughter's whereabouts, saying that she had left California and wasn't coming back.

Gerald Gallego exhausted the appeal process, having his death sentence reaffirmed in 1999. However, unlike his father, he was not to die at the hands of the executioner. On 18 July 2002, seven years after Charlene walked free from prison, Gallego died, aged 56, in the Nevada prison system's medical centre. The cause of his death was given as rectal cancer and he had given instructions that he required no further treatment and no attempts to resuscitate him. He was heavily sedated when he died and made no final statement.

Conclusion

A fascinating example of folie a deux and, like Brady and Hindley, a classic case for those who study the criminal mind.

Born on the wrong side of the tracks, Gerald was the son of an executed serial killer, while Charlene came from honest, upstanding and well-to-do stock. Charlene enjoyed the 'rough' that Gallego offered. The dominant partner, he gave her the thrills she so needed. Charlene loved living 'on the edge', which was already a way of life for her otherwise sexually inadequate partner. And, like Myra Hindley and Rose West, she would do anything to please her man, even if it meant resorting to sado-sexual homicide.

Without the companionship of Gallego, it is inconceivable that Charlene would have committed murder. He, no doubt, would have travelled along Murder Road at some point, inevitably meeting his doom: like father like son.

CHAPTER NINETEEN

RUTH SNYDER AND HENRY JUDD GRAY

The Best-Laid Plans...

The murder committed by Snyder and Gray was, in the words of one crime writer, a 'cheap crime involving cheap people'. But the thrill-hungry 'Roaring Twenties' devoured every sordid detail and made infamous celebrities of this otherwise mundane couple. After murder, their biggest crime was being stupid.

It was in 1925 that Ruth Brown Snyder, a discontented housewife from Long Island, met a corset salesman named Henry Judd Gray while lunching in New York. She was a 32-year-old blonde, tall, good-looking and possessed of a strong personality. He was 34, short and eminently forgettable, with a cleft chin and thick glasses that lent him a look of perpetual surprise.

They seem to have been polar opposites, yet there was an unmistakable sexual attraction at their first meeting and before long they had begun a passionate affair. Ruth's husband, Albert, was at his office every day, working as the art editor of *Motor Boating* magazine, and, when the Snyders' nine-year-old daughter, Lorraine, was at school, the amorous couple would often meet at the family home. At other times the lovers would deposit Lorraine in a hotel lobby and then use a room upstairs. They met as often as they could and it seemed they couldn't get enough of each other.

But it was not long before Ruth Snyder changed from a jaded housewife with torrid sex on her mind to a woman with a devious scheme. Trapped in a loveless marriage, she set about convincing her lover that Albert was mistreating her and must be done away with. Gray rejected the idea, but Ruth kept up the pressure, softening her demands with the affectionate names she used for him: 'Bud' and 'Lover Boy'. In their baby talk she was 'Momsie'.

In time Gray became so unnerved by Ruth's demands that he took to drinking large quantities of Prohibition liquor to calm his nerves. But, despite Momsie's efforts, Lover Boy remained steadfast. Then, on Saturday, 19 March 1927, he yielded. Gray spent most of that cold day drinking, seeking the courage to commit murder for the sake of his lover. The couple had devised a plan whereby he took a train from Syracuse to New York and then a bus to Long Island. After arriving in Queens Village, where the Snyders lived, he hesitated for an hour, drinking from his flask, before making his way to the couple's house and entering by the back door, as planned. The Snyder family were out at a party and would not return home until late that evening. Gray hid in a spare bedroom, where Ruth had left the chosen tools of murder: a window sash weight, rubber gloves and chloroform.

When the Snyders got back, around 2am, Ruth opened the bedroom door a little and whispered, 'Are you in there, Bud, dear?' before leaving briefly, to return wearing only a slip. She and Gray had sex while her husband was asleep in the nearby master bedroom. About an hour later Gray picked up the sash weight and Ruth took him to the room where her husband was sleeping, his head beneath the bedclothes. The two stood at either side of the bed, and Gray lifted the weight and smashed it down awkwardly on to the sleeping man's head. The ill-aimed blow glanced off the victim's skull. Stunned, Albert Snyder bellowed and tried to grab his assailant, who screamed in terror, 'Momsie, Momsie, for God's sake, help!' Gray tried to suffocate Snyder with a pillow. When Albert fought back, Ruth hit him over the head with the sash weight several times. She then chloroformed him and garrotted him with a picture wire.

The pair had been convinced that their plan to simulate a robbery was foolproof, but it failed to convince the experienced detectives who investigated the case. Every one of the items that Ruth claimed had been taken by the burglar was found concealed in the house. Under thorough questioning she made the surprising move of confessing but, less surprisingly, blamed her lover for the whole thing. Gray was found a few hours later, holed up in a hotel in Syracuse. He protested his innocence, saying that he had not been in New York, but, when shown the train ticket stub that he had tossed in the wastebin of his hotel room, he confessed. Like Snyder, however, he blamed everything on his partner in crime.

At the time of their trial the two estranged lovers were still blaming each other for the murder. The trial was a media event, attended by celebrities such as the movie director D.W. Griffith, the mystery writer Mary Roberts Rinehart and the evangelists Billy Sunday and Aimee Semple McPherson. Each defendant had an attorney arguing his client's innocence. Ruth's husband, her lawyer said, 'drove love out from the house' by hankering after a departed sweetheart. He also stated that Gray had tempted Snyder into crime by taking out a $50,000 double-indemnity insurance policy on her husband. His client was a loving wife, he insisted, and she was not to be blamed for the conditions in her home. He followed this by calling the 'wronged woman' to the witness stand. Wearing a simple black dress, Ruth played the part of the long-suffering wife, saying how her husband ignored her nearly all the time, apart from those few occasions when he took her to a movie. It was she who had read the Bible to little Lorraine and made sure her daughter went to Sunday school.

Snyder's lawyer glossed over her romance with Gray and she herself defended their affair by stating that her lover had, like her, been unhappy at home. She added, however, that he had dragged her along to speakeasies and nightclubs, where she had witnessed him drink himself into a stupor. She herself, she swore, rarely drank and never smoked. Then she testified that Gray pressured her into taking out the huge insurance policy on Albert Snyder. 'Once he even sent me poison and told me to give it to my husband,' she told the court.

This caused Gray to whisper to his lawyers. A little later he took the stand and his lawyer described his client's situation as 'the most tragic story that has ever gripped the human heart'. The attorney stated that Gray was a law-abiding citizen who

had been deceived and dominated by a 'designing, deadly conscienceless, abnormal woman, a human serpent, a human fiend in the disguise of a woman'. His client had, he added, been 'drawn into this hopeless chasm when reason was gone, mind was gone, manhood was gone and when his mind was weakened by lust and passion'.

On the stand, Gray acted the victim, looking nervously at his elderly mother, who was attending the trial. Ruth had attempted to kill her husband on several occasions, he testified. Once she added knockout drops to his drink but this plan failed, so she tried to gas him instead. 'I told her that she was crazy,' Gray said innocently, after testifying that Ruth had given her husband poison to cure his hiccups, making him violently ill. 'I said to her that it was a hell of a way to cure hiccups,' Gray claimed, before telling the court of two occasions when Ruth tried to kill her husband with sleeping powder.

Gray's final ploy was to state that Ruth had set up the insurance policy on Snyder. He himself had not done so; nor had it been his idea. He then explained how Ruth had delivered the death blow to her sleeping husband. Gray's claim caused Ruth to sob loudly. The jury took just 98 minutes to return a verdict of 'guilty' on both defendants. Shocked at this pronouncement, Snyder and Gray were even more appalled to learn that death was the punishment for their crime.

On the day of the executions, 12 January 1928, Gray was the first of the two to go to the electric chair. When the warden came to his cell to collect the prisoner, he was sitting smiling, for he had received a letter from his wife saying that she forgave him. He was ready to go, he told the warden, and 'had nothing to fear'.

A few minutes after watching the prison lights flicker – a sign that the switch had been thrown to power the electric chair – Ruth Snyder followed her former lover. Reporters later recalled that, as she was being taken to the chair, she had said that God had forgiven her and that she hoped the world would do so too.

An ingenious *New York Daily News* reporter smuggled a camera into the death chamber by attaching it to his ankle. He got one shot as the electricity entered Ruth Snyder's body and she jerked against the straps holding her in the chair. The picture appeared in the paper the following day, but before long this lurid episode had faded from the public mind, to become no more than a footnote in the history of American crime.

Conclusion

The commanding Ruth Snyder found gullible corset salesman Henry Judd Gray the ideal partner to help her further her plans, but folie a deux this was not! The fool of a man became infatuated with Snyder, who used sex to drag him into her web. Easily led and with no self-esteem, he submitted completely to this dominatrix, who controlled his every emotion and need. It would cost him his life.

For Snyder, motivated by the prospect of financial gain, Gray was merely a disposable tool; had they got away with their crime, it is doubtful he would have seen her again.

CHAPTER TWENTY

REIKO YAMAGUCHI AND KAZUO HOKAO

One Hundred and Thirty-Five Million Yen

The District Court in Nagasaki, Japan, sentenced a woman and her lover to death for killing her husband and later her son, in order to obtain life-insurance payouts. Presiding Judge Keizo Yamamoto ruled that former insurance saleswoman Reiko Yamaguchi, 44, and antiques dealer Kazuo Hokao, 55, drowned Katsuhiko Yamaguchi, 38, by pushing him off a quay in the town of Tara, Saga Prefecture, on 11 September 1992. The couple had mixed sleeping pills into his curry. The pair also drowned Yamaguchi's 16-year-old son Yoshinori in the town of Konagai, Nagasaki Prefecture, on 27 October 1998. The boy was also given sleeping pills, in this case in a drink.

The defendants, residents of Kashima, Saga Prefecture, received some 100 million yen in insurance money by falsely declaring that Yamaguchi's husband had died in a fishing accident. They also attempted to obtain an insurance payment of 35 million yen on the boy's death, but doubts about their claim that the boy had died in an accident similar to that which killed his father prompted police investigations. The two pleaded guilty, but blamed each other for taking the lead in the two murders. Public prosecutors demanded death sentences for both defendants.

Referring to the husband's murder, the judge said Yamaguchi's responsibility was graver than Hokao's but stressed that the roles of both were indispensable in executing the crime and that the same was true for the boy's murder. In mitigation, Yamaguchi said she acted in retaliation for her husband's unfaithfulness and said she thought she would be able to break with Hokao – who, she said, was a gambler and behaved violently – if she agreed to the plot to kill her son. She also testified that it was he who had proposed murdering Yoshinori and, although she had initially refused, she finally agreed because she was in financial trouble. That father and son had both died under identical circumstances was one coincidence, she said. That both of them had taken a large number of sleeping pills before they 'fell' into the water was another.

However, the fact that Yamaguchi had heavily insured both of the deceased merely added to the weight of circumstantial evidence that was piling up against the killers, and a guilty verdict was the result. Even so, had the murderers kept their mouths shut and not turned on each other, they would have got away with the crimes and been very wealthy.

Conclusion

The details of this story are scant because I do not speak Japanese, but the facts as set out here are brutally eloquent. This is not a case of folie a deux by any stretch of the imagination: it is simply a double murder committed by accomplices. And, without doubt, the Black Widow would have disposed of her willing partner in crime as soon as his back was turned.

CHAPTER TWENTY ONE

KENNETH BIANCHI, ANGELO BUONO AND VERONICA WALLACE COMPTON

An In-depth Study of Two Cases of Heterosexual Folie a Deux

For over three years I corresponded with sado-sexual psychopath Kenneth Bianchi and he hates me with a passion. I am his nemesis and I plague his black soul. I am the one who haunts his cell every night, but why? Because I worked my way into his head, ripped out his sick thought processes and threw them back into his face, that's why. This is Kenneth Bianchi's story, a sickening account of one of the most evil sexual predators on earth. I pull no punches, and it will disturb your sleep. But the story also involves a second man, Angelo Buono, and in doing so reveals the dark truth of how two men became beasts when folie a deux joined them.

'I took her into the bedroom and raped and buggered her before killing her. She screamed for her mom, and the last thing she saw was the face of her dead friend lying under the sheets next to her.'

Kenneth Bianchi to the author – on the murder of 14-year-old Sonja Johnson

It takes more than a few homicides to grab the attention of a city the size of Los Angeles. But between 17 October 1977 and 17 February 1978, the best-known part of that city, Hollywood, was thrown into near panic after police revealed that two serial murderers were on the loose. Their modus operandi was always the same: most of the victims, all female, had been involved in Hollywood's seedy nightlife and they had all been strangled with a ligature. Each victim had been restrained by tying up. In all cases the bodies were disposed of in a similar way: they were dumped in secluded areas, usually beside a road, with their legs spread insultingly, as if pointing to the city itself.

At the autopsies it became clear that two men, before murdering the 11 women and two young girls, had also raped them. But then the killings stopped as suddenly as they had started, and it would be a year before one of the murderers struck again. The place was not LA, but the sleepy sea port of Bellingham, Washington, 1,600 kilometres to the north, where two co-eds from Western Washington State University were discovered strangled in a Mercury Bobcat car. And this time their killer was caught within a day. His name was Kenneth Alessio Bianchi.

After four years of continual correspondence with Bianchi,

more often known as one of the evil duo of 'Hillside Stranglers', I was finally granted a rare interview with him. The venue was the notoriously tough Washington State Penitentiary in Walla Walla, a medium-size city that squats in dry flatlands just a stone's throw from the border with Oregon.

During my first visit Bianchi lost his temper, threatening to smash my skull into the wall of the small locked cubicle before he calmed down. At the second meeting, conducted through the steel bars of his cell, he went berserk.

So what does this man look like? Bianchi stands around 1.8 metres tall and is extremely well built. A tough exercise regime has toned his muscles to perfection; with his washboard stomach and powerful shoulders, he is, at 53, a fine specimen of a man. His once rich, black mane of hair is thinning and turning grey, but he still has the drop-dead-handsome looks that women always found so attractive. But it is his eyes that one finds fascinating, if not disturbing. They are small and ink-black. They are the eyes of a Great White shark; unblinking, devoid of any emotion whatsoever, they are the eyes of pure distilled evil.

For all of Ken Bianchi's faults, we are unable to say that he was born evil and he most certainly didn't enter this world with a genetic flaw, a biochemical imbalance. Nor was he an infant spawned by the Devil, for he arrived defenceless, innocent, in need of love and attention, as millions of us do.

He was born on 22 May 1951, in Rochester, New York, the last of the four children of Florence King, an attractive, if not precocious 17-year-old go-go dancer and prostitute. His mother dumped him like an unwanted puppy shortly after giving birth and he never knew his genetic father, so throughout his life he suffered the social stigma of knowing he was a bastard.

Within weeks of his birth Ken was fostered by an elderly woman who had little time for him and loaned him to a number of her friends and neighbours. Every child has a need to be noticed, understood, taken seriously and respected by its mother, and, as Dr Alice Miller says in her book *The Drama of Being a Child*, 'In the first few weeks and months of its life, the child needs to have its mother at its disposal, must be able to use her, and to be mirrored by her.' It is fair to say that, during this crucial period, Ken did not enjoy the necessary presence of a mother. Indeed, he had no one to give him this vital attention. It was quite the opposite, for he was pushed from face to face, home to home, with his minders exhibiting a mix of emotions towards him, ranging from short-term curiosity to hostility towards this unwelcome arrival. So, from day one, Ken was emotionally deprived and damaged.

Frances Bianchi and her husband, Nicolas, a manual labourer in a brake-shoe foundry in Rochester, New York, adopted Ken at the age of three months; he was to be the only child of these Italian immigrants. But Ken's problems had only just begun. Born in 1918, Frances had wanted a child since her late teens, but she could not conceive. Time dragged by and now, at 32, she saw that her only chance was adoption, to which her husband somewhat reluctantly agreed. Frances was a hypochondriac, emotionally insecure and suffered frequent bouts of depression. Nonetheless, she was generally able to conceal her emotional difficulties under a veil of assertiveness, though unfortunately this manifested itself in an over-solicitous and highly authoritarian approach to life.

In order to survive, Frances 'split off' from her weaker self. She relied on denial and repression, putting troubling thoughts out of her mind. This was her mental defence mechanism, one that proved to be vital whenever her husband, an inveterate gambler, further weakened their fragile finances by losing the better part of his wages at the bookies. Although a hard worker and a loyal spouse, Nicolas was weak-willed. And, because he was unable to pay off his gambling debts, the family was always on the move, with loan sharks threatening to shoot him if he didn't pay up.

Each day this combination of mental and financial instability set the tone in the Bianchi household, and it was Frances who felt it the worst, her paranoia soon rubbing off on her adopted son. Faced with this unsettled and worrying existence, what she needed above all was security. However, she mistakenly reasoned that she would be better off if there was someone who really needed her and, to her, a child seemed to be the answer. But Frances wanted a child for all the wrong reasons, with the result that Ken became an object at her disposal, an item that could be controlled, manipulated and made to be totally reliant on her. The security that she couldn't find in her married life could be found in her adopted son, she thought. Ken would have to pay a very high price for this way of thinking, for during his early years he was forced to give Frances his unreserved admiration and full attention in order to secure his own psychological survival. A hint of troubles to come surfaced just a year after he began a new life with the Bianchis.

Recently unearthed adoption-agency records reveal that, although Ken was a 'sturdily-built baby with bluish eyes and wavy brown hair, appearing happy, contended and alert', Frances Bianchi was described as being 'over-solicitous'. A footnote characterised Nicolas Bianchi as 'quiet, unassuming, but very friendly, able to control his incessant stuttering, which has troubled him since childhood, only when Kenneth is around him'.

In 1953, with loan sharks chasing Bianchi for his gambling debts, the family were forced to leave their home on Saratoga Avenue in Rochester, New York, and move to Glide Street, where they kept a low profile. The loan sharks soon caught up with them, so a year later they moved to Los Angeles, lodging with Frances's sister, Jennifer Buono. By now Ken had developed asthma.

Ken attended the Century Park School, where, aged five, he suffered the first of two bad falls: he tripped while running up a flight of concrete steps, cracking open his head. A month later he fell headlong from playground equipment, hitting a number of steel rungs and breaking his nose when he hit the ground. After this accident he started wetting his pants during the daytime. He developed a facial tic that was apparent in stressful situations. Moreover, from now on he was accident-prone and, as he chose to run rather than walk, he was always falling over.

During the family's time in California, Nicolas Bianchi managed to save some money and used this to pay off his gambling debts, so they decided it was now safe to return home to Rochester. After the move, Ken's asthma all but disappeared, although his mother noticed that he had become withdrawn. He would retire to the attic and spend hours gazing vacantly at trains as they passed the house.

Soon Nicolas was once again running up large gambling debts. The family's stay at 529 Lyell Avenue, in Rochester's red-light district, was short-lived. In 1958 they moved to a pink-painted house on Wildwood Drive and in 1959 to Villa Street and then to Campbell Street, and all the while Ken was changing not only any friends he had made, but schools as well.

That same year Ken was examined briefly at the city's Strong Memorial Hospital Clinic. The visit was prompted by a complaint from the Society of Prevention of Cruelty to Children. In a nutshell, evidence provided by his school and the adoption agency suggested that the boy was not being properly cared for. There was, of course, every reason to believe that this was the case. The report that followed Ken's visit stated:

'Kenneth is a very anxious lad who has many phobias and counter-phobias. He uses repression and reaction formation. He is very dependent upon his mother. She has dominated him, and indulged him in terms of her own needs. He is anxious, protective, and this clinging control has made him ambivalent. But, he represses his hostile aggression, and is increasingly dependent upon her.'

So we see signs that Bianchi, as far back as the age of eight, was made up of two opposing sets of emotions. Echoing the psychopathology of his neurotic mother, he was mentally splitting in two. Undeniably, he had for years been the victim of a subtle form of child abuse, and unless something changed he would be emotionally scarred for life. But nothing changed; in fact, matters were worse when two doctors at the DePaul Psychiatric Clinic in Rochester saw Ken in 1960. This time the complaint had come from the monsignor at Ken's school and pointed to the boy's continual absenteeism. The facial tics and enuresis were also cause for concern, as was the asthma, which had returned with a vengeance. Drs Dowling and Sullivan strongly recommended treatment for the nine-year-old, but, after two visits to the clinic, Mrs Bianchi bluntly told the doctors that she saw no need for further treatment. She refused to let them see Ken again and in doing so placed him in great peril.

In June 1965 Nicolas Bianchi died at work from a massive heart attack. He was speaking on the telephone to Frances when his death occurred, and he collapsed with the receiver clutched tightly in his hand. Later that year Frances and Ken moved house yet again, and once more the boy, now 15, was uprooted from his school and enrolled at the McQuaid Jesuit High School in Rochester.

In his unpublished manuscript Kenneth Bianchi devotes just half a page to the subject of his father, whom he says he 'adored'. By contrast, some five pages give explicit details of his early sexual experiences. This is rather sinister in a convicted serial killer who is intent on proving his innocence of a string of sexually related homicides that include the rape and buggery of an 11-year-old and a 12-year-old girl. From his account we learn that this beast refers to young girls aged around ten as women and that he claims to have been sexually active since the age of 11:

'While my hormones increased, it was not until my sophomore year when I had my first sexual experience with a partner. It was when I was about 11 years old when I had my first solo experience. My first love was blonde, of thin build, and easy to speak with. She had a cute way of flirting, head tipped a bit, a beautiful smile across her face. She smelled divine as women do. Our first sexual encounter was at her home, with her parents and sister away. It was brief and I was so nervous my hands shook. I tried my best to be patient and gentle as I assumed a man would be. I'm certain I was hurried and with a touch of experience I wore no protection, which she had insisted on. When we finished, I just held her. It was the most beautiful and memorable experience I'd had up to that point in my life.'

In fact, the girl was just nine years old. Ken goes on to explain that she was not his steady girlfriend. 'We coupled for a week or so,' he claimed, 'but her heart belonged to several other guys in the neighbourhood. She and I had sexual relations twice more before ending our relationship.' Warming to his theme, he admits that he had 'scholastic problems' because his real interest was always on the female sex: 'I was crazy about girls... I dated different women on a regular basis. Romance is wonderful, life was my opiate, women were my fix. I could easily be distracted from my studies by the right woman.'

With equal clarity, he also remembers a girl from his school who was junior to him and one, it seems, who invited him to her home, where there was a swimming pool. At this point in his writing Bianchi launches into a quasi-erotic explanation of a problem that occurred during that same swimming session, and it bothers him to this day:

'She was a little chubby. She had a spinal problem, and [was] bubbly and full-figured. We were in the pool, and I reached out to hug her. She turned and my hand brushed against her breast. I wasn't disappointed, but it was unintentional. We broke up after that. She thought I had touched her breast without her permission. That allegation upset me.'

The girl was 11 years old, but Bianchi did more than touch her breast: he touched just about everything else. Moreover, the pen of the killer himself makes it clear that by the time he was 18 the oldest girl he had had sex with was 14 and the youngest – at least three of them – were all aged nine.

In 1970 Ken set his sights on joining a police academy, so he resumed his studies. Once again he enrolled at the same college, and now, aged 19, he was living with his mother at 105 Glenda Park. Listed below is the sum total of his achievements:

Summer 1970

Basic Algebra	Passed

Fall 1970

English Composition	Unsatisfactory
Elementary French	Passed
Geography	Very good
Modern Maths	Failed
General Psychology	Failed

Spring 1971

English Composition	Unsatisfactory
Physical Education	Failed
Physical Education/PS 11	Average
Administration, Criminal Justice	Average
Juvenile Proceedings	Average
Life Science	Failed
Basic Typing	Failed
Basic Introduction to Sociology	Failed

Fall 1971

Physical Education/Police Science	Withdrawn
Introduction to Law Enforcement	Withdrawn
Law and Public Safety	Failed
Disciplines of Investigation	Failed
Interview/Interrogation	Withdrawn
Highway Traffic Safety	Withdrawn
Criminal Evidence	Withdrawn

Given these poor grades, it is not surprising that Ken not only failed his degree, but was deemed totally unsuitable to become a police officer. He was, however, offered the more menial job of jail deputy, a position he promptly turned down while all of his fellow students were joining the police academy.

Ken was now a laughing stock and he didn't like it one bit. But his narcissistic inclinations were to have much wider-reaching and more dangerous implications than anyone could have predicted at this low point in his life. His abysmal failure at college had been a severe blow to his overinflated self-esteem, for he had promised himself and his mother that he would become a police officer. When this dream was shattered, much of his ego went down the drain, so he took to petty thieving and was dismissed from every part-time job he had.

Ken did, however, have something in common with one small group of people, that sub-culture of society called 'emerging serial killers', for he was a pathological liar. Telling lies was his way of making himself seem cleverer than he actually was. He could not allow himself to be inferior in the eyes of his peers and, looking back at him as he was then, it is clear that he suffered from a manifest grandiosity – and he still does to this day.

On leaving school in 1971 Ken married Brenda Beck. He took a part-time job at Two Guys store and furthered his education at the Rochester Monroe Community College, where he reviewed plays and films for the college newspaper, *The Monroe Discipline*. Ken's enthusiasm then faltered and he failed to finish many of the classes, among them psychology, in which he drew an 'incomplete'. Nevertheless, it was a subject he would return to in less than honest circumstances eight years later.

At the same time as Ken's academic efforts were teetering on the edge of the abyss, his personal life suddenly collapsed around him when his wife caught him in bed with another woman. Brenda threw him out on to the streets and he became the subject of much ridicule among the few friends he had left.

In the early 1990s, Frances Bianchi, now Piccione, told me on audiotape:

'Ken was a blatant liar. You'd catch him doing something, ask him why he did it, he'll tell you, "I didn't do it." I'd catch him in lies, and he would deny everything. And, at the end, you felt like you were the crazy one, and not him. He is such a smooth liar. He tells such lies that you believe him. You really believe what he says until you prove it for yourself.'

So, Bianchi needed to be admired for something he was not. This was his way of compensating for his shortcomings. He *had* to excel in everything he undertook. After all, this was what his mother had drummed into him, expected of him. But, like all grandiose people, woe betide him if something failed him. When that happens to a personality of this kind, the catastrophe of severe depression is imminent, and in Ken's case that catastrophe was immediate and lethal.

The collapse of Bianchi's self-esteem at this time proved that it had been extremely fragile, and this was because nothing genuine that could have given him strength and support had been allowed to develop within his mind. As Dr Alice Miller says, 'The grandiose person is never really free. First, because he is so excessively dependent on admiration from others, and second, because his self-respect is dependent on qualities, functions and achievements that can suddenly fail.'

For Bianchi, these did fail, and looking back through his

history we can see that his relationships, and his efforts to succeed, hung in the air on a very fine thread indeed. His self-esteem, his grandiosity, his psychopathological infrastructure were crumbling away like powdered cement binding the bricks of a wall. Then, when his unstable support mechanism eventually failed, it required just another adverse influence to knock his house down.

At the very time Bianchi's desperate attempts to become a police officer were foundering like a ship in a hurricane, his marriage lay in tatters too. And he soon messed up the relationship which had caused his marital break-up. Then, out of the blue, three horrific child murders shook Rochester. These took place within a 1.5-kilometre radius of Ken's front door, and he soon found himself being interviewed as a suspect.

The media dubbed the case the 'Alphabet Murders', because each victim's Christian name began with the same letter as the surname. The dates of these killings are of some interest. The first murder, of ten-year-old Carmen Colon, occurred on 16 November 1971. This took place within days of Bianchi's learning of his third set of failed exam results and his being kicked out of the marital home. There was a gap of 17 months before the murderer struck again. The murder of 11-year-old Wanda Walkowitz coincided almost to the day of Bianchi's being thrown out in April by the woman he'd had an affair with, because she had caught him sleeping with someone else. Ken's affair with the new woman collapsed in November 1973, and a day later, the Monday after Thanksgiving recess, 11-year-old Michelle Maenza went missing. Two days later her body was found fully clothed on a lonely road in Macedon, Wayne County.

All three young girls had been raped, then strangled to death. Moreover, there were other links between the three murders: all of the victims lived in rundown neighbourhoods; all were walking alone when they were snatched from the street; all were from a broken home – their father gone, their mother on welfare; all had eaten a small meal just before they met their deaths; all had white cat hair attached to their clothing; and each girl was last seen alive in the company of a young, white male who was driving a white saloon car.

All three children were streetwise. They had been warned by their mothers not to speak to strangers, and so investigators reasoned that whoever had abducted them may have been disguised as a police officer or even a clergyman. (When Bianchi later committed the 'Hillside Stranglings' around Los Angeles with his cousin Angelo Buono, the two killers posed as police officers to lure their victims into their car. And indeed the bodies of the 'Alphabet Murders' victims were dumped in exactly the same way: naked, with their legs apart, close to a highway.)

There were other suspects in the frame, of course, and one man committed suicide before the police arrived to interview him. But post-mortem blood tests proved that he could not have been the killer because the culprit was a person whose blood group could be determined from his body fluids. About 20 per cent of Americans belong to blood group AB and do not secrete the antigens characteristic of these blood groups in such bodily fluids as saliva, semen and so on. Bianchi was one of these, a non-secretor.

When interviewed by Rochester homicide officers, Bianchi was as plausible as ever. A natural-born liar, able to sell ice cream to Eskimos, he convinced them that he had watertight alibis for the three murders. However, he refused, as was his legal right in those days, to give body fluid samples, which would have confirmed that he was a non-secretor. Then, amazingly – the more so because Mrs Bianchi owned a white cat and he drove a white car – suspicion fell away, and no one checked to confirm the veracity of Ken's alibis.

Recently I carried out research on these three murders and quickly learned, after speaking to the alibis in question, that Ken's alibis were not worth the paper they were written on. This poses some intriguing questions. Why did Ken lie about his alibis and why did he refuse to give body fluid samples? When I questioned him at the penitentiary, Ken confirmed that his mother had owned a white cat at the time of the murders and that he did own a white car in those days. He stated that it had not been in his interests to give bodily fluids, but that he had been telling the truth about his alibis. In addition he said that the Rochester Police had ruled him out as a suspect. However, Captain Lynde Johnston, head of CID when I visited him, confirmed the opposite. 'Bianchi has always been the chief suspect in these murders,' he said. 'But, without a confession, we can do no more.'

At this point it is appropriate to add what Frances (Bianchi) Piccione told me in interview: 'It seemed that whenever Ken had a fight with a girlfriend, or had a problem, he went out and killed someone. I even told the police the same thing.'

Summing up Bianchi's early life, we see that he is atypical of the serial-murderer type in psychological make-up. He was superficially attractive to women, but when his partners looked deeper they found that he was transparent, immature, unfaithful and a pathological liar. Such men might seem to have many female friends, but they are unable to form and sustain meaningful, lasting relationships with women. Deep down they have formed a growing dislike, even a rage, towards females in general. This is certainly the case with many of the killers discussed in this book.

There is no doubt that, at that period of his life, Ken felt that the world was stacked against him. He would sit for hours asking himself why, if he was so clever, which in his bigoted way he thought he was, he had failed, when all around him were bathed in success. And, as with so many of his breed, it is not what Ken says, or does, that is so important; it is what he will not say, what he patently avoids saying, that is all-important when one is trying to find out why he became such an abominable killer.

For instance, he has always claimed that he is a secretor and therefore could not have been the 'Alphabet Murderer', one of the 'Hillside Stranglers' or the killer of the Bellingham co-eds. He went further by stating in countless letters that he can produce his medical notes to support this claim. However, when pressed to supply these documents, he sidetracked the issue by saying, 'Actually, I am not sure if I am a secretor, or a non-secretor. I just don't know.'

In an attempt to resolve this question, I contacted the FBI, who released a document dated Wednesday, 2 June 1982. In it, Agent Robert Beams, a specialist in blood grouping and body fluids, confirmed that, after taking samples from Bianchi, he was able to say that Bianchi was a non-secretor. More to the point, a recent discovery was made in Bianchi's cell. He had a copy of that very same document and it has been in his possession for 14 years. Obviously Ken believes that everyone in the world is a mug except himself.

But, now, aged 24, Bianchi set off to join a relative in Los Angeles.

With a population of well over five million, Los Angeles is the third-largest city in the United States. It also has one of the highest per capita murder rates in the Western world and its rate of incarcerated felons was given as 369 per 100,000 population in 2002.

Fifteen kilometres north of LA is the suburb of Glendale, where in late 1975 Kenneth Bianchi alighted from a coach at the Eagle Rock Plaza terminal minus his worldly possessions: the two suitcases had been lost during the gruelling trip from Rochester and he wouldn't retrieve them for several days. To meet him at the terminal was his cousin, Angelo Buono, known variously to his cronies as the 'Italian Stallion' and the 'Buzzard'.

Buono was born on 5 January 1934, in Rochester, New York, to Jenny and the brother of Frances Bianchi, Angelo Buono Sr, who drove a truck delivering flowers for an Italian florist. By all accounts, Jenny Buono enjoyed an unbroken string of extramarital affairs, so there was always domestic friction in the house. On one occasion, when little Angelo was two years old, her husband became so enraged by her infidelity that he produced an unlicensed revolver and threatened to shoot her. This got him arrested by the police, but Jenny failed to turn up at court to give evidence against him and the charges were dropped.

As a result of this incident, the Buonos separated for six weeks before agreeing to a semi-reconciliation. Then the Second World War broke out and Buono joined the National Guard, being posted to Hawaii. To support her spouse in his contribution to the war, Jenny moved house to live behind Rochester's busy meat market. This was entirely in line with her morality, for in her husband's absence she turned to prostitution, while at the same time enjoying a long relationship with a butcher who exchanged meat for sexual favours. As Ken Bianchi later said, 'Meat for meat.'

Left with his brother and two sisters at night without a babysitter, young Angelo got bored, and with a little practice he was able to pick the lock of the front door. He began to roam the streets at night, stealing anything that was not nailed down. Soon the boy came to the attention of the police, and at the age of eight he acquired a juvenile criminal record.

Angelo Sr eventually returned home and within days Jenny relieved him of his service back pay and kicked him out. After hopping a bus to LA, she stayed initially with an older brother and then a nephew, before settling down in a rented house on Le Cleyde Avenue.

It is not surprising that Angelo got into trouble with the law. After being convicted of grand theft auto, he was sent to Paso Robles School for Boys. His proclaimed hero and role model was Caryl Chessman, a notorious rapist.

Chessman had demonstrated the possibilities of a cunning ruse. The red light he had attached to his car enabled him to con lovers parked in the hills of Los Angeles into opening their car windows and doors to him, taking him to be a policeman. Showing a .45-calibre revolver, he would force the girl into his car, drive her to another secluded spot and usually make her perform oral sex.

To Angelo Buono, Chessman was a 'heroic combination of guts and brains'. By the age of 18 he was running around with a group of illiterate Mexicans who posed around town in an immaculate Chevrolet coupe which sported oversize chrome exhausts.

In 1955 Angelo impregnated a girl from his high school and married her. He left her less than a week later. Geraldine Vinal gave birth to Michael Lee Buono in 1956. Angelo refused to give her a cent for the boy's support and refused to let him call him Dad.

Angelo's first spell in jail came about when, while cruising the streets with his he spotted a youth wearing an expensive jacket with a dragon emblazoned on the back. Pulling up to the sidewalk, Buono asked if he could try the garment on, and no sooner had he slipped it over his shoulders than the car screeched off, leaving the gullible youngster enveloped in exhaust and tyre smoke.

Once behind bars in Los Angeles County Jail for this crime, Angelo realised that he had little use for his car and sold it. The proud new owner only had it for two months before Angelo, who was still locked up, ordered his gang to steal it back. They stripped it clean, sold the parts and dumped the carcass in Harry Griffen Park.

At the end of 1956 Angelo sired another son, Angelo Anthony Buono III. The following year he married the Mexican mother, Mary Castillo, who then gave birth every year or two: Peter Buono in 1957; Danny Buono in 1958; Louis Buono in 1960; and Grace Buono in 1962.

In 1964 Mary filed for divorce because of her husband's violence and perverse sexual needs, plus she got tired of always being called a cunt. One night during their first week together Angelo tied her, spread-eagled, to the bedposts and raped her so violently she was afraid he was going to kill her. Her pain seemed to give him his greatest pleasure. When she failed to respond to his pinches and slaps and pile-driver poundings, he would tell she was a 'dead piece of ass'. Nor did she share his passion for anal intercourse. But Angelo was not a man to be denied. Although he never drank, he beat and kicked her when she failed to please him and, far from caring whether the children witnessed the beatings, he seemed to want them to watch.

Once again he managed to avoid paying any child support, so Mary was forced to go on welfare to feed the children. When she went to see Angelo about reconciliation, he handcuffed her, shoved a gun to her stomach and threatened to kill her. That was the last time she thought about making amends with her husband.

In 1965 Angelo started to live with a 25-year-old mother of two children named Nanette Campina, who gave him two more sons, Tony in 1967 and Sam in 1969. Nanette was treated just as badly as Mary had been, but she stayed with Angelo because he made it clear that he would kill her if she didn't. Then, in 1971, she decided to risk everything to get away from her husband and took her children away from California for good.

In 1972 Angelo married Deborah Taylor on a whim, but they never lived together nor got round to getting a divorce.

By 1975 Angelo had built himself a reasonable reputation as

an auto upholsterer and he bought a place at 703 East Colorado Street, Glendale, premises he used for his home and workshop. His front porch mat even bore the legend 'The Italian Stallion'.

The Buono tribe of children wanted nothing to do with their father, who, for a man with all the physical and mental attributes of an oversexed, underweight weasel, was extremely adept at attracting the opposite sex. He enjoyed a harem of jailbait girls. A match for his dyed black hair, gold neck chains, large gaudy turquoise ring and red silk underwear was the fast line of vulgar chat he used to compensate for a speech impediment. 'I buh... buh... bet you g... g... some swe... swe... sweet puh... puh... pussy' was Angelo's favourite opener when coming on to a teenager. Ken Bianchi's was a tad more subtle: 'Ya have the most beautiful hair I have seen,' he would say in his well-practised, low tone, his eyes firmly glued to the girl's breasts.

According to Bianchi, the inside of Buono's chalet house on Colorado Street, Glendale, was kept neat and tidy. He claims he was struck, however, by the absence of many of the interior doors, which, apart from those of the bathroom and a bedroom, had been removed. The cooker had never been hooked up and 'the refrigerator was always empty because Angelo always ate out', Ken said in a letter to me.

Behind the house was Buono's workshop, where he repaired car interiors and vinyl roofs. His workmanship was first-rate and he refurbished many of the vehicles owned by Hollywood stars; indeed, Frank Sinatra was among his satisfied customers.

One of Ken's first priorities on arriving in LA was to find a job to help him pay his way with Angelo, and he managed to land himself employment as a real estate customer services clerk with California Land Title (Cal Land). Ken had learned of the vacancy through Buono's female bank manager, who put in a good word for him. At the firm's New Year's Eve party in 1977, he met Kelli Kae Boyd, who worked at the head office in Universal City.

A stunning brunette with large, brown eyes, she fell for Ken's smooth approach and they dated for a month before she decided to end the relationship because of his immaturity and insecurity. 'He was very possessive, and he always wanted to know where I was going, who I was doing what with, and I didn't really like that very well,' she later told Detective V. McNeill of the police department in Bellingham, Washington.

With enough cash to find a place of his own, Ken left Angelo's place and rented rooms at Tamarind Apartments. No sooner had he slammed the door shut than he picked up the phone and started wooing Kelli again.

As was his practice with previous girlfriends, he sent her bunches of flowers and soon he was taking her to the most expensive restaurants he could afford. They began to live together and at the beginning of May 1977 Kelli announced that she was pregnant with Ken's child.

Life with Ken was always a rough ride. The couple argued frequently and more than once Kelli turned him out. Each time he returned to Angelo's place, where he slept on the floor, or he would call his mother, who mediated a reconciliation.

Throughout all this and despite being heavily pregnant, Kelli continued to work at Cal Land. Ken earned considerably less than Kelli and, although he had now been promoted to

Assistant Title Officer, he decided to earn a little more cash on the side. He would become Dr Bianchi, with a doctorate in psychology, and published here for the first time is his account of how he set up a bogus counselling service:

'People in California are big on widow dressing. Joining the *Psychology Today* book club, I took in books to decorate my shelves. I was introduced to Dr Weingarten, and I asked him if I could rent part of his offices at night. I sounded literate, and he accepted me on the reference of a mutual friend. There was no extraordinary effort to fool the doctor, and if he'd asked me just some basic questions about psychology, he would have seen right through me. Placing ads in the *Los Angeles Times*, I received credentials from other psychologists and students applying for a job with me. A diploma replacement service supplied more decorations for my walls and shelves. Also, I had several basic psychology books from back east. I knew I was doing wrong, but I took every precaution to not harm anyone.'

So now we find 'Dr' Bianchi obtaining genuine diplomas by sleight of hand from students who applied for a post with him: as soon as they dropped into his mailbox he altered them to suit his name. To add authenticity to the phoney venture, he forged letters from various well-known institutions which thanked Dr Bianchi for his 'generosity' and for the 'small, cash donations, and his valuable time in giving such enlightening lectures'.

The whole scam was a figment of Ken's overactive and crooked imagination, but then he went way over the top when he told Kelli that he had earned his psychology degree way back in Rochester and that he was helping two colleagues, one of whom was the unwitting Dr Weingarten, with their overload of patients. But then, like all of Bianchi's schemes, it all fell apart.

During a visit to California to see her son, Frances could not fail to notice the many fraudulent diplomas which he also proudly displayed in his apartment. Impressed she was not, and she berated Ken, explaining that he would find himself in hot water if he were to be exposed as a cheat. But the warning went unheeded and was like water off a duck's back to the resilient Ken, who continued to pour money into advertising until his funds dried up. Patients failed to materialise, and when Kelli heard the truth from his mother he dumped the fabricated sideshow. And, yet again, she threw him on to the streets. This time she had had enough.

'I've got a growth on my lung,' Ken whined to Kelli on the phone. 'I haven't got long to live,' he said, crocodile tears running down his cheeks. 'Please, please take me back, Kelli.'

She fell for it hook, line and sinker, as she explained later in a statement to the police:

'Those days were very fretful for me. I took time off work to be with him. He had appointments at the hospital, and I drove him there to make sure he was OK. But he made me wait in the car. He had many bad ways, and very good ways. He was bad at paying the bills, and he was always skipping off work. On balance I loved him, and I didn't want him to die without seeing our child. Yet, all the time, he was lying to me about the cancer. Then he got dismissed from work for having drugs in his desk drawer. That's when I kicked him out for good.'

Poor old Ken was now falling apart like a cheap suit. This guy, who was so bent he couldn't lay straight in bed, had lost his job with Cal Land; his phoney counselling business had flopped; Kelli was heavily pregnant; he had no home and the bills were mounting daily. So, apart from wrecking his own life, he was destroying Kelli's, and perhaps she made the wisest move of her life by moving in with her brother at 200 East Palmer on the day after Thanksgiving 1977. Within a week she moved again, this time to Adelaide Avenue, but shortly afterwards she travelled north to Bellingham, Washington State, where her parents put a secure roof over her head. Tragically, however, a soon-to-be cold-blooded serial killer would follow in her tracks.

A week after Kelli left him Ken bounced back when he was introduced to a drop-dead-gorgeous blonde at a party. Just 16, she was an aspiring model with all the physical attributes to match her ambitions. She was the stuff of *Baywatch*. For his part, Bianchi was loveless and penniless and Angelo was sick and tired of handing out cash to his immature cousin, so, within minutes of meeting the girl, the quick-thinking con man came up with another scam that would raise money and please Angelo into the bargain.

After placing a drink in her hand, Ken slipped his arm around her waist and gently steered her into another room, where he explained that she was the most beautiful woman he had ever seen. 'I ought to know,' he said. 'I'm a doctor with friends in the modelling business and they are always on the lookout for lovely starlets.' Ken told the teenager that she could easily earn $500 a week from the outset and that this figure would rise when she became better known. By now a little the worse for drink, she was lured to the Buzzard's nest, where Buono's eyes lit up when he saw the slim-figured, busty teenager. 'We use this as a studio,' he told her. 'I do the film work, and often we sleep over.' As the hours drifted by, the young girl fell asleep, totally unaware of the scheming cousins whispering together in another room. Yes, this time Ken had come up with a great idea. The two men would force her into prostitution, and before the week was out she was left under no illusion that they would kill her if she attempted to leave, for by then she was already their sex slave and soon to be their hooker. The folie à deux was about to begin.

Fearing for her life, she was now coerced into introducing her 15-year-old friend to the cousins. This girl was also forced into prostitution, and every night both men sodomised the two teenagers so much that they had to wear tampons in their rectums to stop the bleeding. Life for the girls then took an unexpected turn for the better.

After a fortnight of this living hell, one of them was summoned to a wealthy lawyer's apartment for sex. On her arrival she looked so downhearted that her client asked her how she had become involved in prostitution. With tears flooding down her face, she explained that Buono and Bianchi subjected her to degrading sex acts and sadistic cruelty. She said that the two men had threatened to track them down and kill them if they ran away. To his credit, the lawyer acted immediately. He drove her to the airport, bought her a ticket to her home in Arizona and just before she boarded the aircraft he stuffed a large wad of notes into her pocket. Then he kissed her on the cheek and said goodbye.

As might be expected, Angelo went ballistic when his younger hooker failed to return home, so he made several threatening phone calls to the lawyer, stammering, 'Give me her fuckin' address, or I'll fuckin' shoot you.' However, this was the type of threat to which the attorney had the answer, for among his clientele was the local chapter of the Hell's Angels, and he asked them to pay Buono a visit.

Still fuming with rage, Angelo was fitting new mats into a customer's car when he was tapped smartly on the shoulder. At first he ignored the leather-clad bikers, which was not exactly the diplomatic thing to do. Then, as one biker produced a sawn-off, pump-action shotgun, the largest of the group reached through the car window and extracted the struggling Buono by his shirt front. 'Do we have your attention, Mr Buono?' he asked. Unfortunately, there is no record of the discussion that followed, and all that remains to be said is that the cousins didn't bother the lawyer again.

This incident was certainly the crucial turning point that led the perverted Buono to become a serial murderer. Word of his humiliation flashed around the neighbourhood like a bush fire. He lost face with his cronies, and the intensely macho crook was outraged that he had been proved to be a weakling in front of Bianchi. At Buono's favourite eaterie, Henry's, regular customers and staff alike sniggered behind his back. It was rumoured out loud that the Italian Stallion could no longer control his women.

When I questioned Bianchi about his role in the stable of hookers, he denied that he ever touched the girls. He added that he was only their driver, and responsible for collecting the cash.

With the girls gone, Buono's pimping income dried up, so the two men had to find more teenage girls. They tried to abduct one girl until they realised that she was Catherine Lorre, the daughter of actor Peter Lorre. Eventually they found a young woman and installed her in their lair. They also bought from a prostitute a 'trick list' of men who frequented prostitutes. But this turned out to be merely a list of men who wanted to visit one particular good-time girl in her own apartment. To make matters worse, this prostitute already had a pimp and had no intention of going into business with the likes of Buono and Bianchi. The list was useless; the dirty duo had slipped up yet again, and of the effect this rip-off had on the two men Bianchi wrote in a letter: 'We went off in search of the vendor, madder then hell.'

The police have always maintained that Bianchi and Buono never found the seller of this list, and that the vendor's best friend, Yolanda Washington, was the first victim of the Hillside Stranglers. However, during my correspondence with Bianchi, he said this is not the case. Ken argues that Laura Collins had sold them the phoney list, and that is why she was the first to die. Also of interest is the fact that, after the Hillside Stranglings task force was assembled during the weeks to come, in December 1977 Laura Collins's name was erased from the list of victims and it was not until the following month that the then Assistant Chief of Police, Darryl Gates, publicly indicated that she was indeed a victim of the Hillside Stranglers. Further, it has recently been established that among Laura Collins's clients were a number of well-known figures.

Twenty-six-year-old Laura was last seen alive just after noon at Ventura Freeway and Lankershim Boulevard, on Sunday, 4 September 1977. Her partially clad body was found near the Forest Lawn drive-off ramp of the Ventura Freeway in Burbank at 10.30am on Friday, 9 September. She had been strangled, and this homicide became the blueprint for all of the subsequent killings.

At 1.34pm on Monday, 18 October 1977 a naked body was found perversely sprawled on its stomach alongside Forest Lawn Drive, close to the famous Forest Lawn cemetery and just south of Ventura Freeway. Lying in a crucifixion posture, with the right hand crooked over, the female corpse appeared to have been dragged from a vehicle by two men and dropped near a pile of broken road-surfacing concrete just a metre from her head. Behind the body was a yellow 'No Trespassing or Loitering' sign. Tall and leggy, the black woman was immediately recognised by vice officers as Yolanda Washington, a particularly attractive 19-year-old who had almond-shaped eyes and black, medium-length hair. She was a part-time bar waitress and hooker who was known to have touted for business along with Laura Collins.

Enquiries soon established that Yolanda had last been seen alive just before midnight the previous day as she solicited for business at Vista and Sunset Boulevards. On a good night she could earn over $300, which helped her support her 30-month-old daughter, Tameika.

The autopsy showed that she had had sex with two men shortly before her death, one of whom was a non-secretor. She had been strangled with a piece of cloth while she was lying down with her killer kneeling over her. There were marks around her wrists, and she had also been anally raped. Bianchi confirmed all the details, saying that he had killed her in the back seat of his car.

Just after midnight on Monday, 31 October 1977 a white female was abducted from the Howard and Wilcox area of Hollywood. Unattractive, with reddish-brown, medium-length hair, 15-year-old Judith Ann Miller lived in a ramshackle hotel which was her base as a part-time hooker. From trailer-park stock, she had a mother who was wanted in connection with a welfare fraud and a father who had jumped bail for a similar offence.

It was a grim sight that Halloween morning at Alta Terrace and La Crescenta. Judy's naked body lay close to the kerb in a middle-class residential area, covered by a tarp by a property owner so as to shield the corpse from local children. Bruises on the victim's neck showed that she had been strangled. She had ligature marks on both wrists and ankles as well as her neck. Insects feasted on her pale skin. On her eyelid was a small piece of light-coloured fluff that Sergeant Frank Salerno of the Los Angeles County Sheriff's Department saved for the forensic experts. It did not appear that Judy had been murdered at this location. The coroner determined that she had been strangled to death around midnight, some six hours before she was found. It was also clear that she had been raped and sodomised.

Bianchi says that Judy was taken back to Buono's house, where she was raped. Bianchi sodomised her, then strangled her. He finished her off by suffocating her with a plastic supermarket bag. 'She involuntarily urinated after death, just as Washington had done,' Bianchi claimed, an evil grin playing across his mouth. 'We made her go into the washroom before we killed her to stop it happening, but it didn't work. She was tied by the arms, legs and neck to our special chair in Angelo's bedroom. She didn't like dying one bit.'

The murderous duo's fourth victim was 21-year-old Teresa Kastin, known as Terri or Lissa, a waitress at the Healthfair Restaurant near Hollywood and Vine and a part-time prostitute. White, moderately attractive, with a Roman nose and dark, bushy hair, Terri was stopped by Bianchi and Buono, who were posing as police officers, at 9.15pm on Saturday, 5 November 1977. They ordered her into their black-over-white sedan, at the 1600 block on Vine Street. Like Miller, she was taken back to Buono's home for what Bianchi called 'questioning'. There she was tied to the special chair and her striped sweater and short skirt cut off with scissors. The two men were repelled because she had hairy legs, and Bianchi was reduced to raping her with a root-beer bottle as he throttled her. When she kicked out in her death throes, Buono sat on her legs, shouting, 'Die, you cunt, die.' Terri was allowed to suck in lungfuls of air many times before she lost consciousness for the last time.

At 1.15am the next day Terri's body was found at Chevy Chase and Linda Vista. Identification was made swiftly after a news broadcast reported the murder and her father telephoned the police to report that his daughter was missing.

At autopsy, no semen was present in the vagina or anus, which supported Bianchi's confession that neither of the two men had physically raped this victim.

Jill Barcombe was an 18-year-old white hooker who had moved to Hollywood following a string of prostitution convictions in New York. She was last seen alive at Pico and Ocean Boulevards around 7pm on Wednesday, 9 November 1977. She was found naked and strangled at 5.50 the following morning at Franklin Canyon Drive and Mulholland. Clearly she had put up a fierce fight for her life, for severe head trauma was present.

A 28-year-old aspiring actress and part-time model, Jane

King was rated by the Hollywood set as a stunning blonde bombshell who had exploded on the scene when she was just sweet 16. Over the years she had raised the eyebrows of every hot-blooded male and film producer who saw her. Jane was a student of L. Ron Hubbard's Scientology and Dianetics. Police claimed that she was a part-time hooker, but my own enquiries contradict this view.

Jane was last seen alive outside 9500 Lemona, at 10.10pm on Wednesday, 9 November 1977. Posing as police officers, Buono and Bianchi cruised up to her, arrested her on suspicion of prostitution and took her back to Buono's home. She was dragged screaming through the living-dining area into the east bedroom, where she was stripped naked. Bianchi confessed that they 'were delighted to find her pubis was shaven'. However, because she struggled while she was being raped, the two men decided to teach her a lesson. A plastic bag was placed over her head while Bianchi sodomised her. She pleaded desperately for her life during four hours of terror before she was allowed to suffocate to death as Bianchi climaxed.

Jane's naked body was found in undergrowth at the Los Feliz exit ramp of the Golden State Freeway on Wednesday, 23 November.

All crimes like this are pure evil, but the murders of Sonja Johnson and Dolores 'Dolly' Cepeda must be the most heinous. Sonja, 14, and Dolly, 12, were both pupils at the Saint Ignatius School in Los Angeles. They were last seen on Sunday, 13 November, boarding a bus at the Eagle Plaza stop, half a kilometre from Buono's home. The two men followed the bus and, when the girls got off near their homes, Bianchi, again posing as a police officer, approached them and accused them of shoplifting. They were taken 'downtown' and interviewed in Buono's house. Sonja was raped and murdered in a bedroom by Buono, while Dolly sat outside with Bianchi.

'Where's my friend?' asked the girl when Buono came out alone.

'Oh, don't worry,' said Bianchi. 'You'll be seeing her in a minute.'

The last thing Dolly saw on this earth was the dead face of Sonja as Bianchi raped and sodomised her. Children playing on a rubbish tip at Landa and Stadium Way found the girls' bodies naked at 4pm on Sunday, 20 November.

Landa Street is set deep into a rich, green hillside south of Hollywood, and I visited the scene in 1995 with impeccably dressed Detective Leroy Orozco of the LAPD's Homicide Squad. On a clear day one can follow the eye over the Golden State Freeway, across the Los Angeles River flood control channel, to the sprawling, haze-covered mass of Hollywood in the distance. But on this particular day the weather had closed in. A grey mantle of low cloud and drizzle covered the hill and a slight wind was rising in the swaying trees, heralding a storm. Back at my hotel that evening I pondered over the scenes-of-crime photographs showing Dolly and Sonja sprawled out among the discarded beer bottles and tin cans. There was a rotting mattress, a used tampon, and the girls seemed as close in death as they had been as playmates in life.

Sonja rested almost on her right side, her left hand tucked up under her breasts, nudging her chin. Her right arm, the hand gripped tight in a death spasm, was outstretched and underneath her right side. The legs were almost straight, the left foot draped over the neck of Dolly, who was on her stomach, her torso slightly crooked and leaning to the right of her legs, which were parted. Dolly's left arm was also tucked underneath her body, the hand covering her mouth as if to stifle a scream. The right arm, bent at the elbow, was outstretched. There were a set of human bite marks on her left buttock.

Only when one sees such terrible things, can one truly understand the profoundly evil nature of Kenneth Bianchi and Angelo Buono.

Like Jane King, 17-year-old Kathy was an attractive blonde who was well known around the hotspots of Hollywood. Her flowing blonde hair caught the attention of the Hillside Stranglers at 9.30pm on Wednesday, 16 November. She was walking towards her car, parked near Pico and Ocean Boulevards, when Buono and Bianchi drew up alongside her. Flashing a phoney police badge, they ordered her into their car. She was found fully clothed, strangled with her throat cut, at Burnside and Curson at 8.30am the next day.

Twenty-year-old Kristina Weckler was a quiet honours student at the Pasadena Art Design Center. She lived at Tamarind Apartments, 800 Garfield, Glendale. This was the apartment block where Bianchi had once resided, and he knew the young woman and had pestered her for a date. Kristina, who knew that Ken was living with the pregnant Kelli Boyd, had rejected his advances.

Kristina's naked body was found at Ranon's Way and Nawona on Sunday, 20 November. Detective Sergeant Bob Grogan immediately noticed the ligature marks on her wrists, ankles and neck. When he turned her over, blood oozed from her rectum. The bruises on her breasts were obvious. Oddly enough, there were two puncture marks on her arm, but no signs of the needle tracks that indicate an addict.

Bianchi told me that around 6pm on Saturday, 19 November he knocked on Kristina's door, telling her that he was now a police officer and that someone had crashed into her car, which was parked outside. Once in the parking lot, she was bundled into his car and driven to Buono's home, where the pair tried to kill her using a new method. They had intended to inject Kristina with caustic cleaning fluid, but when this barbaric method of murder failed, they covered her head with a plastic bag and piped coal gas into her lungs. Bianchi raped Kristina, ejaculating into her at the moment she convulsed into death. She died as the result of strangulation by ligature.

A promising lead in the hunt for the killers came on Monday, 28 November, the day after a student and trainee secretary disappeared from 9500 Lemona, Sepulveda, in the San Fernando Valley. The father of Lauren Rae Wagner found his 18-year-old daughter's car parked, with the driver's door open and the interior light on, near his house and directly in front of the home of an elderly woman named Beulah Stofer. Mrs Stofer told police how she had seen the young redhead abducted by two men. They were driving a black-over-white sedan, and at first she had thought that it was a police car.

At 7.30am the following day a driver on his way to work found the naked body at 1200 Cliff Drive, in the Mount Washington area. Lauren was lying on her back, her left arm outstretched, her left lower leg just touching the road. Her mass of rich, red hair framed her pretty face and her eyes were peacefully closed in death. But there was something different: it looked as though she had burns on her palms. Like the strange puncture marks on Kristina Weckler's arms, these wounds suggested that the killers were experimenting – possibly with methods of torture. There was also something else that was different: a track of a shiny, sticky liquid that had drawn a column of ants to it. If this was semen or saliva, it was possible that the killers' blood types could be determined. Tests on semen found in earlier victims had revealed that only one of them was a secretor, the other a non-secretor.

Bianchi told me that, at Buono's house, Lauren pretended to enjoy being raped in the desperate hope that her attackers would allow her to live. However, they tried to electrocute the woman by attaching live electrical wires to the palms of her hands, but, this only caused extreme pain and superficial burns. Bianchi then raped her and Buono strangled her to death with a ligature.

The two killers now realised that they had been seen by Mrs Stofer, so they obtained her telephone number and called her from a kiosk in the North Ivar Street Public Library in Hollywood. Despite being subjected to death threats, Mrs Stofer was undeterred and furnished police with an excellent description that matched Bianchi and Buono in every respect.

On Monday, 14 December police raced to a vacant lot on a steep slope at 2006 North Alvarado Street, arriving at 7.03am. The sun had just come up, and it was a clear day with very few clouds in the sky. Rampart Divisional patrol unit 2-A-47, consisting of officers Lewis and Akeson, had responded to a radio call alerting them to a dead body lying beside the road, which ran through the floor of the canyon, splitting Lakeshore Drive and Alvarado. When homicide detectives Oakes and Crotsley arrived, they noticed that the tall, blonde victim was lying on her back in the now usual spread-eagled position and that post-mortem lividity had started to form in her toes. The young woman was Caucasian and in her twenties. There were ligature marks around the wrists, ankles and neck. On her left forearm she had a tattoo: a square cross with four dots within its border. The right ankle bore a second tattoo of faint design bearing the name 'Kim'. With no other identification to be found, she was labelled as 'Jane Doe # 112', and the stranglers' penultimate victim was on her way to the morgue.

Using documents furnished by the LAPD and having had the facts confirmed by Bianchi himself, I am now able to plot the last hours of Kimberley's life in some detail, and, using this previously unpublished material, we can see for the first time the cunning of the Hillside Stranglers as they entrap a victim.

At precisely 8.30pm on Tuesday, 13 December 1977 the phone rang at Climax Nude Modelling of 1815 Serrano Avenue, and Michelle Elaine Rodriguez answered it. The call was from Kenneth Bianchi, using the name 'Michael Ryan', and this is a transcript of the recorded conversation:

Rodriguez: Hello, modelling service.

Bianchi: Hello, yes. Can you get me a girl?

R: That depends where you are located, sir.

B: I'm in Hollywood.

R: That will be no problem. I can have a girl with you in about 15 minutes.

B: How much does it cost?

R: Forty dollars for a modelling service.

B: OK. My wife has left town for the first time in two years, so I would like you to send me a pretty blonde model if you could. Possibly wearing black stockings and a dress.

R: That will be no problem, sir. May I have your name?

B: Michael Ryan.

R: And could you spell your last name, please?

B: R-Y-A-N.

R: May I have your phone number?

B: 462-9794.

R: Sir, that is a payphone.

(Bianchi was again using the phone kiosk in the library in North Ivar Street.)

B: Ha, ha, ha. You know it's funny. A lot of people seem to think that this is a payphone. It must be a digit in the number, or something.

R: That must be what it is. The reason I thought it was a payphone is that the fourth digit of the number is a 'nine' – it's a payphone.

B: That must be it, or the fact that you hear my TV in the background. Would you like me to turn it off?

(The 'television noise' was the conversations of people using the library.)

R: Oh, no. I'll verify it.

B: All right.

R: And what is your address, sir?

B: 1950 Tamarind.

R: Sir, could you spell that for me?

B: T-A-M-A-R-I-N-D.

R: Is this a house or an apartment?

B: This is an apartment. Number 114.

R: Sir, how are you going to pay?

B: Cash.

R: May I ask where you found our advertisement?

B: The *Freep* [a local free paper].

R: OK, sir. I'll have a girl out to you shortly.

This ended their first conversation and Michelle then rang the operator to verify the number. She always followed this practice to ensure that she didn't send a girl out to a prank caller. First she asked the operator if the number was a payphone. If so, under normal circumstances the operator would confirm it, but, if it was a private number, the operator would advise the caller that it was not permitted to provide this information. On this rare occasion Bianchi had luck on his side. The operator spoke to her supervisor and came back to say, 'No. My supervisor won't allow me to give out that information.' Naturally, Michelle understood this to mean that her client had booked one of her girls from a private address, even though this wasn't the case, and that therefore the call was genuine.

She phoned back 'Mr Ryan', who picked up the handset immediately 'as if he was waiting for the call', Michelle later told the police. Unwittingly, Michelle had now sealed the fate of Kimberley Martin. The call went as follows:

B: Hello.

R: Hello. Michael?

B: Yes.

R: This is just the modelling agency calling to verify your call.

B: OK. Thank you. How much longer will it take before the girl will call me?

R: Very shortly.

B: OK. Thank you. Goodbye.

Michelle then phoned Kimberley Martin, who worked under the name of 'Donna':

R: I have a call. It's a cash call out in Hollywood in an apartment. Do you want it?

D: Yeah. Give me the information.

R: Michael Ryan. Phone number 462-9794. 1950 Tamarind, Hollywood. Cash. Apartment 114. Sounds like a good call to me. It's an apartment. It's near your location, but always be careful and make sure he's not a cop.

D: Sounds good to me. I'll give him a call.

R: Phone me and let me know whether you'll go on it?

D: OK. Goodbye.

Kimberley Martin called her prospective client, then she rang the agency back:

D: Sounds good to me. I'm going right on it.

R: Call me when you get there. Goodbye.

From the library on North Ivar Street to 1950 North Tamarind Avenue is 1.3 kilometres, taking some five minutes to drive. Bianchi was seen sitting on the library steps by a witness around 9pm. Then he suddenly stood up and walked off; Buono was picking him up.

At around 9.05pm Kimberley left her apartment, 1105 at 8440 Sunset Boulevard, and took the elevator to the ground floor. In the parking lot was her white-over-bronze 1963 Oldsmobile Cutlass. It was a two-door convertible, licence-plate number QIM 073, and she shared the leased car with her flatmate.

It took Kim 15 minutes to drive the six kilometres to Tamarind. She parked and walked into the lobby, where several people saw her at 9.25. Shortly afterwards residents heard a woman screaming, 'Please don't kill me', but all of them thought that this was a domestic dispute. Minutes later, however, they found the contents of a woman's handbag strewn along a hallway.

Bianchi claims that he and Buono dragged the woman out through a rear entrance and into the underground car park, where they had left their car. They drove her to Buono's home, where she was tortured, raped and killed. 'We killed her,' he said, 'because she was fuckin' useless in bed.'

Even though 84 officers were assigned to the Hillside Stranglers investigation, the general public now thought that the police were helpless – and they were about right. There were 10,000 leads to follow up, thousands of fingerprints to be processed and a reward of $140,000 had been posted for information that would lead to the arrest of the Hillside Stranglers, yet the task force were no nearer catching them than they had been on day one.

After press headlines suggested that the killers were posing as police officers, the public trusted no one and it was even asked if two renegade policemen were running amok on some kind of sick vendetta. It got to the point where nobody could be certain of the true identity of a man wearing a uniform or waving a silver badge, and citizens were simply not stopping when requested by any cop, uniformed or not. So the police implemented a new policy, allowing motorists to drive to a police station with a flashing patrol car following them, and this prompt action partly put people's minds at rest.

On Friday, 17 February 1978 the crew of an Angeles National Forest helicopter spotted an orange Datsun car parked precariously close to a ravine by the Angeles Crest Highway. On opening the trunk, police found the body of 20-year-old Cindy Lee Hudspeth, who worked as a telephonist. The brunette was also employed as a part-time waitress at the Robin Hood Inn, a restaurant frequented by Angelo Buono.

In his statement to police, Bianchi claimed that he had arrived at Buono's auto upholstery shop, where he found Cindy's car parked outside. 'She had called to enquire if Angelo could make new mats for her,' he said. The two men spread-eagled Cindy on a bed, hog-tied her and raped and strangled her for almost two hours. Then, with the dead body in the trunk, Bianchi drove her car, closely followed by Buono in another vehicle, to the ravine, where they tried to push the Datsun over the edge. It rolled some 15 metres and stopped, but by then the killers had fled and Cindy proved to be the last victim of the Hillside Stranglers.

The two men now fell out. Ken, like the fool that he was, still insisted that he wanted to become a police officer and went for rides with officers in squad cars to see just what this part of the job entailed. Buono was furious. 'You dumb fuckin' asshole,' he screamed at him, 'you'll draw heat down on us. Fuck off!' With that he pointed a loaded revolver at Ken's head.

Within a day Bianchi packed his bags and left Los Angeles. Buono went back to refurbishing cars, and did not kill again, while Ken headed north to Bellingham, Washington, leaving 13 dead bodies, countless broken lives and a mountain of debt behind him. The folie a deux was over.

The small seaport city of Bellingham has a population of about 60,000 and lies 32 kilometres due south of the Canadian border, on the north-west seaboard of Washington State. Bellingham is the gateway of the Mount Baker recreational area, which offers one of the most magnificent vistas in the area: the pine-clad slopes of San Juan, the Vancouver Islands and the Strait of Juan de Fuca.

When I visited Bellingham for the second time in 1996, the place was well wrapped up in an icy coat, which typifies winter in these parts, and my thoughts travelled back in time to January 1979, when the weather was similar but laced with the cold chill of murder most foul. Violent crime in this neck of the woods was such a rarity in those days that, when Bellingham's Chief of Police, Terry Mangan, was informed one Friday morning that two young women had been reported as 'missing under suspicious circumstances', his first thought was they had left town for an early vacation without telling anyone. Co-ed roommates 22-year-old Karen Mandic and 27-year-old Diane Wilder both studied at Western Washington University, and several friends were concerned about their welfare.

Chief Mangan was a former Roman Catholic priest who

had a close friend, Sister Carmel Marie. At one time she ran the Saint Ignatius School in Los Angeles, and she had introduced Mangan to the bookkeeper of her diocese, one Tony Johnson. In November 1977, when the Hillside Stranglings were at their peak, Mangan had read in a paper that Johnson's 14-year-old daughter, Sonja, was one of the victims. Now, in January 1979, after an amazing sequence of tragic circumstances and coincidences, Mangan would secure the arrest of one of the Los Angeles killers in his own 'back yard', some 1,700 kilometres from Tinsel Town.

Karen Mandic was a beautiful student with long, blonde hair. She had last been seen alive at 7pm on Thursday, 11 January, when leaving the Fred Myer department store on Interstate 5, where she worked as a part-time cashier. Earlier in the week she had told two boyfriends, Steve Hardwick and Bill Bryant, that a man who had recently asked her for a date had offered her a house-sitting job for that Thursday evening that paid $100 an hour. In fact, he had asked her out several times and his name was Kenneth Bianchi.

Bianchi, who by now was back living with Kelli and their son, Ryan, had previously worked at Fred Myer as a security guard and was now employed as a security officer with the Whatcom Security Agency (WSA), a local company that provided mobile and static security patrols throughout an 80-kilometre radius of Bellingham. Bianchi had pledged Karen to secrecy; nevertheless, she was thrilled with the opportunity to earn some extra cash.

On learning of the offer to Karen, Steve Hardwick was suspicious from the start. Karen, however, would have none of it and insisted that everything was OK. She explained that the house, owned by a Dr Catlow, was in an upper-class area. The doctor was going on vacation with his family but the burglar alarm was not working, she said, and she had asked her friend Diane Wilder along for company. It was easy money, she told Hardwick. All they had to do was wait until the repair people turned up later in the evening to fix the alarm, and then she could return to Fred Myer and cash up. Besides, Bianchi worked for WSA, which was a highly regarded firm, and even Hardwick knew that.

But he was still highly suspicious and pressed Karen further. 'Don't worry,' she snapped back, 'it's only for two hours, and I'll be back to finish up at the store by 9pm. Everything will be OK. I'm taking Diane with me. Besides, Ken has given my name to the insurance company who are paying the bill. I can't change anything now.'

When Karen failed to return to Fred Myer later in the evening, the manager telephoned Hardwick, who immediately drove to Dr Catlow's house at 334 Bayside. The split-level property appeared deserted. Although he could not recall Bianchi's name, Hardwick did remember WSA, so he telephoned the night dispatcher, Wendy Whitton, and requested any information on the Bayside account. Wendy, who was not authorised to reveal details of her employer's business, promised the anxious Hardwick that she would call the firm's co-owner, Randy Moa, and, as soon as she did, alarm bells started to ring.

Moa and his partner, Joe Parker, had just completed a somewhat belated security check on Bianchi's resume, and in doing so they had spoken to a Susan Bird, an attractive woman who lived locally. Susan had been shocked to hear that

Bianchi had obtained work in the security business because he had recently suggested to her that, because of her stunning figure, she would make a good prostitute, and he could become her pimp. She was all the more concerned because she knew that Bianchi had applied to the Bellingham Police Department for a job as a cop.

At first Moa and Parker didn't believe Susan Bird, so she put them in touch with a girlfriend named Annie Kinneberg. Annie and her pal, Margie Lager, confirmed what Susan had said, adding that Bianchi had also wanted to photograph lesbian models for clients he had in LA. 'He's a kinky bastard,' Annie explained. 'He's living with a woman called Kelli, and they have a little boy. That guy is real weird, you know.'

On receiving the call from Wendy Whitton, Moa sprang into action. First he radioed Steve Adams and ordered the night patrol officer to check out the Bayside address himself. Unfortunately, Steve went to the wrong address, 302 Bayside, where the bleary-eyed owners knew nothing at all. Then, having realised his mistake, he called the office and waited in his truck until the police turned up.

In another effort to solve the problem, Moa telephoned Bianchi at home. Ken, who could sell sand to the Arabs, denied knowing about any house-sitting job. He denied knowing Diane Wilder or Karen Mandic and bolstered his protestations of innocence by claiming that he had been to a Sheriff's Reserve first-aid meeting that evening.

By now Moa was not only confused but also increasingly alarmed, so he summoned Bianchi to the firm's office. Then he contacted the instructor of the Sheriff's Reserve to confirm what Bianchi had told him, and learned that Ken was lying through his back teeth. Told that Bianchi had failed to turn up for the class, Moa then rang the police.

When they arrived at WSA, officers asked Bianchi if he knew the two young women. At first he flatly denied the suggestion, but realising that he was painting himself into a corner, he backtracked, saying, 'Maybe Karen.' A gut feeling told the police that Bianchi was lying because he wouldn't look them straight in the face and appeared shifty and nervous. However, with little evidence to take him into custody, they allowed him to return home.

At 6am Bill Bryant, a university campus cop, obtained a key to Karen's apartment. By the telephone, written in red ink, was a message in Diane's handwriting. It read: 'Karen. Ken B. called. Phone 733-2884.' Picking up the scrap of paper, Bill called the number. It turned out to be WSA and, lo and behold, it was Bianchi who answered. 'I know your voice,' said Bryant. 'You called Karen's apartment on Tuesday and I told you that she wasn't in.' Once again Bianchi denied knowing Karen Mandic, saying that anyone could be using his name.

Bryant then called his father, also a police officer, and he in turn called the Bellingham Police Department, who re-interviewed Bianchi later that morning. Officers Geddes and Page confronted him with the note, and Bianchi reacted angrily. 'I'd sure like to know who has been using my name,' he snapped. 'I'm well known. I was in the newspaper when I left Fred Myer to come here in charge of operations.'

But, even though Bianchi was now the chief suspect for the girls' abduction, and despite the evidence mounting against him, the officers could do little more than allow him to carry on with his work.

At 4.40pm the same day Karen's green Mercury Bobcat was found. The car, parked 1.6 kilometres from the Bayside address, in a cul-de-sac in Willow Drive, contained the fully clothed bodies of Karen Mandic and Diane Wilder. At autopsy it was determined that both young women had been raped and strangled with a ligature.

After this grim discovery an order went out for Bianchi's immediate arrest, but first the police needed the help of Randy Moa. Knowing that Bianchi might be armed and dangerous, he radioed him in his truck, instructing his unwitting employee to check out a disused guard shack at the South Terminal, a remote area of the docks. Moments after Bianchi arrived at the location, Detective Terry Wight, brandishing a pistol, arrested him.

With Bianchi now in custody, the investigation moved up a gear. While officers broke the tragic news to Karen's father, Detectives Nolte and McNeill and Field Investigator Moore made a thorough search of Bianchi's home, where they found in the bedroom a pair of blue uniform trousers with the crotch ripped. Kelli confirmed that these were the trousers that her common-law husband had been wearing the previous evening. She also pointed to a red plaid shirt, and there was an identical one lying underneath it. Kelli said that Ken had been wearing one of these shirts the night before, and fibres, identical in every respect to those of these shirts, were later found in Dr Catlow's home. The officers also took possession of a pair of cowboy boots, and the sole tread pattern was soon found to match imprints found at both Willow Drive and Bayside.

Hanging in the bedroom closet was a .357-calibre Highway Patrolman's revolver, complete with a standard Sam Browne belt and holster. In the same closet Nolte discovered a shoulder holster and several cameras. The firearm was licensed and in extremely good condition. The cameras, along with other photographic equipment, were of professional quality, and the discovery added veracity to the claims of Susan Bird, Annie Kinneberg and Margie Lager.

Next the officers turned their attention to Kelli's dressing table, where they found a quantity of jewellery and seven watches. Kelli explained that Ken had given her most of these items as presents, but in fact these were dead women's trinkets, for he had stolen them from the bodies of his Hillside Strangling victims.

The property was now searched from bottom to top, and in the basement officers found several thousand dollars' worth of brand-new tools, all in their original boxes but with not a price tag or sales receipt to be found. It was soon discovered that this handyman's treasure trove had been stolen from Fred Myer when Ken had worked at the store as a security guard. However, the stash of stolen goods didn't end with the tools, for on a shelf there were enough medical supplies to supply a doctor's surgery. These Bianchi had stolen way back, from the Verdugo Hills Hospital in Los Angeles. And when Moore made the mistake of prising open a cupboard, he was buried under a shower of scores of tins of crab meat. Ken had taken this lot from a cold storage company to which WSA had assigned him as a guard. And then came the last of the swag. A large box was found to be jammed full of brand-new jackets and touchtone telephones. These had been misappropriated from the Uniflite Corporation, whose offices were at the South Terminal. However, all this merely proved that Bianchi was a thief, not a murderer, and at the time there wasn't the merest hint that he was one of the Hillside Stranglers.

Bianchi's two vehicles, one private and the other his work vehicle, were impounded at Bellingham Police Station, where Detective Knudsen waited for Kelli Boyd to arrive before he could search them. Meanwhile, at 2am on Saturday, 13 January, he started by looking for clues on Karen's Bobcat. Crawling underneath the car, he noted that the gas tank had a fresh dent on the driver's side. It appeared, from the angle of the damage, that this was a 'back-up' dent, and later that day the investigator found paint on a dislodged rock in the driveway of 334 Bayside. This evidence was solid proof that at some time the Bobcat had been on Dr Catlow's property.

When Kelli eventually arrived at the car pound, Knudsen went through Ken's battered VW with a toothcomb, and in the front passenger footwell a brown leather attache case was found. Tipping the contents of the case on to a table, officers found that every document tied a 'Dr Bianchi' to a psychiatric counselling service in Los Angeles. Taken together, these were unusual items to say the least, so Nolte and Knudsen moved into a huddle. It seemed they had captured a double murderer, thief and bent security guard cum pseudo cop and psychiatrist.

Nolte decided to make further enquiries, so he picked up the phone and called the LAPD. 'We've got a real fruit under arrest here in Bellingham,' he explained. 'We got him in on suspicion of two homicides, and rape. Do you know the name Kenneth Alessio Bianchi?'

Within the hour the LAPD called back with electrifying news. 'Sure,' said the breathless voice, 'we got a Bianchi, K.A., on our list. He applied to join the Force; he even had a ride-along in a squad car. Yeah, his name has come up several times during the Hillside Strangler investigation, but, ya see, no one has gotten around to speaking with him yet. We can wire you an ID FIT of our suspects if you need it.' This he did, and one face from the printout was Bianchi to a tee.

At the time of his arrest Ken had been in possession of a large bunch of keys, which were now in a police property box. Detective Nolte had overheard Randy Moa saying that a ring of keys, along with several client account cards for Bellingham's south-side district, were missing from the office, so Nolte went to the box and retrieved them. Moa identified them as belonging to those accounts for which Bianchi was solely responsible. One key in particular fitted Dr Catlow's front door. Indeed, the account card was tied to this key and this proved that Bianchi had had access to the Bayside address.

With the very real prospect of them having arrested a cold-blooded serial killer dawning on them, the police then searched Bianchi's WSA pickup, call sign 5. However, the only item of note recovered from Bianchi's truck was a striped towel. Tests later proved that it was stained with the semen of a non-secretor and, as we now know, this category was Bianchi's.

On Monday, 15 January 1979, Nolte and his colleagues searched Karen Mandic's apartment for the second time. In a drawer, Nolte found a business card in Ken's name indicating that he was the self-styled 'Captain Kenneth A. Bianchi' of Whatcom Security. Nolte spoke to Moa, who reported that no such title had been authorised by his company.

A few days later police carried out a thorough search of the South Terminal, where Bianchi had been arrested. Here they found a coat belonging to Diane Wilder and in one of the pockets were the keys to Karen's car. Since the two young women couldn't have dropped the coat off at the docks, the killer must have done. The noose was tightening around Bianchi's neck.

It was now crucial for the police to establish Bianchi's movements for the times in question because, if he produced a solid alibi to say he couldn't have committed the murders, the police would have been back to square one. Kelli Boyd was positive that Ken had arrived home on Thursday evening at about 10.30pm. She told officers that she noticed that he had ripped the seat of his denim trousers, which she thought was 'kinda comical', but she was surprised when he threw the garment into a trashcan. She had retrieved the trousers because she thought that the cloth might come in useful as her mother was making a rug and needed all the denim she could lay her hands on. Kelli also recalled that Ken had been sweating profusely when he walked through the door, and this was unusual. 'He smelled kinda strange,' she said.

When asked about a little gold Italian good luck horn on a chain that had been found on her dressing table, Kelli explained that it had been a gift from Kenneth way back in Los Angeles. Later this item of jewellery proved to be identical to one belonging to Yolanda Washington.

With Kelli placing Bianchi at home around 10.30 on the night of the murders, the police looked elsewhere for witnesses who might have seen him out and about. First they spoke to a Mrs McNeill, who lived at 327 Bayside, almost opposite Dr Catlow's home. She reported that at around 9.30am on Thursday, 11 January she had seen a yellow WSA pickup truck enter Dr Catlow's drive. At noon she saw an identical vehicle enter and leave the property and around 7pm or shortly thereafter she heard a vehicle enter the drive but did not see it. When questioned about the sound of the engine, Mrs McNeill said that it had sounded like the vehicle that had made the earlier visits.

On Saturday, 13 January a vital witness came forward in the form of Raymond Spees, who said that late on the evening of the murders he had been at church. Between 10 and 10.30 – he could not be precise about the exact time – he said that he was returning to his home at 517 Fern Road, and in doing so he took the new Willow Road, which was now the quicker route. This journey took Spees past the cul-de-sac where the bodies were found in Karen's car. However, more to the point was the fact that, as he passed the entrance of the cul-de-sac, a vehicle came out rapidly, and he had to swerve to avoid it. Spees described the vehicle as a yellow WSA pickup truck with a flashing light bar on the driver's cab. He was positive about this identification because he knew the firm and had noted its emblem on the cab door. Spees also noticed that the driver was shielding his face with his hand.

With overwhelming evidence mounting against him, Bianchi consistently refused to admit guilt, and then he asked for legal representation. Attorney Dean Brett advised his new client not to talk to the officers again without his being present, and initially Ken found Brett, 'a shining example of an energetic champion of justice'. This flowery accolade was withdrawn a week later, after Bianchi started to sum up his predicament. He was furious that Kelli had held a yard sale to dispose of his property, then he accused her of having an affair with Brett and later of 'humping a police officer'. Bianchi was also worried about the lies he had told police about his movements during the time of the murders. He had told them, Randy Moa and Kelli that he had attended a Sheriff's Reserve meeting, and this was blatantly false. Some years later he wrote to me with a pathetic excuse for telling the lie:

'I hate confrontations. People only have their whereabouts checked when they are suspected of doing something wrong. So, knowing I hadn't done anything wrong, and nothing to hide, I had given the original, short answer, about going to the Sheriff's Reserve class. That was a simpler than the longer, true explanation. Besides, if I had killed the girls, I would have remembered it. I didn't, and that's what I kept telling the police.'

Yet another example of deep-seated psychopathic denial, this illustrates Bianchi's thinking process around the time of the murders, and indeed today. Of course, the 'true explanation' to which he refers tongue in cheek is that he had just raped and strangled two innocent young women. Now that would have taken some explaining away.

When Bianchi was charged with the two counts of murder, he pleaded 'not guilty'. An Affidavit of Probable Cause set out the allegations in detail, and this was the first opportunity for Bianchi and his legal team to study the case presented by the state. It was also the chance for Ken to embark on the first of his many 'fly-specking' exercises, where he examines every dot and comma of a problem, and for which he has become notorious ever since.

The main thrust of the prosecution was to file for the death penalty, but there was a plea-bargain offer on the table: if Bianchi pleaded guilty, the state wouldn't press for the death penalty, and he would live. This somewhat rocked Ken's boat, for he had no intention of simply throwing his hands in the air and admitting guilt, but Brett was quick to point out that protestations of innocence would no longer wash. Moreover, Ken had failed the lie-detector test to which he had agreed. Nevertheless, he tore up the plea-bargain offer and returned to his cell to sulk.

In the United States, the moratorium on capital punishment was lifted in 1976, and Brett was anxious that his client would not be the first killer to be hanged in Washington State, so he attempted to mitigate Bianchi's culpability for the Bellingham murders by suggesting that he should plead 'not guilty by reason of insanity' (NGI). To this end, the attorney felt obliged to inform his client of the horrors of death by hanging, going on to paint a morbid and terrifying picture of this form of execution. 'Most go to the gallows screaming,' he told Ken.

'Some collapse and have to be strapped to a board. An' hanging is goddamn painful if it don't work out right. That meeting scared me straight,' Bianchi said in a letter. 'I was in a corner not of my own making, an' I had nowhere to run or hide.' So now, confronted with the stark choice of death or a life behind bars, he finally agreed to plead NGI.

With their client's permission in their pocket, Ken's legal team employed the services of an investigative social worker named John Johnson, who started to probe Bianchi's history right back to day one. Johnson was an excellent researcher, and before long he reported back to Bianchi and Brett. It was good news, for it was suggested to Ken that he might have been abused as a child and this would have unhinged his mind. In fact, the defence team went even further: Ken's failure to have remembered killing the co-eds could be due to some form of amnesia. With this information now to hand, there was the possibility that Ken would receive a reduced custodial sentence with a specific period before parole, or better still, his time could be served in a psychiatric institute, where the silver-tongued killer could work his ticket to freedom.

But he never will. After pleading guilty to seven murders, including the Bellingham slayings, Kenneth Alessio Bianchi was sentenced to serve life in prison on Friday, 19 October 1979. Three days later Angelo Buono was arrested in Los Angeles and charged with ten murders. On 1 April 1984 Buono was sentenced to life in prison, only escaping the gas chamber because a deal had been done to spare Bianchi's life if he gave evidence against Angelo. It was thought it would not be 'fair' to execute one and not the other, nevertheless, the Grim Reaper eventually claimed Buono. He died from a heart condition at the Calapatria State Prison on Saturday, 21 September 2002. He was 64. 'He had assigned duties at the prison, and he was singled-celled because of the nature of his crime,' Martinez said. 'There was nothing exceptional about his conduct in prison.'

To complete the story, we should now look at a related case of folie a deux: that of Bianchi and 'VerLyn', Veronica Wallace Compton. Veronica told me in conversation: 'Let's deal with our mutual friend, Bianchi. Ken's not stupid. Ken is the slickest criminal I've ever met in all of my years, and I've met a few criminals. But, without doubt, Ken is the master of them all. He is very circumspect – um, that's where his brilliance lies, in his ability to premeditate things, and to protect himself. He is very good at that.'

While held in custody at Los Angeles County Jail during

Buono's trial, Bianchi almost engineered his freedom when a beautiful young actress and budding screenplay writer fell in love with him. Veronica was a statuesque, sultry beauty with raven hair. She had a figure that made most men, and many women, drool and, as one woman observed, 'VerLyn has a figure that most women would die for.'

Veronica was and still is highly intelligent, but it would be fair to add that she has never fully applied her many abilities to any studies or goals and around the time of the Hillside Stranglings she was deeply locked into a downward spiral of cocaine and sexual perversion, the second of which would bring about her downfall.

In the waning days of 1979 Veronica was into the S&M trade, practising as a dominatrix. Partying every night, she was living a constant quest for the high from the white powder that fuelled her fantasies and energised her huge bisexual appetite, an appetite that drove her to wield a whip on the flesh of the rich and powerful of Los Angeles.

When I met Veronica at the Western Washington Correctional Center for Women at Gig Harbor, she explained, 'In those days I was inexorably slipping deeper and deeper into the nether world of the leather and the lash scene. The more lurid, the more wickedly cruel the fantasy, the better.'

She also explained that back then she had had aspirations of becoming an actress and a screenplay writer. In fact, she had penned a number of frantic, blood-dripping fiction pieces, far too extreme for any mainstream publisher. One of those stories was called 'The Mutilated Cutter' and it concerned a female serial killer who injected semen into her victim's vagina to make police think that a man was the murderer.

The trial in Los Angeles of Bianchi and Buono was in full swing at this time, so Veronica wrote to the handsome Ken, asking him to help her research the story. Soon they were meeting frequently in the county jail, and Veronica fell in love with Bianchi, who had now convinced her that he was an innocent man.

Week after week they shared fantasies and intimate love letters, and quick to take any advantage that came his way – the plot of 'The Mutilated Cutter' appealed strongly to Ken's agile mind – he persuaded VerLyn to carry her literary plot into real life in, of all places, Bellingham. This, he said, would prove that the Hillside Strangler was still at large. 'If you can do this,' he told her, 'I will be let out of prison and be free to marry you.'

The first and most important part of the scheme was to obtain Bianchi's semen and smuggle it out of the jail. Bianchi soon solved that problem when he cut the finger from a stolen kitchen rubber glove. He masturbated into it and then tied the open end with the cord from a string of rosary beads that he had acquired from a visiting Roman Catholic priest. This small package he stuffed into the spine of a law book that had been loaned to him by Veronica, and, when she called to visit him a week later, she walked out of the jail with the book tucked under her arm.

With the first part of the plot a success, they now had to establish alibis for the times of the Los Angeles murders, for even Bianchi could not be in two places at once and, if he could prove that he was elsewhere when the murders took place, he reasoned, he would be home and dry. To resolve the problem of alibis, VerLyn travelled outside the state of

Washington, staying at hotels where she granted sexual favours to the staff in return for blank bar tabs and backdated receipts for rooms Ken and she never used. On these documents she would forge Ken's signature, but, to add even further credence to the plan, she stole gas station receipt books and filled them in. The idea was that in the weeks to follow she would miraculously uncover this 'new evidence' and present it to the police, in the hope that this would ensure her lover's release from prison.

In 1980, completely under Ken's hypnotic spell, VerLyn flew to Seattle, from where she drove up to Bellingham. In an audiotape she sent to me, she had this to say about the lovers' plot:

'The task would be settled in mere hours. The victim would fit the needed requisites. I would arrive in Bellingham, Washington, on a fall afternoon. Another woman's body would be discovered shortly afterwards. The method of killing would be familiar to the Whatcom County Homicide team. Their worst nightmare would be relived; a serial killer had apparently returned to town to continue the reign of terror he had enjoyed only 20 months previously. What they were not to know was that this individual was not a serial killer, neither was it a man.

'The peculiar murder tools remained undisturbed in the luggage I retrieved from the airport conveyor. There were no suspicious glances; and, with a small pillow under my clothes, I was just another pregnant woman, dressed perhaps a bit too "California", with my long, blonde hair held back in a silk scarf, a muslin dress, and designer sunglasses, more suited to a beachside patio than the gloomy rain forest of Washington.

Still, even with the clothes, I could hardly qualify as anyone noteworthy.

'My purse contained plenty of cash, and a cache of narcotics; both would be essential in my work ahead. A taxi took me to my destination, a small motel off the town's main boulevard. I signed the register with a fabricated name, the same one as I had used for my plane tickets, to keep my real identity a secret. Without taking off my gloves, I picked up the room key, and said, "Thank you", in my best-affected Southern drawl. It, like everything about me, was a performance. A creation. A fiction.

'The motel room was standard, but it held everything necessary for my purpose. There was a queen-size bed, a mirrored vanity area, and a small bathroom. Still keeping my gloves on, I unpacked the one suitcase, and arranged the items in a vanity drawer. I carefully laid out two pieces of rope, one with a pre-tied noose, the other loose to be used to tie the victim's wrists.

'Satisfied with my organisation of the items, I started the ritual of medications: tranquillisers, cocaine, and alcohol, to be taken as he [Bianchi] had directed. Finishing with them, and with my addictions sated for the moment, I felt hopeful that the hallucinations would be kept at bay, so I settled into tending the blonde wig and adjusting the padding that made my flat stomach give the appearance of pregnancy under my dress. All part of the fictitious creature partly of my making and partly of Ken's.'

During her first evening in Bellingham, VerLyn met Kim Breed in a local bar. After a few drinks, and using the promise of drugs, VerLyn invited Kim back to her motel room. Once there, she slipped the noose over the unsuspecting woman's head, then tried to tie her wrists. However, Kim was a martial-arts expert, so she athletically threw her assailant over her head and rushed into the street, leaving VerLyn dazed and scared on the bedroom floor. When she recovered, VerLyn fled back to Los Angeles, with the police, who had traced her airline ticket, in hot pursuit.

When she was arrested and returned to Bellingham, she knew that she was in a serious predicament. In this conservative town where wearing a garter belt was considered 'kinky' and drug addicts thought to be the curse of the nation, she was about to stand her trial with the odds a million-to-one in favour of a guilty verdict. Subsequently, VerLyn was sentenced to 15 years for trying to duplicate a Kenneth Bianchi murder in an effort to free one of the most hated men in American criminal history. After one failed escape bid in which she climbed under the wire and almost got clean away, VerLyn is now a free woman, married and living near Seattle.

In 1995 I saw Ken Bianchi in the flesh for the last time. He was lying on the bunk of cell number 12 in the Special Housing Unit, where he is kept for his own protection. The very sight of me peering through the bars of his cage infuriated him. He went berserk and immediately threatened to sue the Department of Corrections for allowing me to violate his civil rights. But this threat was not hot air. For a start, it brought down a mountain of paperwork for the DOC to deal with, and with his appeal against the Bellingham convictions, Petition C95-0934, filed on 11 June 1995 in the United States District Court of Western Washington, in the pipeline, we have not heard the last of Kenneth Bianchi.

Conclusion

It is highly probable that Kenneth Bianchi had killed before he met up with Angelo Buono. We also know that this sexual sadist committed a double murder after he and Buono split up and that therefore he was the more likely of the two to commit homicide on his own.

Although Buono was cast from a similar mould, the two men sharing the same perverted delusions and fantasies, he had not committed murder before he and Bianchi teamed up and most certainly he did not kill again after they parted company in acrimonious circumstances.

This interesting heterosexual folie a deux came about because of a complex of fateful circumstances that allowed the two men to enjoy and act out their shared sadistic tendencies to the limit. In doing so they became extremely dangerous creatures. Had they not met up in California, the Hillside Stranglings would not have occurred.

But what makes Bianchi unique among cases of folie a deux is his subsequent such partnership, in which he was joined by Veronica Wallace Compton. Such was VerLyn's fixation on the man, she was prepared to kill for him in an effort to have him released into her arms. Their story brings together a convicted double killer in custody awaiting his trial for a number of other murders and a beautiful young woman who walks into his life and falls for him. Both soon learned that they shared the same fantasies. Today Veronica freely admits this, while, as might be expected, the devious Ken still denies all. Yet, as clear as day, the conspiracy between them was intended to win Bianchi his freedom, and to do this VerLyn would have committed murder by proxy. In this intriguing case we have the potent ingredients of the self-sacrificing accomplice and a conspiracy between two warped individuals who share a fantasy and pursue a common goal.

CHAPTER TWENTY TWO

CAROL BUNDY, JACK MURRAY AND DOUGLAS CLARK
A Triple Shared Madness

'I used to be a good-looking guy, ya know. But see what they done to me in here. My hair is falling out, my teeth are rotten and still they want to kill me. Still we all gotta fuckin' die sometime. I've outlived the judge, and the prosecutor; it's just they're killing an innocent man.'
Douglas Clark to the author at San Quentin State Prison, 1995

Perhaps one of the most fascinating examples of 'shared madness' we will ever find is the terrifying and unique case of Carol Bundy, Jack Murray and Douglas Clark.

It all began during the summer of 1980, when a string of horrifying murders rocked Hollywood. All of the victims were hookers working the notorious Sunset Boulevard, which prompted the press to dub the as yet unknown serial killer the 'Sunset Slayer'. But first allow me to introduce you to the three principal characters, all distinctly unappealing.

Carol Mary Bundy – no relation to the serial killer Ted Bundy – is a short, overweight, potato-faced woman who is as blind as a bat. If we could place her alongside Rose West and several other large murderesses featured in this book, they would all seem like fat peas from the same pod. And, like so many serial killers, Carol had an extremely dysfunctional childhood.

In this story of a triple shared madness, we see two fairly intelligent and well-educated men drawn to this woman like moths to a flame – to join with her in committing brutal murder.

Carol's mother, Gladys, was part Algonquin Indian and her father, Charles Peters, a French-Canadian, was of a build that might be described as roly-poly. Carol once remarked, 'He was a male version of me with a bald head. He had blue eyes, a pleasant appearance and a dynamite personality. He was a good father. He worshipped me because I was bright.'

Born in 1943, Carol was the second of three children and the family lived in various cities across the USA. She claims to have attended 23 different schools before the ninth grade. By the age of 11 she had already started shoplifting and stealing money from her parents and neighbours.

Gladys Peters died of a heart attack on 10 June 1957. The following night, Carol said, she was in bed with her father, who 'performed oral sex on me and sexually abused my 11-year-old sister'. One night just after her sixteenth birthday her father sent her out to a local store to buy provisions. When she arrived home, she claimed, she found 'globs of blood everywhere and a rifle on a chair'. She explained that her father, who was remarried by then, couldn't take life any more and had planned to commit murder. 'That's why he sent me to the store,' she said. 'He was going to kill his new wife while I was gone, then kill me when I got home.' Apparently the plan literally backfired when he and his wife wrestled with the rifle, which discharged and blew off his thumb.

After this incident Carol's stepmother arranged for the children to be taken to a foster home. This was a temporary arrangement, for then they were packed off to Indiana to live with an uncle. Two years later Charles Peters hanged himself, aged 52.

Carol was married in 1960 to a 33-year-old pimp whom she had known for two weeks. The marriage ended after six days, when Carol left because her husband apparently wanted her to have sex with his friends. She was not prepared to tolerate that sort of treatment, although she later told psychiatrists that she had been involved in sex for gain before marrying and also claimed to have been a prostitute in Portland, Oregon, in the mid-1960s.

Following her divorce from the pimp, Carol said, she tried to pull her life together by attending the Santa Monica City College, where she studied to become a vocational nurse. The college is unable to support her claim that she graduated in 1968.

In 1969 Carol married a hospital orderly called Grant Bundy. This marriage lasted for most of the 1970s and the couple had two boys. But Grant was a women beater, and court records show that in January 1979 Carol sought refuge in a women's shelter before leaving him and going on welfare. Twice she attempted suicide. After taking a job as a licensed vocational nurse at the Valley Medical Center in Los Angeles,

Carol, now overweight, moved with her two children to Valerio Gardens, an apartment block in Van Nuys, which was managed by Jack Murray.

John ('Jack') Robert Murray was a 41-year-old Australian who lived on the site with his wife and two children. He had a reputation as a ladies' man and in no time at all he and Carol were in the throes of an affair. Recently divorced from her second husband, Bundy received half the proceeds from the sale of her previous home. This was a substantial amount and Murray soon got wind of her good fortune. Lavishing love, care and attention on Carol, he encouraged her to have her eyesight examined. Her vision was so poor was that she was subsequently declared blind and therefore eligible for monthly disability payments from Social Security, and there is no doubt that her disability payments found their way into Murray's pocket.

The man was not known for being a philanthropist or even charitable, for he conned money out of his friends and repeatedly cheated on his wife. On one occasion he was caught pocketing wads of notes from a Telethon charity collection with which he had been involved.

After Murray learned of Bundy's sizeable bank account, the relationship changed direction, becoming one of prostitute and punter in reverse. Now completely infatuated with her lover, Carol started paying him for sex and by the end of 1979 he had wheedled $18,000 out of her on the bogus grounds that he needed the money to pay for a cancer operation for his wife. In reality he used half to pay off the outstanding debt on his Chevrolet van, which he often used as his mobile sex den. The balance was used to refurbish the van's interior.

By Christmas 1979 Carol was so obsessed with Murray's sado-sexual performances with her that she approached his unsuspecting wife and offered her $1500 for her husband. The woman was so furious that she insisted that Bundy vacate the apartment complex. Meanwhile, Jack timidly agreed to keep the peace. For him it was a matter of selfish economics, as his wife cooked his meals and laundered his clothes, services he could not afford to lose. Also, from his purely cynical viewpoint, Carol was simply his subservient sex partner. Now that he had got most of her money she was of no further use to him. Nevertheless, he did arrange for her to move into an apartment on Lemona Avenue, Van Nuys, some five kilometres from his home.

On arriving at her new home in May 1980, Carol was immediately attracted to an 11-year-old girl. She was mentally and physically well developed, and the unlikely pair established the relationship by trading adult jokes. Inevitably, this arrangement took on a sexual dimension and Bundy encouraged the minor to cross the bridge from gentle petting and cuddling to full-blown lesbianism.

Despite their apparent split, Jack and Carol continued their clandestine affair but in a less evident manner. The sex turned increasingly deviant and the couple tried to encourage other young girls to indulge in three-way sessions with them. However, they were all put off by Bundy's unsavoury looks. By now totally dejected, she took her two sons out of school and sent them to the Midwest to live with their father's parents.

'Carol Bundy, that half-blind bitch? She shit-canned her kids and sent them in a hand basket to Hell,' Douglas Daniel Clark told me during our 1995 interview at San Quentin State Prison.

Clark had been born Daniel Clark in 1948 in Pennsylvania, where his father, Franklyn, was stationed in the Navy. He was the third son of five children. In the third grade he decided that he wanted to be called Doug instead of Daniel. The family moved repeatedly, living in various parts of the USA and in other countries all over the world. In 1958 Franklyn retired from the Navy as a lieutenant commander. The following year he moved with his wife, Blanche, and their children, Frank Jr, Carol Anne, Doug, Walter and Jon Ronlyn, to Kwajalein, an atoll in the Marshall Islands, where he took up a civilian position running the supply department for the Transport Company of Texas. Blanche worked as a radio controller.

They spent two years in Kwajalein, enjoying a life of colonial privilege, in a housing complex that was built specifically for the many American families who lived on the atoll. When they returned to America they lived in Berkeley for a short time before moving to India. The Clarks lived in a manner reserved for only the very wealthy back in the States, with servants who waited dutifully on parents and children alike.

Other Americans living in the area described the Clarks as pleasant people who kept themselves to themselves. As for Doug, no one could remember any startling behavioural problems, although they had found that, if the boy ever got into trouble for any of the usual childhood pranks, his father would defend him aggressively, refusing to acknowledge his son's responsibility for his behaviour.

Later Walter and Doug were sent to Ecolat, the International School in Geneva attended by the children of UN diplomats, international celebrities and European and Middle

Eastern royalty. Unlike Walter, who was popular and out-going, Doug was considered sullen and arrogant and made few friends. He did not do well in his studies, as he couldn't be bothered to do the work or complete assignments. Doug claimed that he had developed his preferences for kinky sex during his time in Geneva, and it was for this very reason that he was expelled from Ecolat.

After Geneva, 16-year-old Doug was sent to Culver Military Academy in Indiana. Frank Jr and Carol Ann had already left home by this time and Walt was sent to a boarding school in Arizona; Jon Ronlyn joined him there later. Doug's parents continued to move around the world, first to Venezuela, then to Perth, Australia.

Although intelligent, Clark was happy to scrape through his schooling, expending minimal effort. He was involved in a number of sports and played saxophone in the dance band. In the three years that he attended the academy, he had no close friends, but instead hung around with a group of kids who shared his contempt for authority and his 'I don't give a fuck' attitude. Doug would boast of his family's wealth and his sexual exploits, oblivious to his friends' annoyance and boredom. The fact that most of his classmates refused to socialise with him and in many cases avoided contact with him altogether did not seem to bother him at all.

Doug's behaviour and attitude led to many meetings with the academy's therapist, Colonel Gleeson. Despite the fact that Gleeson had written many letters informing the Clarks of their son's bad conduct, they showed no concern. In the time he was there, he only received one visit from his mother. The only visit his father made occurred while the lad was on holiday.

Like many teenage boys, Doug and his classmates were obsessed with teenage girls and sexual fantasies, but for Doug it went further than fantasy. He would often take a girl to his room and record her moans and groans as he had sex with her. Playing the tapes to his classmates, he revelled in their obvious jealousy.

Doug claimed to have met the love of his life at the age of 17, at a dance in Culver, where he took her away from another boy. Despite his claims to have been in love with Bobbi, he would take photographs of them having sex and pass them around the school, savouring the notoriety that they brought him.

In 1967, at 19, Clark graduated from Culver and went to live with his parents, who were now retired and living in Yosemite. When he was drafted, he enlisted in the Air Force in radio intelligence to ensure that he would not end up in the front line in Vietnam. He would first go to Texas and then Anchorage, Alaska, where he was given the job of decoding Russian messages.

The military discipline in Anchorage reminded Doug of Culver and he resented his senior officers' corrections, but the city life made up for it. He spent most of his time in the many dancer bars, where he nurtured his ego by leaving each night with one of the dancers hanging on his arm. Before his term was up, Clark left the Air Force with an honourable discharge, a National Defense Service Medal and his benefits intact. What the events were that led up to his leaving are unknown, as his story is different every time he tells it and the Air Force will not reveal anything. He claims that he had witnessed the murder of a black man by a white man and that he had fled after being called in for questioning.

With over $5,000 to hand, Doug planned to drive from Alaska to the Mexican border, but stopped when he got to Van Nuys, in Los Angeles, where he moved in with his sister, Carol Ann, who was living with her husband. At 24 he met 27-year-old Beverley in a North Hollywood bar and two years later they married. Blonde and heavy, Beverley saw herself as fat and ugly, but felt that Doug, with his big dreams and ambitions, would always try to build her up.

They bought a car-upholstery business, which Doug ran while Beverley had a job and did the books at weekends. He insisted that he was the one with the intelligence and refused to listen to any advice she gave about the business. Whenever they began to get ahead financially, Doug would quickly blow it. During the seventies the business began to falter, so they sold it. To pay off the debts, Doug worked in a gas station and as a security guard before he started buying goods at auctions to resell at swap meets. Beverley had the job of loading and unloading the truck because, in Doug's opinion, he was a better salesperson than her.

Although Beverley could not exactly say what went wrong in the marriage, she did say that Doug was lazy. She would not consider the fact that he liked to wear her underwear as any more unusual than his desire to try wife-swapping or three-way sex. As Beverley gained more weight during their marriage, Doug spent less and less time at home, preferring to go to bars. According to Carol Ann, her brother drank heavily and would become overanxious and angry when drunk. Beverley would deny that Doug drank to excess, even though she had persuaded him to join Alcoholics Anonymous as a condition of their staying together. He kept off the booze for two years.

Doug was ambitious but could not commit himself to the work required to achieve the success he longed for. It had been Beverley's suggestion that he apply to work for the city as a steam-plant trainee. He agreed and actually completed the training course.

In 1976, after a marriage that had lasted four years, Doug and Beverley separated and later divorced, although they remained close friends.

Three years later Clark began work at the Jergens soap factory, where his duties as stationary engineer required him to tend the large boiler. While the job did not befit his level of education, he enjoyed the sense of power controlling the three-storey structure gave him. In February 1980 Clark set fire to his car outside the factory while he was working the night shift, in order to claim the insurance.

By the time he met Carol Bundy, Clark had developed quite a talent for insinuating himself into the lives of fat, unattractive women who would willingly provide him with free accommodation, food and money in return for the attention he gave them. But, when a woman demanded more in return, he would quickly leave her and move on to the next lonely soul.

Clark was handsome, had an incredibly smooth manner, was well read and liked to sprinkle his conversation with quotations from Shakespeare and French phrases. On top of all this, his soft, slightly European accent was a gift that enabled him to take the pick of women he wanted. This leech-like sexual hedonist enjoyed nothing more than to have a variety of eager girlfriends willing to share their home with him. At times he was so much in demand he would even forget where he was living.

Just after Christmas 1979, 36-year-old Bundy met Clark, five years younger than her, at the Little Nashville Country Club in LA and afterwards they spent the night together. On learning that Doug had rent problems with his landlady, Carol offered him lodgings in her apartment. For a short time the arrangement was mutually satisfactory. To put it simply, Clark traded his body and sex for a roof over his head. Eventually, however, he came to the view that cash for sex would be more agreeable to him. During his brief stay at Lemona Avenue, Bundy introduced him to her sexual playmate, the 11-year-old-girl.

The proximity of the sexually advanced youngster, along with Carol's keenness for the three of them to have sex together, proved irresistible to Clark. Bundy photographed him simulating sex with the made-up child – a shot that would later prove to be his undoing. During our interview at San Quentin State Prison, Clark ranted on about the subject: 'I had sex with Bundy about three times in all our relationship, although Carol will say otherwise. Murray was her intense S&M lover. She and Jack had sex with the 11-year-old. He tried to orally and vaginally rape the kid. They repeatedly tried to engage my roommate, Nancy, in three-way sex. Carol even tried to get Nancy to join her and the girl in three-way female sex. She told them not to let me know she was busy with Jack trying to have sex with them since I would not like her and her lover fuckin' around with one of my girlfriends.'

The first confirmed victims of the 'Sunset Slayer' were 15-year-old Gina Marano and 16-year-old Cynthia Chandler. The naked bodies of the two attractive teenage prostitutes were found on an incline off the Ventura Freeway by a Caltrans street cleaner on Thursday, 12 June 1980. The medical examiner established that they had died the previous day. Cynthia was killed by a single .25-calibre gunshot wound to the back of her head, which had left the bullet lodged in her brain, and a second shot had penetrated her lung and burst open her heart. It was also determined that both shots had been fired at point-blank range. Gina had likewise been shot twice. One round entered behind her left ear, exiting near her right eyebrow, and the second bullet blasted through the back of her head, also exiting behind the left ear.

From my investigations I can say that the killers were, without doubt, Carol Bundy and Jack Murray.

Around 8pm on Saturday, 14 June, a woman called the LAPD Northeast Division at Van Nuys. She told a detective that she thought her lover was a murderer. 'What I'm trying to do,' she said, while officers recorded the call, 'is to ascertain whether or not the individual I know, who happens to be my lover, did in fact do this. He said he did. My name is Betsy.' Later in the call she changed her name to Claudia. The police were anxious to learn the full name of the alleged killer. The informant refused to give out this vital information, but, when pressed, she did give a brief description. 'He has curly brown hair and blue eyes. His Christian name is John, and he's 41 years old,' she added.

She was, of course, referring to Jack Murray.

'I've found a duffel bag in his car full of bloody blankets, paper towels and his clothes.' This description matched Murray perfectly, and not Clark, who was only 32 at the time. Warming now to her theme, the woman added, 'He tells me he fired four shots. Two in one girl's head and virtually blew her head away. One shot in the head and one shot in the chest of the other girl. He used a .25-calibre pistol. Does that square with what you've got?'

When the caller hung up, a detective wrote on the tape cassette: 'Either the killer, or one who knows the killer!'

Over the following days investigators compiled a list of people who had purchased .25-calibre pistols in recent months. Carol Mary Bundy's name came up, for she had purchased two .22-calibre Raven automatics in Van Nuys on Friday, 25 April. In fact, she was the only female on the register. The gun shop provided the police with her address, vehicle registration and social security number. Amazingly, the police chose to ignore this crucial information, despite the previous telephone call from a woman indicating a connection with the double murder. Quite why they chose to act this way would remain a mystery for some time. Meanwhile, on Saturday, 22 June, Bundy moved to Verdugo Avenue in Burbank. Clark, among others, helped her by taking her furniture and other possessions across town to her new home, which was a stone's throw from his place of employment at the soap factory.

At 3.05am the next day a Burbank police officer found the fully clothed body of a prostitute named Karen Jones lying in the gutter of a residential street near NBC's Hollywood studios. She had been shot in the temple with a .25-calibre pistol and there were indications that she had been thrown from a moving vehicle. Ballistic tests on a bullet retrieved from her head at autopsy proved that it matched, in every respect, the bullets that had killed Chandler and Marano.

Again the killers were Carol Bundy and Jack Murray.

Later that same morning and just a few kilometres away in a Sizzler Diner parking lot, police found the headless corpse of another hooker, Exxie Wilson. The body, which had been dragged behind a trash dumpster, was naked and lying in a pool of congealing blood. Wilson and Jones shared the same pimp, and he reported that he had last seen them both alive shortly before midnight. The women had been together.

During the late hours of Thursday, 26 June, a resident pulled into the driveway of his home in Studio City and found an ornate wooden chest obstructing his access. 'I thought I'd found some treasure,' he later told police, but on opening the chest the man was horrified to find a severed head wrapped in a T-shirt and jeans. At autopsy it was determined that Exxie had been shot with a .22-calibre bullet, the head had been washed and make-up roughly applied. It had also been refrigerated after decapitation, which had taken place while she was still alive. There were traces of what appeared to be semen in the victim's throat. The recovered bullet matched, in every respect, the bullets that had been used to kill Chandler, Marano and Wilson.

The killers were Carol Bundy and Jack Murray.

Snake hunters were out looking for trophies in a ravine in the hillside country near foothill Boulevard in Sylmar on Sunday, 29 June, when they found the body of a 17-year-old prostitute named Marnette Comer. Partially naked and covered with scrub, the corpse, which had been dehydrated and mummified in the summer heat, was lying on its stomach. At autopsy it was determined that Comer had been shot three times in the chest with a .25-calibre pistol and her belly slit open. She had last been seen alive on 31 May. The bullets recovered matched, in every detail, the rounds that had killed all of the other previous victims.

By now the police had traced the ornate chest to a Newberry's store in Reseda, where the sales clerk remembered the customer being an overweight woman – 'She was dumpy, and kinda ugly,' the clerk told them – who wore glasses with thick lenses and short, black gloves. The witness especially remembered the gloves because it had been a very hot day.

The clues floating around as to the identity of the mystery informant 'Claudia' were starting to adding up. Five prostitutes had been shot with the same .25-calibre pistol, and the description of the buyer of the chest matched in detail that of Carol Bundy, the only woman in the whole of California who owned two Raven automatic pistols. Yet still the police couldn't match up these leads.

On 29 July Bundy started to implode mentally. She phoned Clark and begged him to shoot her. When he refused, telling her to 'Fuck off', she attempted suicide. She sat in her Datsun car and injected herself with insulin and Librium before swallowing a handful of sleeping pills. Despite her knowledge of drugs, gained from her nursing experience, the suicide attempt failed and she was found and taken to hospital.

The next day her first action was to call Murray from her hospital bed and ask him to pick her up in his van. When they met he had with him a woman named Nancy Smith. Now feeling rejected by both Clark and Murray, Bundy was so furious she refused to get in the Chevy and, seething with rage, walked home. Yet none of this prevented her and Murray from having three-in-a-bed sex with the 11-year-old four days later.

On Sunday, 3 August, Bundy made arrangements to meet Murray again in the parking lot of the Little Nashville Country Club. Her timing let her down, though, for when she turned up at the rendezvous as planned she found he was already in his van and having sex with a woman named Avril Roy-Smith. Carol banged on the door and Avril left.

This chance encounter with yet another woman was to be the straw that broke the camel's back. Bundy and Murray drove away from the club together and parked a few blocks away, where they prepared for sex in the back of the van. Now undressed, Murray lay on his stomach while, crouching behind him, Bundy parted his buttocks and pushed her tongue into his anus. As Murray groaned with delight, she reached into her overextended waistband and drew out one of her Ravens. With her tongue still in place, she touched the muzzle of the pistol to the back of Murray's head. He felt the cold steel and froze for an instant before she fired a single shot into his brain. Bundy checked for a pulse and ascertained that he was still alive, so she fired again. Still his heart kept on beating.

After throwing the gun to one side, the killer pulled out a heavy boning knife from her bag and repeatedly drove it into her lover's back. After a dozen stabs he finally died. To complete her gruesome work, Bundy then slit open Murray's buttocks and mutilated his anus before hacking off his head. After rummaging through the van's cupboards, she scattered pornographic videotapes and magazines around the body. Emptying Murray's briefcase, she removed several Polaroid sex shots and took his keys and his gun, before placing his head in a plastic bag. She then returned to her own car, which was still parked at the club. Now, in the early hours of

Monday, 4 August, she drove to a call box and telephoned her own apartment, where Clark was sleeping.

Clark was in bed with Nancy Smith when the shrill ring dragged him out of a heavy sleep. 'Carol was whispering and giggling on the phone,' he explained, and, as the call continued, Nancy, who suffered from epilepsy, started to have a seizure. Clark told Bundy to shut up and get back home, and then he called for an ambulance.

When Bundy arrived at the apartment five minutes later, paramedics were already on the scene. After the ambulance left, she took Clark to her car, where, in the well of the front passenger seat, lay Murray's head in the plastic bag. The ragged and bloody stump was exposed, causing Clark to fall back and vomit. What with Nancy's fit and now this, it was all too much, but then Bundy coolly asked him if he would help her dispose of the mess. Like a complete fool, he agreed, despite the fact that he was due to start his shift at the soap factory within the hour. They drove off in the direction of the factory, with Bundy cradling the plastic-wrapped head in her lap. As they passed a pile of rubbish, she wound down the window and tossed out the grisly article. Murray's head was never seen again.

Three days later, on Tuesday, 7 August, the sexually insatiable Bundy invited Tammy Spangler, one of Murray's former girlfriends, over for dinner. Clark knew that Carol was trying to initiate another three-way sex session and declined to take part. In any case, he fancied the attractive woman himself, and he also feared for Bundy's state of mind.

'If she could do that to Jack,' he told me, 'what the fuck could she do to someone else. What about my fuckin' head?' After the meal Tammy left to go to work, and Bundy and

Clark were now alone. Her sexual expectations had not been met, so she convinced Clark that they should drive into Hollywood and find another girl who would treat him to a hooker's blow job. This was to be his birthday present from Bundy and reluctantly he agreed.

They drove to Highland Avenue, where they saw a suitable whore. She was called over and a deal was agreed. The girl's name was Cathy, but before she took payment, she said, 'I don't do nothing with no woman.' Her concerns were allayed and she climbed into the back seat, followed by Clark, who left the driver's seat tilted forward. This enabled Carol, sitting in the front passenger seat, to have a grandstand view. She gloated at the unedifying sight through her thick spectacles. Clark described what happened next:

'I was on the left an' Cathy was on my right, and twisted around with only her left buttock on the edge of the seat. She was working me up with her mouth, an' stuff like that. Then I noticed Carol fidgeting in her seat. She began heaving herself up and down, craning her neck to view the area around the car, like she was looking to see if there was anyone around. I saw Carol's hand reach around the seat, like she was gonna grope Cathy. Then I saw the fuckin' gun. For an instant, I thought she was going to shoot me, like she did Murray. But Carol placed the pistol to the back of the hooker's head and pulled the trigger.'

The bullet passed clean through the girl's head and struck Clark in the lower side of his stomach. Fortunately, it was only a flesh wound but blood flowed on to his work shirt. 'I was shocked and freaking out,' he explained. 'Carol told me to drive the fuckin' car while she climbed in the back, tore the clothes of the dead girl and sexually assaulted her, all the while ranting that she was sure the dead girl would have liked it.' When the body had been dumped, the two drove back to Bundy's apartment, where he changed his soiled clothes. He wouldn't see them again until the police arrested him.

On Saturday, 9 August the Van Nuys Police received a complaint about a Chevrolet van that had been left unattended on Barbara Ann Street. The caller also mentioned a foul smell emanating from the vehicle. Within minutes a squad car arrived to investigate and a police officer, looking through one of the van's windows, saw a body in the rear. As the scene was being cordoned off, Detective Roger Pida climbed in to conduct a preliminary investigation and, among the documents scattered about, he found a wallet that identified the male victim as John Robert Murray. Checking through their computer, the police learned that Murray's wife had reported him missing several days earlier, and officers were able to ascertain that he spent a lot of time with a woman called Carol Mary Bundy.

The following morning two detectives called at Bundy's apartment in Burbank. She invited them in and they were introduced to Clark and Tammy Spangler. Clark and Bundy were taken downtown for further questioning while Spangler followed in her car to bring them home after the interview.

At the police station the couple offered different alibis for the time of Murray's murder. Clark told the truth and said that Bundy had come home later that night. In a separate interview room, Bundy lied, claiming to have been at home all evening. She was adamant that she had not gone out. Asked if she owned any firearms, Bundy said that she had recently sold a pair of pistols to a tall guy with red hair and a scar. The only name she could conjure up at short notice was 'Mike Hammer', which provided the officers with a moment's amusement. Then Tammy Spangler piped up. She told the detectives that she had seen Murray with a woman called Avril Roy-Smith on the night of the murder. 'Perhaps you'd better go talk with her,' she suggested.

With no solid evidence with which to hold Bundy, the detectives allowed her and Clark to leave while they went in search of Avril, who subsequently gave a verifiable alibi to account for the time encompassing Murray's death. She said that, when she left the Chevy van, Murray was very much alive. As Avril departed, heading for a club where she spent the next three hours drinking with friends, she saw Carol Bundy climb into Murray's van.

The homicide cops were now very interested in Bundy. The next day, while they were completing their paperwork for the arrest warrant, Bundy walked off her job at the hospital after confessing to colleagues that she was responsible for murdering and decapitating her lover. She told them that she was going back to her apartment to 'clean out the evidence before Doug gets home'. As soon as she left, a senior official at the hospital reported Bundy's extraordinary allegation in a frantic call to the police.

On her way home Bundy called in to see Clark at the factory. She asked the gatehouse security officer to summon him. When he came out, she told him that she had told the police everything. Clark was livid. 'You crazy cunt,' he snapped, 'get the fuck away from me.'

With Bundy now off the premises, Doug stormed back into

the factory, where he tried repeatedly to phone Detective Pida, who was not in his office. 'Bundy was trying to fit me up with murder,' Clark has said many times while protesting his innocence of the 'Sunset Slayings', 'an' who the fuck is gonna believe a woman is doing all this murder stuff. An' she had incriminating photos of me and the 11-year-old hidden away. Blackmail. Yeah. That's what it fuckin' is.'

Just after 11 o'clock that morning Bundy called the LAPD's Northeast Division without identifying herself and asked to speak to homicide detectives. When Officer James Kilgore picked up the phone, she said, 'Sometime way back you were having a string of murders involving prostitutes in Hollywood.'

'We still are,' replied Kilgore, totally unaware that the caller was recording their conversation.

'Do you still have a code name on the girl by the name of Betsy/Claudia?'

Kilgore said he wasn't sure.

'All right, never mind,' said the caller. 'Would you like your man today?' She talked about the murders and said that the weapon was a .22-calibre automatic. She said her man had told her he had 'hit over 50 people'. Then she said that she had killed a man named Jack Murray, and admitted her involvement with several of the other murders. 'The one, he cut her head off. Well, I played around with that one... and the fat girl [Karen Jones] that he dumped off near the NBC studios, I was involved with that.'

Kilgore asked how many murders there had been.

'Probably 12 or 14 total,' came the reply. 'But I can't verify all of them. I can only verify about eight or nine.'

'And you helped him on some of them?'

'Yes, I did,' said Bundy. 'Specifically how I got involved with it was a case of being scared to death because I knew that he had done these things. I felt I had to get involved. If I was involved he'd have no reason to kill me.'

She then said she was calling to give herself in, and that her real name was Carol Bundy. Finally, referring to the killer, she blurted out, 'He's my boyfriend and his name is Douglas Daniel Clark.'

'Doesn't it make you feel bad that you killed somebody?' asked the detective.

Bundy replied with an amazing statement: 'The honest truth is it's fun to kill people, and if I was allowed to run loose, I'd probably do it again. I have to say, I know it's going to sound sick; it's like going to sound psycho, and I don't really think I'm psycho, but it's kinda fun. It's like riding a roller coaster. Not the killing, not the action that somebody died, because we didn't kill them in any way that they'd suffer. It was just killing them straight out.'

Spurned by two men, Bundy had killed the first, her accomplice in serial murder, then involved the second in a homicide, and now she was going to turn him in.

After making the call she started rearranging her apartment in the belief that she had a few hours to get things in order. She was bent on doing everything she could to incriminate Clark, but she had just minutes, because detectives were about to arrive on her doorstep and arrest her. When they did, they conducted a careful search of the place.

Almost immediately Bundy held up a cardboard box that contained a pair of panties and assorted clothing. These items later proved to belong to an as yet undiscovered murder victim who would later be tagged 'Jane Doe 28'. The box also contained a purse belonging to another unidentified victim, 'Jane Doe 18'. 'This box belongs to Clark,' Bundy said. 'And do you want to see what kind of guy Doug Clark is?' she asked as she reached for her handbag on a table.

An officer stopped her because he suspected that the bag might contain a gun, but inside was her keyring. She selected a key and offered it to one of the police officers to open the cabinet in Clark's bedroom. The cupboard contained a photo album of Clark with his numerous lovers, including photos of his poses with the 11-year-old. Also, hidden among various papers, was a firearm sales receipt made out to a Juan Gomez, which later proved to be false.

Meanwhile, Detective Pida had taken Clark in for questioning to Van Nuys Police Station, where he was held for hours without water and food and denied the use of the toilet. This treatment was illegal, especially as Clark had not even been told of the reason for his arrest. Indeed, at the time he believed the arrest was all about Murray. When finally he was asked what he knew about this murder, to his credit he admitted everything he knew. When Clark was asked why he hadn't gone straight to the police, he truthfully answered that Bundy had dozens of incriminating pictures of himself and the young girl, which she had used as a threat.

When Pida produced the photograph album taken from his bedroom cabinet, Clark started to feel decidedly uneasy. The detective showed him a mugshot of the dead Cynthia Chandler, and Doug explained that he knew her personally. They talked about the prostitute murders, to which Clark retorted, 'Someone is tryin' to lynch my ass, and I have a hunch I know who it is.'

With little else to book him with, the police initially detained Clark on a holding charge of child molestation. This was a stopgap measure, for they had wider ambitions as far as he was concerned. There was certainly no evidence to say that Clark had been involved with the Sunset Slayings, other than Carol Bundy's wild accusations. Nevertheless, he was held without having his legal rights read to him for a further eight hours because he demanded to see an attorney.

It was now late at night and, when the police finally acceded to his request for legal representation, they informed him that all the lawyers had gone home and it would take hours before one could be recalled. Then he was illegally moved to another police station 50 kilometres away. When an attorney did turn up at Van Nuys Police Station, Clark was no longer there and no one seemed to know where he had been transferred.

If the police were being 'unco-operative', Clark was quite the opposite. He gave them permission to search his apartment, his motorcycle and his place of work. 'I gave them everything,' he railed on to me. 'I gave them my fuckin' boots, my fuckin' saliva, my fuckin' blood. I offered to take a polygraph, but changed my fuckin' mind 'cos I ain't never trusted the cops. I could see a fit-up coming from a mile off.'

While Clark was being grilled, Bundy was unloading her story on the detectives interviewing her. She corroborated Clark's denial of guilt for Murray's murder, saying that, although she had shot Murray, another man, 'a psycho', had hacked the head off to remove the evidence of traceable bullets. Questioned as to why she had left the cartridge casings in the Chevy, she gave conflicting answers. At first she stated that she didn't realise that the weapon automatically ejected the cases. Then, in a complete reversal, she said that she did realise that the cases had ejected from the weapon but had simply forgotten to pick them up.

During the initial, extremely thorough search of Murray's van, there was no record of any shell casings being found. Sometime later, though, a detective said that he had found a single shell casing in the van and that it had been fired from Bundy's chrome-plated Raven. This discovery took on a more sinister aspect when it transpired that a police evidence envelope, sealed and marked '2 x shell casings found at unspecified sources', had been torn open and one of the shell cases was missing.

When she was asked why she had shot Murray, Bundy gave four vague reasons in rapid succession. The first was that he had stolen money from her; the second, that he had jilted her; the third, that she had shot him as he had planned to rape and kill the very young girl; and finally, that he was going to report Clark to the police, accusing him of being the deadly Sunset Slayer. None of this made any sense whatsoever but, incredibly, the police seemed inclined to believe her. However, which of the four stories they believed, they didn't seem to know.

With an attentive audience of good-looking police officers surrounding her, Bundy went on to say that she had been involved with the murder of the hooker named Cathy, who had been shot while sitting in her Datsun. When the police told her that there was no forensic evidence of a shooting in the car, let alone a murder, she changed her account, saying that the crime had taken place in her Buick, which she had loaned to Clark. For his part, Clark maintains that it was most certainly the Datsun because the car only had two doors and he had to push the driver's seat forward to let the girl in.

Bundy went on to say that she had paid Cathy to give Clark a blow job as a birthday present, but claimed that it was agreed that he would give her a signal as to when to shoot the prostitute in the head. Clark vehemently denies this, arguing, 'No man, I don't care who he is, would let a half-blind bitch reach over, shoot at the head of a hooker suckin' his cock and hope like hell she didn't blow a hole in his knee or chest. I mean, what if her jaw locked shut?' And perhaps he has a valid point.

When questioned about the Chandler and Marano murders, Bundy claimed that she had not been involved. She had merely learned of the crimes through Clark. It was he, she said, who had told her that he had shot both women in the head while they were giving him oral sex. During the interview at San Quentin, Clark was asked to comment on Bundy's claim. 'You are pulling my pecker,' he declared. 'Do you think I'm fuckin' crazy, man? Some broad is blowin' me off an' I stick a gun to her head and blast them away. What about the fuckin' blood, man? What about my dick, man? I'd have been covered with the shit and it would have been painted all over the inside of the fuckin' car.'

Bundy told the police that Clark 'dragged the bodies from the Buick and into his lockup garage where he had sex with them'. She added, 'And it was because of this bloody mess in the car that Doug put it through a car wash.' Clark has never denied washing the Buick and indeed he even volunteered this information to the detectives, who confirmed that he had been to the car wash on 21 June, exactly a week after Bundy made her 'Betsy/Claudia' call to the police. He had this to say about washing the interior of the car: 'Everyone who saw or rode in the Buick from 14 June to 21 June, and there will be many who testified to this, will say that the car was dry and right after the car wash on 21 June it was soaked and damp with steamy air for a full week. The point is, what fucking vehicle was she washing out just before the taped call to the police on 14 June? The Datsun was broken down, the Buick was dry, and only Murray's Chevy van fits the details she made in that call.'

It later proved to be the case that Murray's van had indeed been washed out after the first three murders, although the police chose to ignore this vital evidence that would prove beyond doubt that Bundy was lying once again to save her own skin. Yet all of this begs the question of why Clark washed the Buick in the first place. The answer lies in supporting evidence given by four other people who confirm that he is telling the truth.

During the evening of 20 June, Clark visited Joey Lamphier, one of his many girlfriends, and when he left her apartment he accidentally reversed over an alley cat, crushing its hindquarters. He lifted the badly injured animal into the Buick, where it crawled under the front passenger seat. Clark is known for his love of cats and in the past had taken in several strays. He rescued many more from animal pounds and found new homes for them. As any cat lover will confirm, it would therefore have been in his nature to have been very concerned about the cat's welfare after the accident. Unfortunately, the cat died before he could reach a vet, so he placed its body in a cardboard box and left it by a garbage skip.

After work on the 21 June, Clark drove Bundy and Timmy, the young son of his current landlady, in the Buick to the car wash. Bundy was pressing for the return of the car in preparation for her move to Burbank. Clark hosed the cat's blood, urine and excrement from under the seat and vacuumed the excess water away. Later Timmy told police that the small amount of blood was still wet when he got into the car, which totally contradicted Bundy's claim that the blood had been there for some ten days. And, Clark explained, 'If this car wash had a sinister motive, why would I have taken a mouthy kid along?' Police evidence technicians did find a small amount of what appeared to be blood under and around the front seat of the Buick, yet in no way was the back seat contaminated in a manner which would have been consistent with Bundy's claim that three brutal and bloody murders had been committed in the vehicle.

In mid-1991 Carol Bundy changed her story yet again, this time for the benefit of a journalist who was writing a book about the Sunset Slayings. She now said that the car wash on 21 June followed the murder of Cathy (Jane Doe 28), which had been committed the night before. Now, according to her latest claim, the blood was no longer that of Chandler and Marano, nor was the Cathy murder committed in the Datsun. This time it was someone else but, once again, the police seemed to ignore these contradictions.

When questioned about the murders of Karen Jones and Exxie Wilson, Bundy denied any involvement in these crimes and merely related an account allegedly given to her by Clark.

'There were three hookers working together,' she said. 'Clark picked up Exxie and shot her in the head before decapitating her behind the Sizzler Diner.' (Witnesses heard a vehicle racing away from this precise location at about 1.15am.) Bundy went on to say that Clark returned to pick up Karen Jones and he shot her while she was giving him oral sex in the car. 'He killed her and dumped the body,' she said. (Witnesses heard a scream around 2.40am and Karen's corpse was discovered at this location less than an hour later.)

Bundy alleged that, after these two murders, Clark brought Exxie's head back to her new apartment in Burbank, where he placed it in the freezer before phoning her at her old apartment at Lemona, where she was still living. Telephone records show that this call was made at 3.08am. But is Bundy's story true? She claims that it was Clark who called her to explain what he had done. He says that it was Bundy who phoned him. The difference is that his account can be verified, for he had an alibi that night.

Tammy Spangler confirmed that Bundy had called Clark around 3am at the Lemona apartment, where they were sleeping on an old mattress. 'Doug was in a lot of pain because he had hurt his back while moving Carol's stuff,' she said. 'He was in agony and pretty wild that Carol had got him out of bed.'

Once again the detectives ignored Clark's story and chose to believe Bundy, who, at best, was a pathological liar. But was there any other evidence to support Clark and Tammy Spangler's claim that they had spent the night at Bundy's old apartment? There was, and Clark has this to say: 'I argued with Cissy Buster on the Sunday. She said, "Leave me if you don't want to live with me." I said, "Fuck it," and lugged my stuff down to the Buick. Carol had complained about the dampness and lingering smell of the cat faeces from the previous day's car wash. I had offered to dry it out 'cos I needed the car. I promised to dry it out and return it in time for Carol's move to Burbank. I then drove to Lemona about 1.30am to 2.30pm. The movers came about 3pm to 4pm and moved her into Burbank in two trailers and pickup loads. I rode with them and Carol had a slew of kids to help her put the kitchen shit in the Buick. At the other end the movers moved it all up. I helped and strained my back and ended up nearly unable to move. I left early and rode my bike to Van Nuys. I called Al Joines, my assistant at Jergens, around 6pm. I told him that I'd hurt my back, and asked him if he would start up the boiler the following morning. I then drank several beers. Tammy came over and we crashed on a mattress in the now empty Lemona apartment. I was woken from my sleep by a call from Carol at a time I know to be 3.08am, because the police confirmed that such a call was made.'

Every detail of this statement was later shown to be true.

Most prostitutes are reluctant to 'trick' alone, preferring to work in pairs for safety. Bundy claims that, contrary to this practice, Exxie Wilson allowed herself to be picked up by Clark, who killed her and then returned to the red-light district on his own with the intention of enticing the now dead girl's colleague into the Buick. Furthermore, it was later shown at autopsy that Wilson was still very much alive during her decapitation and that it would have been impossible to accomplish this act of mutilation without Clark being sprayed with arterial blood, which was not the case. Even more startling was the statement of the coroner, who claimed that both Murray's head, which Bundy had admitted cutting off, and Wilson's headless body had been decapitated by the same hand, using knives that had been found in Bundy's apartment.

The time interval which elapsed between the murders of Exxie Wilson and Karen Jones is also of interest, for it has the Bundy–Murray modus operandi written all over it. Bundy confirmed her MO when she offered Clark his birthday present and shot the hooker into the bargain. That Exxie had been decapitated by the same skilled hand that had cut off Murray's head, and that it had been Murray's van that had been washed out several times just after the murders, both point to Murray and Bundy as being the real murderers of Wilson and Jones.

Then there is Bundy's telephone call to the police on Saturday, 14 June, in which she described the killer as a man called 'John' and gave a description that matched that of John 'Jack' Murray right down to his age.

During her tape-recorded interrogation on Monday, 11 August, Bundy made reference to Clark murdering another hooker (Jane Doe 18) 'two weekends ago', and she was adamant about the date. Somewhat curiously, she was allowed to change this all-important date when the police ascertained that Clark was over 600 kilometres away, attending his brother's wedding, on the weekend pinpointed by Bundy. Eventually Bundy could only say 'sometime in July'. But, if this female killer was allowed to change a specific date to any one of her choosing in a given month, it paled into significance when she added that the crime committed on that date had been 'Doug's last murder'. 'He told me nothing about it,' she explained to the detectives. 'Absolutely nothing at all, and if he won't tell me, then he won't tell you, so you might as well forget it.'

But, within minutes, she changed her tune yet again by giving a full description of the crime, including the nickname Clark had supposedly given to the victim, 'Water Tower', and then offered up the location of the body. She even described Clark placing the girl's body on the bonnet of her Datsun and having intercourse while the motor ticked over and he simulated what she called 'coital movements'.

With Bundy lying and changing her story at every twist and turn, it may come as no surprise to learn that she also told police that the handbag they found in her apartment belonged to 'Water Tower'. In fact, the bag belonged to someone else. It contained a woman's business cards, telephone numbers and a driving licence, yet the police made no effort to check out these vital details or to find the true owner.

Quite rightly, Clark believes that, if Jane Doe 18 had been identified, that information could have established a date when she was last seen alive and probably murdered, thereby giving him the opportunity to confirm an alibi. More recently, he has also commented on the nickname he allegedly gave to this victim: 'I have never named anyone by that name, dead or alive. The police say the body was found by an oil tank. I am a four-year-educated engineer, and tanks are not towers, and oil is not water. This location was probably in the oil-pumping area of those hills, and I would never nickname a girl "Water Tower". Only a layman who didn't know the difference might do that.'

Even when confronted with her lies, which the police anxiously accepted as 'truths' to suit their case against Clark,

Bundy continued to lie and lie again. She further confused the already vexed situation by claiming that the cosmetics she had used to transform Exxie Wilson's head into a Barbie doll had been taken from the purse belonging to Jane Doe 18. She insisted on this, despite the obvious fact that Wilson had been killed a month earlier than this victim, ruling out Bundy's possession of her purse.

During her trading of accusatory testimony to escape execution, Bundy insisted that Clark was a necrophile. She said that he shot the prostitutes through the head as they performed oral sex on him. In such an unusual case anything is possible, but commonsense suggests that even the most deviant sexual psychopath would be deterred from such perverse activity. Not only was there the real danger of exiting and ricocheting bullets, as in the murder of Cathy, but also the very real peril of reflexive, death-spasm bites on the penis, and Doug Clark was very proud of his manhood.

While there was no evidence to support Bundy's claim that Clark was a necrophile, there was strong evidence to say that *she* was. She had admitted to having her tongue in Jack Murray's anus when she fired the bullets into his head. Furthermore, when her Datsun was stored after it had been released from the police pound, a letter was discovered that seemed to have eluded the first search of the vehicle. In Bundy's handwriting and signed 'Betsy', the pseudonym she had used in her first call to the police, the letter contained sexually explicit details of 'vaginal death spasms'. She continued by describing in sexually graphic detail how Clark had taken the severed head of Exxie Wilson from the freezer and into the shower, where he performed oral sex with the icy remnant.

Yet again, Bundy's account is a pack of lies and a testimony to the power of her grisly imagination. This is not about a 'chilled head': the object of Clark's alleged sexual outrage was not simply 'chilled', but frozen solid. The severed head had become a solid block of ice, as both Bundy and the police confirmed when it was discovered and it took several days to thaw out. When interviewed, Clark said, 'The cops said it was froze solid, and Bundy says the same fuckin' thing. The jaw was locked shut. So, how do you get a penis into that mouth? Give me a fuckin' break, will ya?'

This argument, nevertheless, could be missing the obvious. There was nothing to say that the head had been used as a sexual receptacle before it had been frozen. Despite Bundy's claim that Clark ejaculated into the mouths of both Chandler and Marano, internal swabs taken from the bodies showed no traces of semen. Traces of blood and sperm were found, though, on Exxie Wilson's body and Chandler's external vulva area. When tested, this was shown to be blood type A, the same grouping as Murray's, and distinct from Clark, who is type O. Traces of acid phosphates were found in Wilson's throat, but this probably came from her spinal fluid, although the prosecution later insisted it was Clark's semen, even though it did not match his blood group.

Shortly after her arrest for murder, detectives took Bundy for a meal. During this break in proceedings she was given the freedom to empty her bank safety deposit box while the police stood by making no record of the contents. She also took officers to Clark's private post box, where, without a search warrant, they unlawfully ordered the clerk to hand over the mail it contained. Then Bundy was allowed to return to her apartment so that she could arrange the sale of furniture, despite the fact that much of it belonged to Clark. Clark stated quite correctly that, 'They [the police] then let her have her car back before it was tested by the defence team,' emphasising, 'They never let murder cars back, never.'

A citizen who was storing the Datsun for Bundy after her arrest found the death spasm letter and a bloodstained jacket, which has never been forensically tested or blood grouped. The garment did not belong to either Clark or Bundy, or to any of the known victims. Subsequent research identified the true owner as Jack Murray. When his wife was shown a photograph of the jacket, she unequivocally identified it as having belonged to her late husband.

Incredibly, the generosity shown by the police to their star witness knew no bounds, even though she was shown to be a pathological liar. On 29 August, only 18 days after her arrest, they allowed Bundy access to Jack Murray's bank deposit box and allowed her to remove $3,000. This was cash to which Mrs Murray had lawful title. The money simply vanished into thin air. For many years the police adamantly denied that this incident took place. It was only when Clark finally proved in court that this was a lie that the police agreed that the deposit box was opened in their presence.

If mystery after mystery surrounds the lies and false accusations of Carol Bundy, the firearms involved in this case are a veritable minefield of problems and enigmas. It was established that she had purchased two .25-calibre Raven automatic pistols on 16 May 1980. These guns were similar, but not identical, in appearance. They were distinguishable insofar as one was chrome-plated while the other was nickel-plated. Ballistic tests identified the nickel-plated pistol as the weapon used in all of the murders, with the exception of those of Cathy, Jane Doe 18 and Jack Murray. In the latter case, no ballistic evidence was possible, for the very good reason that his head was never found. By now both of the two cartridge cases allegedly found in his truck had mysteriously gone missing in much the same manner as Mrs Murray's cash. Not to be beaten, Bundy now came up with the explanation that the nickel-plated gun actually belonged to Clark. He denied it and other people, whom the police chose not to believe, corroborated his denial.

During the Memorial Holiday weekend, which began on 24 May, Clark and a girlfriend, Toni, had made arrangements to travel north to Yosemite with the intention of visiting his parents. He planned to make the journey on his motorcycle and, just in case Toni was too nervous to travel by this means, he telephoned Bundy to see if he could use her Buick should the need arise. It was during this call that Bundy told him that she had recently bought the Ravens, and she asked him if he could check them over because one kept jamming. When Clark took possession of the pistols, they were unloaded but they came with a two-thirds-full box of shells.

On his return from Yosemite, Clark told Bundy that the chrome-plated gun was still jamming. She retained the nickel-plated pistol, which was later proved to be the murder weapon, and gave the malfunctioning chrome-plated one to Clark as a gift. She confirmed as much to the police. On 16 June Clark gave the gun to Joey Lamphier, showing her how to clear it if it jammed again. Early in July, Bundy demanded the return of this gun. There was an argument following which

Clark returned the Raven to Bundy. The next time he saw it was on the night of 7 August, when Carol used it to shoot Cathy through the head.

The two pistols surfaced again on 9 August, after the police discovered Murray's headless corpse. Bundy handed the firearms to Clark, saying, 'Get rid of these where they'll never be found.' He took them to the soap factory, where police officers eventually discovered them still in Bundy's make-up bag, which was hidden on the top of a boiler.

Police investigators had had a field day combing through Bundy's apartment. In her bedside cabinet they found 29 rounds of .25-calibre ammunition. Also in the living room, investigators found several film reels of 'super' pornography and a book that contained an illustration of a severed head. All of this material was owned by Bundy, but at his trial it was all attributed to Clark.

During her lengthy interviews with the police, Bundy told them that Clark had had sex with the dead bodies of Chandler and Marano in his garage, where he stored wood, along with his motorcycle and several boxes of his personal belongings. The detectives' ears pricked up and they obtained a search warrant for the place. No sooner had this accusation poured from Bundy's mouth than she frantically insisted that they wouldn't find any evidence there. 'We scrubbed the place out,' she said. Nevertheless, officers found Clark's boot print on the floor and they were keen to ascertain if the stain was blood.

Forensic experts carried out a 'presumptive' blood test, which gave a positive indication that the stain was organic in origin. Further tests were required to determine the true nature of the stain. This was never done, and the reason, according to the police, was to 'preserve the boot print for identification and comparison'. This was a relatively lame excuse as the print was recorded photographically and there was no reason why a positive blood test could not have been completed after photographs had been taken. Another possible explanation lies in concern that the stain might fail the test and so prove, for the umpteenth time, Bundy to be a liar.

Police also claimed to have found a further bloodstain, measuring 0.6 metres by 2.5 metres, on the floor of Clark's garage. They concluded from this that heavily bleeding bodies had been dragged across the floor. Hence, they reasoned, this corroborated Bundy's testimony about the necrophile orgy that had supposedly occurred in the garage with the bodies of Chandler and Marano. As with the boot print, only a presumptive test was carried out, and again the test proved inconclusive. Furthermore, when examined, the girls' bodies showed no signs of blood smears or streaks, as would have been the case if they had been dragged in such a manner. Postmortem abrasions on Chandler's back were attributed by investigators to the act of dragging the body across a rough surface. On the other hand, the medical examiner argued that these marks could have been the result of the body being dumped into the ravine.

Clark was astonished that the police should be so surprised to find his boot print in his garage, and with his usual droll sense of humour, he commented, 'What the fuck am I supposed to do? Levitate around my garage!' He also provided an explanation for the large drag marks in his garage: 'There was a track where the bike went in and out over a period of six months right down the middle of the garage. I stored raw wood, ply and particleboards there. There were four woodworking shops within a 50-foot radius that directly dusted the area. The door allowed leaves and dust to blow in, round and under it.'

This would certainly explain why the drag mark was organic in origin.

After careful investigation of Clark's garage, the police could only say that there 'might have been blood on the floor'. There was certainly not a shred of evidence to support Bundy's allegation that he had had sex with two dead and heavily bloodstained bodies there. Moreover, Bundy's other statement, that they had scrubbed the place clean, proved to be another of her lies, for it was patently obvious, even to the police, that the place had not been cleaned out for years.

If anything could save Clark from the death sentence, it lay in establishing solid alibis for at least a few of the murders. But alibis seemed to be lacking, especially for 11 June, the date of the Chandler and Marano killings. Clark argues that he could not even remember where he was living on that day, let alone what he did after work, when Bundy says the crimes were committed. It soon became apparent that he was lodging with Cissy Buster, one of his many on-and-off girlfriends. She told detectives that he arrived home around 8 o'clock that evening, but timekeeping records from the factory suggest that he finished much earlier, at 1pm. Buster added that Clark had phoned her to say he would be home late, and she remembers this because it was her son's graduation party. It was subsequently shown that these events actually took place on Friday, 13 June, and not on the day of the murders.

One thing that could clinch the case against Doug Clark would be a survivor who could identify him. While he and Bundy were under lock and key, a regular jailbird, named Charlene Anderman, a mentally unhinged woman who had been frequently arrested on drug and prostitution charges, was also behind bars. Around the same time as the Sunset Slayings occurred, a series of savage knife attacks and robberies were committed against hookers. In April, Charlene had fallen victim to one such assault. She had joined a punter in his car when the man pulled out a knife and stabbed her several times in the back before kicking her out on to the street.

Police arrested Jerome Van Houten, whom Charlene Anderman identified in a line-up, but her recollection of the attack was hazy because she had been high on cocaine at the time. She told the police that the attack had taken place in a motel room, then she changed her story to say that she had been stabbed in a car, the colour and make of which constantly changed. Understandably, the police deemed her identification unreliable, but they had enough on Van Houten to secure his conviction on the basis of positive identification provided by other victims.

Locked up in jail, Anderman started bragging about Clark being her assailant, so the police decided to interview her again. They showed her a photograph of him and suddenly she decided that he was the knifeman, adding that she was willing to testify to this in court, provided that the police would free her from custody after the case was over. Fortunately for Clark, the court thought that Anderman was totally unreliable and her evidence was thrown out. The police had to honour their part of the deal, and Anderman, whose sister had said that she was 'a liar who would say or do anything to get out of trouble', was released almost immediately.

Clark has always maintained that Bundy and Murray killed most of the victims while driving around in Murray's Chevy van. During the forensic investigation of this vehicle, a vital piece of evidence was found hanging from the roof vent hatch. It was a sliver of human scalp with strands of blonde hair attached to it. This gruesome item was approximately five centimetres in length, dehydrated and probably detached from a head as the result of a gunshot blast. As most of the victims had been blonde and Murray was dark-haired, it would seem evident that at least one of the prostitutes had been killed in the van, which would support Clark's claim. The state, however, desperately needed to convict Clark. After all, Murray was dead, and, if he had been the Sunset Slayer, the crimes had been allowed to run their bloody course. None of this would have gone down well with the police departments involved. The skin tissue, with hair attached, was taken away and no investigation was carried out to determine its origin. Clark was also refused the right to have it submitted as evidence at his trial.

With all the cards stacked against him, what luck Clark had remaining totally evaporated as, from the outset, it was patently obvious that the state was determined to get a conviction against him. He couldn't develop a relationship with his lawyer and became ever more despondent about his chances of success. Occasionally he would burst out with angry rants and accusations. One afternoon he was manacled and tied to a chair in which he was gagged with a leather strap and a sanitary towel. At other times he was escorted from the courtroom and locked up in a small holding room equipped with speakers so that he could listen to his right to live being eroded, all the while failing to understand his lawyer's tactics as the details were unfolded.

Understandably anxious that his case should be fully and clearly presented and the judge should only intervene when absolutely necessary, Clark saw a change only as the trial reached its mid point. Judge Torres acceded to his insistence that he should be allowed to represent himself.

Despite this being exactly what the defendant had wanted from day one, nothing improved. Indeed, things became far worse, for he was denied co-counsel, advisory counsel and the services of a law clerk, and the judge, illegally, told him to 'go it alone'. At one point Clark gave the court a list of items he required as evidence, including the items found in Murray's van. Some of these were sex toys and home-made pornographic videos. (Bundy had bought Murray a video camera, and it has always been suspected that they may have been recording their murders as snuff movies.) Needless to say, the judge blocked Clark's request. The accused man was astounded, screaming, 'If I had a colour movie with the sound of Carol and Jack committing these murders, you would not let me bring it in?'

The judge said, 'You are right, Mr Clark. I would not.'

At another stage of the trial it became evident that Clark did indeed have an alibi for the night that Exxie Wilson's head was deposited in the ornate chest. Several people recalled that he had been partying with a go-go dancer who was about to return home to New Zealand. Clark had also written her a cheque that night, and he was able to provide banking documents to support the fact that it had been cashed the following day. Not even the most adept serial killer can be in two places at the same time, and Bundy had told police that it had been Clark who had dumped Wilson's severed head, so this provided a problem for the prosecutor. The dancer even offered to return to the USA to give her evidence if her airfare was paid. Clark asked for this dispensation, rightly arguing that the District Attorney had flown in scores of witnesses. One of these had been an FBI agent brought from Virginia, to confirm that the boot print found in Clark's garage was indeed Clark's, something that he had admitted from the outset. Indeed, the prosecution spent over $10,000 on travel for their witnesses, and Clark was allowed just $20 – which amounted to his entire defence funding – in dimes for a single telephone call. In a last-ditch effort to get the dancer to testify, he begged that she be allowed to give her evidence over the telephone. This is a legally accepted procedure if the witness is positively identified and sworn in at a local court. But, once again, his request was denied.

Meanwhile, another problem surfaced when the court began hearing about the discovery of Wilson's head, and the clothing it was wrapped in. The police had made efforts to identify the jeans and T-shirt, and detectives Stallcup and Jaques of the LAPD, who were working on the Marnette Comer murder, telephoned the Sacramento Police Department. Stallcup required contact with known associates of Comer, such as co-hookers and pimps, and also wanted to interview her sister, Sabra, who was also a prostitute. Sabra categorically told the two investigators that the T-shirt and jeans had belonged to a hooker called Toni Wilson, a Caucasian, aged

19, with natural blonde hair and blue eyes, slim, 1.7 metres tall, with freckles. This was a positive identification and one that was supported by numerous other characters, including a pimp named Mark. These witnesses even told Stallcup that the last time they saw Toni Wilson she had been wearing the very same clothing described by Comer's sister.

In his handwritten report, timed and dated 4pm, 9 August 1980, Stallcup made a careful note of this information. Later that evening he inexplicably reproduced an 'official' version in typewritten form, the substance of which somewhat changed the testimony of Sabra Comer to read that she had identified the T-shirt and jeans as belonging to her deceased sister, which was not the case. During the trial the prosecution called Sabra Comer as a witness to identify the clothing, and she did identify the items as belonging to her sister, Marnette. Somewhere there was a major discrepancy and Clark picked it up. He called Stallcup to give evidence.

He asked the detective about the handwritten notes he made from replies given by a Sabra, and enquired whether it was his usual practice when typing them up to turn the details around 180 degrees. Stallcup answered, 'No. I would put myself in a very bad spot of jeopardy there. The crime for doing such… something like that, if it ended up to be a capital case, I would be under the same problem that you have got sitting there.' Stallcup knew that for a police officer to falsify evidence and to commit perjury in a capital case left that officer open to a capital charge himself. After being pressed on this issue by Clark, the detective agreed that he made the handwritten notes. Stallcup 'thought' the typed version was his too, but only after his signature was pointed out to him on the page. This incident was allowed to pass without a stain on Stallcup's character.

A similar situation to the one Clark found himself in occurred in the more recent case of Alton Coleman (see Debra Brown and Alton Coleman, page 37), who continually protested his innocence for murder. When Coleman's defence submitted solid proof of innocence for a retrial, it was deemed too late, but he was given the benefit of doubt and offered a polygraph test, which took place just a few hours before his execution. This test, which simply detects any slight heartbeat increase or sweat secretion when the vital questions are asked, was unsurprisingly failed by Coleman, who was about to die an agonising death, and he was escorted to the electric chair on 21 May 1992.

Like Clark, Coleman had solid alibis, witnesses and forensic evidence suggesting he had not committed murder. Furthermore, a woman claimed that another man, who was a known killer, had confessed to her that he had carried out the murder attributed to Coleman. This witness was found dead on the day following her 'On Air' statement. Also, in the Coleman case, the state offered a fellow inmate freedom to repeat evidence in court that Coleman had told him that he had committed the crime. He talked and walked, while Coleman died. On his subsequent release, the jailhouse snitch retracted his admission.

Douglas Daniel Clark was found guilty on six counts of first-degree murder and sentenced to death. Carol Mary Bundy was found guilty on two counts of first-degree murder, that of Jack Murray and Cathy (Jane Doe 28), and she was sentenced to two terms of life imprisonment. But is Clark really a serial murderer?

He had alibis and witnesses for all the murders except one. The police obtained statements from many of these witnesses, some of whom were allowed to make several contradictory statements which helped to incriminate Clark.

The weapons and vehicles associated with all the murders belonged either to Bundy or Murray.

Bundy lied at every turn.

Most of the prosecution witnesses had criminal records. Indeed, one of the young girls forced into prostitution has recently said that she felt she had to tailor her evidence, otherwise she feared she might be 'put out of business' if she didn't co-operate with the police.

The judge refused to allow the jury to hear tape-recorded evidence of Bundy confessing her involvement and pleasure in the murders.

Murray's van was returned to his wife before the trial began, thus denying Clark any opportunity to have the interior independently examined.

Vital trace and ballistic evidence was either mislaid or 'lost' by the police.

The state's Attorney General admitted that Bundy had been given a deal to testify against Clark in return for her life.

Today Clark awaits his appointment with San Quentin's executioner. As his time has just about run out, it is perhaps unfair to criticise him for being a very angry man who is full of contempt for the police and the US system of justice.

Without doubt Doug Clark was a fool. He most certainly was an accessory after the fact in the case of Jack Murray, for he has admitted that he was with Bundy when she threw her former lover's head out of her car window. And he was certainly present when Bundy shot a hooker through the head as she gave him oral sex in a car. He did not report this murder either, which would have bought at least a life sentence when he was arrested.

Clark's early years remain something of a mystery, and he is loath to discuss this part of his life when he has far more pressing matters on his mind. Unlike Bundy, it is known that Clark came from good stock and enjoyed a healthy childhood and a first-class education.

Clark used to be a handsome man, well read, and he spoke, most agreed, beautifully. He was a philanderer who wooed a different woman almost weekly and was a Don Juan of almost epic proportions. But all of his lady friends say he treated them well and he has never been accused of using violence against them even though his sexual interests were hardly conservative. Clark also used women to provide him with lodgings, often in return for sexual favours, a practice which ultimately proved to be his undoing when he fell in with Bundy. So, in every respect, and even by the FBI's own reckoning, Doug does not fit the psychological profile of a serial killer.

Like so many serial killers, Carol Bundy had had a troubled upbringing. She was an ugly, duck-shaped woman who could hardly see. She paid men to have sex with her and Murray was a willing partner who satisfied all of her perverse sexual needs. By her own admission she was a necrophile and a hedonist killer.

Hedonist killers may be divided into sub-types. Lust murderers kill for sexual enjoyment. Thrill killers kill for the excitement of a novel experience. Both of these sub-types may show evidence of sadistic methods, mutilation, dismemberment and pre- and post-mortem sexual activity. Bundy fits both categories extremely well.

There is little evidence to contest the view that it was Bundy and Murray who killed at least five of the Sunset prostitutes. Following these murders, Bundy, spurned and embezzled by her lover and accomplice in serial sexual homicide, killed and decapitated him in a fit of jealous rage. Indeed, the 'Betsy/Claudia' telephone call to the police, when she pointed an accusatory finger at Murray, proved beyond any doubt that the seeds of anger and resentment had already been planted well before she shot him.

Clark distanced himself from Bundy at this time and, in an act of spite, she turned him in. She cast herself in the role of the state's only witness, yet, totally untruthful in her testimony, she engineered a life sentence for herself and a death sentence for Clark. Good luck, Doug Clark. As for Bundy, she died on 9 December 2003 of heart failure at the Central California Women's Facility (CCWF), Chowchilla.

The above account is based on exclusive videotaped Death Row interviews between myself and Douglas Daniel Clark held in 1995 in San Quentin State Prison, California, and on extensive correspondence.

Conclusion

It is very unlikely that Carol Bundy would have committed serial murder without pairing with Jack Murray and later Douglas Clark. But whereas it was genuine folie a deux between Bundy and Murray, I believe that it was not so between Bundy and Clark. In my view, rather than a killer, Clark is a fool who allowed himself to become an unwilling accomplice to a murder committed by a devious and psychopathic woman.

SUMMARY

Many of the cases in this book suggest that genuine folie a deux most often exists between those murderers who share a sexual motive for committing their crimes. There is no doubt that Carol Bundy and Jack Murray gained deviant sexual thrills from their relationship, as did Fred and Rose West, Ian Brady and Myra Hindley, and Debra Brown and Alton Coleman.

With a slight variation on this theme, the same can also be said of Kenneth Bianchi, Angelo Buono and Veronica Wallace Compton. Bianchi, who had probably murdered three times before he met up with Buono, and definitely killed twice after they parted company, was the more intelligent and devious of the duo. Bianchi would have continued to murder until he was caught, but in the case of Buono it is doubtful, even taking into account his abysmal history, that he would have killed had he not fallen in with Bianchi.

Veronica Wallace Compton, call her a dumb patsy if you will, met Bianchi in jail on just a handful of occasions, which tells us just how enthralled she was with this Lothario and how quickly she fell under his spell.

And what a bizarre little world we live in, for later Veronica writes to Doug Clark suggesting that the two of them, if they were to be released from prison, enter into a relationship and open up a mortuary to have sex with the dead. Sick and twisted minds, and a folie a deux indeed.

Lawrence Bittaker teamed up with Ray Norris to commit sexually related homicides, as did Gerard and Charlene Gallego. All of these, I would argue, are genuine cases of folie a deux.

Debra Brown and Alton Coleman also provide us with a genuine folie a deux. Although Coleman (see Carol Bundy, Jack Murray and Douglas Clark, page 221) claims he was totally innocent, this was a heterosexual serial killing team formed by a classic folie a deux relationship, for the two offenders enjoyed the same delusions before they paired up to become sexual sadists, committing murders for sexual thrills.

Of widespread interest are the parallels between the Wests, Myra Hindley and Ian Brady, and Marc Dutroux and Michelle Martin (formerly Dutroux). The first two couples are definitely examples of folie a deux, and given that in all three cases the modus operandi appears identical, we can safely say that genuine folie a deux of a sexual nature existed between the Dutroux too.

Let's move away from clear-cut cases of folie a deux and look at some of the other pairings discussed in this book. As we have seen, contrary to the view of many criminologists that genuine folie a deux existed between Christine and Lea Papin, no persuasive evidence has emerged that the sisters plotted together to kill their employers, the Lancelins. The disturbed Christine was the prime mover and her psychosis would surely have pushed her to murder at some point, regardless of her relationship with the younger and weaker Lea.

I would also suggest that, although deeply in love, there existed no genuine folie a deux between Freddie Bywaters and Edith Thompson. Of course, they were immature young people, and Edith did write a number of implicating letters to her lover, as well as making a few injudicious remarks. But closer examination produces no evidence that she conspired with her lover to kill her husband, so to label the relationship as folie a deux is wrong.

We now may look at the case of Kelly O'Donnell and William Gribble in a similar light to that shone here on Bywaters and Thompson. There seems to have been no motive other than Gribble's jealousy for the murder to have taken place. Yes, they eagerly shared the spoils, but this was no shared madness. It was an unpremeditated murder linked to post-crime robbery, an aggravated homicide that earned the two lovers the death sentence, but most certainly not a folie a deux.

Ruth Snyder was a bullying woman, and a greedy one. Besotted with her, the weak-willed Henry Judd Gray became merely a tool, an accomplice, at her disposal so that she could get her hands on ill-gotten gains. Had she succeeded, she would have dumped him without delay; as would have Reiko Yamaguchi treated Kazuo Hokao in the Orient.

We could place Susan Minter and her accomplice Michael

White in the same non-folie a deux category. Minter's motive was to collect on her murdered husband's insurance policy and White was, like Gray and Hokao, merely a tool at Minter's disposal.

Renuka Shinde and Seema Gavit, our two hard-pressed female serial murderers from India, were two of four accomplices who killed solely for financial gain.

And finally, Lynda Block and George Sibley, two crooks on the run who murdered to avoid arrest, but with not a hint of folie a deux in their tragic story.

This book has looked at the little-known phenomenon of folie a deux from a criminological point of view. And, staying with this focus, from a police interrogator's perspective it is evident, as the few examples of genuine folie a deux included here demonstrate, that in most cases the more dominant partner is the male. We might assume that an interrogator armed with this knowledge would find the female the easier partner to crack when trying to obtain a confession and bring a pair of killers to justice. But we would be wrong. For such women have become so psychologically dependent on their male partners that they will readily sacrifice their lives to imprisonment, even execution, in order to protect them.

In non-folie a deux relationships between men and women, the opposite seems to be the case. The women, using their sex as a manipulative tool, seem to hold the upper hand, while the men become slaves to their bidding. Indeed, when the game is up and they are under arrest, the woman will confess and do all she can to implicate the male partner as the prime mover – a final twist in the power struggle between the sexes.

Now you can buy any of these other books by Christopher Berry-Dee from your bookshop or direct from the publisher.

Free P+P and UK Delivery
(Abroad £3.00 per book)

Gangland UK
ISBN 978-1-84454-832-3   PB   £7.99

Dead Men Talking
ISBN 978-1-84454-714-2   PB   £11.99

Dead Men Walking
ISBN 978-1-84454-592-6   HB   £17.99

Prime Suspect
ISBN 978-1-84454-612-1   PB   £7.99

Murder.com
ISBN 978-1-84454-517-9   PB   £7.99

Talking With Serial Killers
ISBN 978-1-90403-453-7   PB   £6.99

Face to Face With Serial Killers
ISBN 978-1-84454-367-0   PB   £7.99

Monster (with Aileen Wuornos)
ISBN 978-1-84454-237-6   PB   £7.99

TO ORDER SIMPLY CALL THIS NUMBER
+ 44 (0) 207 381 0666

Or visit our website
www.johnblakepublishing.co.uk

Prices and availability subject to change without notice